걸프 사태

재정지원 공여국
조정위원회 회의 2

걸프 사태

재정지원 공여국 조정위원회 회의 2

| 머리말

  걸프 전쟁은 미국의 주도하에 34개국 연합군 병력이 수행한 전쟁으로, 1990년 8월 이라크의 쿠웨이트 침공 및 합병에 반대하며 발발했다. 미국은 초기부터 파병 외교에 나섰고, 1990년 9월 서울 등에 고위 관리를 파견하며 한국의 동참을 요청했다. 88올림픽 이후 동구권 국교 수립과 유엔 가입 추진 등 적극적인 외교 활동을 펼치는 당시 한국에 있어 이는 미국과 국제사회의 지지를 얻기 위해서라도 피할 수 없는 일이었다. 결국 정부는 91년 1월부터 약 3개월에 걸쳐 국군의료지원단과 공군수송단을 사우디아라비아 및 아랍 에미리트 연합 등에 파병하였고, 군·민간 의료 활동, 병력 수송 임무를 수행했다. 동시에 당시 걸프 지역 8개국에 살던 5천여 명의 교민에게 방독면 등 물자를 제공하고, 특별기 파견 등으로 비상시 대피할 수 있도록 지원했다. 비록 전쟁 부담금과 유가 상승 등 어려움도 있었지만, 걸프전 파병과 군사 외교를 통해 한국은 유엔 가입에 박차를 가할 수 있었고 미국 등 선진 우방국, 아랍권 국가 등과 밀접한 외교 관계를 유지하며 여러 국익을 창출할 수 있었다.

  본 총서는 외교부에서 작성하여 30여 년간 유지한 걸프 사태 관련 자료를 담고 있다. 미국을 비롯한 여러 국가와의 군사 외교 과정, 일일 보고 자료와 기타 정부의 대응 및 조치, 재외동포 철수와 보호, 의료지원단과 수송단 파견 및 지원 과정, 유엔을 포함해 세계 각국에서 수집한 관련 동향 자료, 주변국 지원과 전후복구사업 참여 등 총 48권으로 구성되었다. 전체 분량은 약 2만 4천여 쪽에 이른다.

2024년 3월

한국학술정보(주)

| 일러두기

· 본 총서에 실린 자료는 2022년 4월과 2023년 4월에 각각 공개한 외교문서 4,827권, 76만 여 쪽 가운데 일부를 발췌한 것이다.

· 각 권의 제목과 순서는 공개된 원본을 최대한 반영하였으나, 주제에 따라 일부는 적절히 변경하였다.

· 원본 자료는 A4 판형에 맞게 축소하거나 원본 비율을 유지한 채 A4 페이지 안에 삽입 하였다. 또한 현재 시점에선 공개되지 않아 '공란'이란 표기만 있는 페이지 역시 그대로 실었다.

· 외교부가 공개한 문서 각 권의 첫 페이지에는 '정리 보존 문서 목록'이란 이름으로 기록물 종류, 일자, 명칭, 간단한 내용 등의 정보가 수록되어 있으며, 이를 기준으로 0001번부터 번호가 매겨져 있다. 이는 삭제하지 않고 총서에 그대로 수록하였다.

· 보고서 내용에 관한 더 자세한 정보가 필요하다면, 외교부가 온라인상에 제공하는 『대한 민국 외교사료요약집』 1991년과 1992년 자료를 참조할 수 있다.

| 차례

정 리 보 존 문 서 목 록

기록물종류	일반공문서철	등록번호	15251	등록일자	1999-10-26
분류번호	772	국가코드	XF	보존기간	영구
명　　칭	걸프사태 재정지원 공여국 조정위원회 회의, 1990-91. 전6권				
생 산 과	북미1과/경제협력2과/중동2과	생산년도	1990~1991	담당그룹	
권 차 명	V.4 제5차. Luxemburg, 1991.3.11 : 기본문서				
내용목차	* 수석대표 : 이정빈 외무부 제1차관보 * 1991.3.6-9 이정빈 외무부 제1차관보 미국 방문				

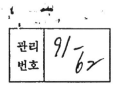

관리
번호 91-6?

외 무 부

종 별 : 지급

번 호 : USW-0628

수 신 : 장관(미북,중근동)

발 신 : 차 관 (주미대사 경유)

제 목 : 걸프사태 재정공여국 조정위 제 4차 회의

표제회의는 예정대로 2.5(화) 10:00-13:00 간 재무부 회의실에서 28 개국(3 차회의 참석국에 호주, 놀웨이, 아이스랜드 추가)및 EC, GCC, IMF, IBRD 대표 참석하에 MULFORD 재무차관과 KIMMITT 국무차관 공동 주재로 개최되었음. 아측은 소직이 이정보 국장, 최영진 참사관, 허노중 재무관, 이윤재 과장을 대동 참석한바, 요지 하기 보고함.

1. 개회벽두 KIMMITT 차관은 하기 내용의 발언을 하였음.

가. 이락에 대해서는 정치, 경제및 군사적 차원에서의 종합적 대응이 필요한바, 금번 걸프만 전쟁은 이락의 쿠웨이트로 부터의 철수라는 목적을 달성하기 위한것이지 이락 자체의 파괴를 목적으로 하고있는것이 아니라는것을 강조하고자함. 이러한 고려때문에 군사시설만을 공격 목표로 삼고 있음.

나. 오늘 회의 참석국가중 18 개국이 연합국에 참전하고 있고, 군사적 동맹은 계속 결속이 강해지고 있으며, 경제적 차원의 결속을 다지기 위한 데 오늘 회의의 주요 목적이 있음.

다. 요르단의 경우 요르단의 정치적 성향에 대해서 실망을 금할수 없으나, 요르단이 경제 봉쇄에는 계속 참여하고 있기 때문에 요르단에 대한 재정 지원을 계속할 필요가 있다는것이 미국의 입장임.

라. 전선국가 이외에 걸프 사태로 피해를 입고 있는 국가로서 동구권 국가들에 대한 관심을 기울이지 않을수 없음.

KIMMIT 차관은 대표단과 인사하는도중 소직에게 와서 어제 자신의 사무실을방문하여주어 감사하다고 말하였을뿐 작일 사무실에서는 금일 회의전 대화를 계속하자고 하였으나, 그이상의 대화를 추구하지 않았음.

2. 이어서 IMF, IBRD 의 전선 3 개국 경제상황 및 피해액에 관한 설명이 있었음.

미주국   장관   중아국   청와대   안기부

PAGE 1   검토필(1991. 6. 30.   91.02.06 16:52

외신 2과 통제관 BN

0002

3. MULFORD 차관은 별첨 I 도표와관련, 현재까지 전선국가에 대한 원조 약속이 110 억불, 원조 이행액이 40 억불로서 미 이행분이 70 억불이나 되어 이에 대한 조속한 시행이 요청된다고 언급하고, 터키의 경우 30 억불, 요르단의 경우 35 억불 총 65 억불이 부족한 상태이고 미할당분 26 억불이 이들국가에 할당된다고 할지라도 39 억불이 부족한 상태이기 때문에 오늘 회의에서는 조속한 원조 이행, 및 미할당금액의 할당 및 추가 약속등 3 가지 문제에 중점을 두어 진행하자고 하면서, 사우디, 쿠웨이트, UAE, EC 불란서, 독일, 일본 및 한국을 특히 지적하여 발언을 요청함.

4. 이에 대해, 소직은 한국 입장을 아래와갈이 설명함.

가. 한국은 금번 회의 참석 국가중 유일한 비산유 개발 도상국가로서, 한국은 재정 지원국가 그룹의 일원으로 걸프 사태 해결에 기여하게 된것을 기쁘게 생각함.

나. 도표에 한국의 총기여액이 100 백만불로 되어 있으나 115 백만불로 수정되어야 하는바, 이는 이집트 등 일부 국가가 군수물자 대신 생필품 현물지원을요청하여 15 백만불이 재정지원에 추가 되었기 때문임.

다. 재정 지원 총(115 백만불)중 (95 백만불)은 이미 한국 국회에서 예산조치가 끝났기 때문에 원조를 시행하는데 아무런 문제가 없게 되었음.

라. 약속금액의 조속한 집행을 위하여 본인이 작년 11 월 한국 조사단을 이끌고 이집트, 요르단, 터키, 시리아를 방문하여, 이들 국가들과 구체적인 원조 필요 분야에 대해 협의를 시작한바 있으므로, 이에 따라 대부분의 집행이 금년 1/4 분기중 가능할것으로 예견됨.

마. 또한 걸프 사태로 피해를 입고 있는 동구권 국가중 헝가리, 폴랜드, 루마니아 및 불가리아에 대하여는 한국이 별도의 광범위한 경제 협력 사업을 시행하고 있음을 밝히고자 함. (헝가리, 체고)

바. 비재정분야 군사지원에 있어서는 지난주 한국이 280 백만불의 추가 군사지원을 약속하여 총원조액이 500 백만불에 달하게 되었으며, 그외에 150 여명의 의료단을 사우디에 기 파견하였고, 5 대의 C-130 군수송기 지원이 원칙 결정되었음.

5. 원조 집계의 언론 공개와 관련, 상세내역은 계속 대외비로 하고 별첨 도표 II (원조 약속 총액 141 억불, 전선 3 개국 110 억불, 기타국 31 억불)및 현재까지의 집행액 72.8 억불의 대략적 내역만 미측에서 언론에 발표키로 하였음.

6. 차기 회의는 룩셈브르크 대표 (EC 의장국)의 제안을 받아들여 유럽에서 하기로 하고 시기는 3 월 전반기로 잠정 결정됨.

PAGE 2

0003

첨부:1.USW(F)-0462
2.USW(F)-0463
(차관-장관)
예고:1991.12.31 까지

TABLE A

GULF CRISIS FINANCIAL ASSISTANCE *

($ Billions – as of 2/5/91)

Donor/Creditor	Commitments
GULF STATES	9.3
EUROPEAN COMMUNITY	2.3
JAPAN	2.1
OTHER	0.4
TOTAL	14.1

* Includes all commitments to date for extraordinary economic assistance in 1990 and 1991. Does not include contributions to the multinational force, existing bilateral assistance, or funds made available by the IMF and World Bank.

TABLE B

GULF CRISIS FINANCIAL ASSISTANCE *

($ Billions – as of 2/5/91)

Donor/Creditor	Total Commitments	1990–91 Commitments		Other States
		Egypt/Turkey/Jordan	Unallocated	
GULF STATES	9.3	6.1	0.2	3.0
EUROPEAN COMMUNITY	2.3	2.0	0.2	0.1
JAPAN	2.1	2.0	0.1	0.0
OTHER	0.4	0.2	0.2	0.0
TOTAL	14.1	10.3	0.7	3.1

* Includes all commitments to date for extraordinary economic assistance in 1990 and 1991.
Does not include contributions to the multinational force, existing bilateral
assistance, or funds made available by the IMF and World Bank.

0006

TABLE C

GULF CRISIS FINANCIAL ASSISTANCE *

($ Billions – as of 2/5/91)

Donor/Creditor	Commitments	Disbursements
GULF STATES	9.3	5.4
EUROPEAN COMMUNITY	2.3	~~0.5~~ 0.68
JAPAN	2.1	0.4
OTHER	0.4	0.1
TOTAL	**14.1**	~~6.4~~ 6.6

* Includes all commitments to date for extraordinary economic assistance in 1990 and 1991. Does not include contributions to the multinational force, existing bilateral assistance, or funds made available by the IMF and World Bank.

발신전보 USW (기) -0462

유선 : 정리

발신 : 韓 차관 (국영 北美)

제목 : USW 별 첨부 (3매)

GULF CRISIS FINANCIAL COORDINATION GROUP

February 5, 1991

AGENDA

I.   Introduction by Chair

II.   Political Overview

III. Presentation by IMF and World Bank

    A.   IMF/World Bank Responses to Gulf Crisis

    B.   Economic Developments in and Status of Discussions with Egypt, Turkey, and Jordan

IV.   Status of Commitments and Disbursements

    A.   Report of Working Committee on Commitments and Disbursements

    B.   Prospects for Acceleration of Disbursements

    C.   Additional Commitments for 1991

V.   Next Steps

0462-1

(Millions of U.S. Dollars)

Balance of Payments	Grants	In Kind	Loans	Project Financing	Co-Financing	Unspecified	TOTAL
GCC STATES	1075	1420	100	1050	0	2703	6348
Saudi Arabia 1/	1000	1160		500		188	2848
Kuwait	75	10	100	550		1765	2500
UAE		250				750	1000
EC	662	6	111		7	1397	2183
EC Budget	78					682	760
Bilateral	584	6	111		7	715	1423
Belgium	*21*					*12*	*33*
Denmark						*30*	*30*
France						*200*	*200*
Germany	*414*		*13*			*468*	*895*
Ireland		*6*					*6*
Italy	*88*		*62*				*150*
Luxembourg	*4*						*4*
Netherlands	*56*				*7*		*63*
Portugal	*1*						*1*
Spain			*36*				*36*
U.K.						*5*	*5*
OTHER EUROPE/AUSTRALIA	45	1	0		0	179	225
Australia		1				13	14
Austria						11	11
Finland						11	11
Iceland						3	3
Norway						32	32
Sweden	45						45
Switzerland						109	109
JAPAN 2/	90	1	648	194	157	1026	2116
CANADA	66						66
KOREA		60	23				83
TOTAL	1938	1488	882	1244	164	5305	11021

• Does not include contribution to multinational force. Totals may not equal sum of components due to rounding. Includes assistance to Egypt, Turkey, and Jordan. Based on data submitted to the Coordinating Group.

1/ Project financing for Egypt is on grant basis. 2/ Balance of payments loans are 30 years at 1% interest. Project financing is loans, terms not yet specified.

1/31/91

GULF CRISIS FINANCIAL ASSISTANCE *
1990-91 COMMITMENTS AND DISBURSEMENTS
(Millions of U.S. Dollars)

	TOTAL			Egypt			Turkey			Jordan			Unallocated 1/			Other States			GRAND TOTAL		
	Commit.	Disb. to Date	Future Disb.	Commit.	Disb. to Date	Future Disb.	Commit.	Disb. to Date	Future Disb.	Commit.	Disb. to Date	Future Disb.	Commit.	Disb. to Date	Future Disb.	Commit.	Disb. to Date	Future Disb.	Commit.	Disb. to Date	Future Disb.
GCC STATES 2/	6348	3012	3336	3123	2263	860	2060	682	1378	0	0	0	1165	67	1098	2950	2129	821	9298	5141	4157
Saudi Arabia 3/	2848	1570	1278	1688	1288	400	1160	282	878	0	0	0	0	0	0	1503	1103	400	4351	2673	1678
Kuwait	2500	855	1645	1015	555	460	550	300	250	0	0	0	935	0	935	1184	763	421	3684	1618	2066
UAE 3/	1000	587	413	420	420	0	350	100	250	0	0	0	230	67	163	263	263	0	1263	850	413
EC	2184	515	1669	1125	194	931	431	87	344	452	168	283	176	66	110	108	0	108	2292	515	1777
EC Budget	760	78	682	254	15	239	240	2	239	214	10	204	51	51	0	0	0	0	760	78	682
Bilateral:	1424	437	987	871	178	693	191	85	106	237	159	79	125	15	110	108	0	108	1532	437	1095
Belgium	33	7	26	16	6	10	7	0	7	10	1	9	0	0	0	0	0	0	33	7	26
Denmark	30	4	26	20	0	20	0	0	0	10	4	6	0	0	0	0	0	0	30	4	26
France 4/	200	0	200	50	0	50	30	0	30	20	0	20	100	0	100	30	0	30	230	0	230
Germany	895	362	533	673	154	519	74	74	0	148	134	14	0	0	0	69	0	69	964	362	602
Ireland	6	6	0	6	6	0	0	0	0	0	0	0	0	0	0	0	0	0	6	6	0
Italy 5/	150	4	146	75	0	75	49	0	49	27	4	23	1	1	0	9	0	9	159	4	155
Luxembourg	4	1	3	1	0	1	1	0	1	1	1	0	1	0	1	0	0	0	4	1	3
Netherlands	63	45	18	18	18	0	18	11	7	18	16	2	9	0	9	0	0	0	63	45	18
Portugal	1	0	1	0	0	0	1	0	1	0	0	0	0	0	0	0	0	0	1	0	1
Spain	36	9	27	12	0	12	11	0	11	9	9	0	4	0	4	0	0	0	36	9	27
U.K.	5	5	0	0	0	0	0	0	0	0	0	0	5	5	0	0	0	0	5	5	0
OTHER EUROPE/AUSTRALIA	225	49	175	13	2	11	9	2	7	37	18	19	165	27	138	21	21	0	246	70	175
Australia	14	3	11	1	0	1	0	0	0	0	0	0	13	3	10	0	0	0	14	3	11
Austria	11	1	10	0	0	0	0	0	0	9	0	9	2	1	1	0	0	0	11	1	10
Finland	11	0	11	0	0	0	0	0	0	0	0	0	11	0	11	0	0	0	11	0	11
Iceland	3	2	1	0	0	0	1	0	1	1	1	0	1	1	0	0	0	0	3	2	1
Norway	32	14	18	2	2	0	5	2	3	2	2	0	23	8	15	21	21	0	53	35	18
Sweden	45	21	24	10	0	10	4	0	4	26	16	10	6	5	1	0	0	0	45	21	24
Switzerland	109	9	100	0	0	0	0	0	0	0	0	0	109	9	100	0	0	0	109	9	100
JAPAN 6/	2116	445	1671	444	0	444	320	218	102	266	167	99	1086	60	1026	0	0	0	2116	445	1671
CANADA	66	17	49	22	0	22	4	0	4	23	0	23	17	17	0	0	0	0	66	17	49
USA	83	5	78	23	0	23	20	5	15	15	0	15	25	0	25	17	2	15	100	7	93
(a) TOTAL COMMITMENTS	11021	4043	6978	4751	2459	2292	2844	994	1850	793	354	439	2634	237	2397	3096	2152	944	14117	6195	7922
(b) EST. EFFECT OF GULF CRISIS 7/	13580	13580	-	3375	3375	-	5910	5910	-	4295	4295	-	-	-	-	-	-	-	-	-	-
DIFFERENCE (a minus b)	-2559	-9537	-	1376	-916	-	-3066	-4916	-	-3502	-3941	-	-	-	-	-	-	-	-	-	-

* Does not include contributions to the multinational force. Totals may not equal sum of components due to rounding. Based on data submitted to the Coordinating Group. 1/ Unallocated among Egypt, Jordan, and Turkey. Includes general humanitarian assistance. 2/ GCC financing for "Other States" is for Syria, Morocco, Lebanon, Somalia, and Djibouti. 3/ Grant oil to Turkey: $1160 million from Saudi Arabia and $250 million from the UAE. 4/ Protocols for $130 million of grand total were topped by end-November. Aid to "Other States" is for Morocco. 5/ Italian aid to "Other States" is for Somalia. 6/ All GOJ procedures for $322 million to Egypt completed; awaiting parliamentary approval in Egypt. 7/ IMF/World Bank estimates (oil at $31/barrel) circulated to Group shown for illustrative purposes. Not intended to represent precise figure of impact.

報告畢

1991. 2. 22.
美 洲 局
北 美 課(9)

報 告 事 項

題 目 : 걸프전 관련 주한미대사관 통보내용

1. 쏘련-이라크 종전안

o 미측은 현재 쏘련-이라크 종전안에 명시된 내용 및 함축적 의미를 분석.
  검토중에 있음.

o 미국으로서는 현재 제시된 종전안에 대해 우방국 정부들이 지지 성명을
  발표하는 등의 성급한 조치를 취하지 않기를 바라고 있음.

2. 제5차 걸프사태 재정지원 공여국 조정위 회의

o 91.3.11(월) 룩셈부르크에서 개최될 예정임.

  - Kimmitt 국무부 정무차관, Mulford 재무부 차관 공동주재

o 한국 정부가 고위 대표를 파견하여 줄 것을 요청함. 끝.

0011

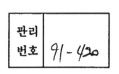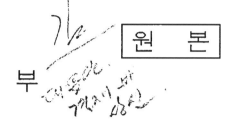

관리
번호 91-420

외 무 부

원 본

종 별 : 지 급

번 호 : USW-0968

일 시 : 91 0227 1914

수 신 : 장관(미북)

발 신 : 주 미 대사

제 목 : 걸프 사태 재정 지원 공여국 조정위 제 5차 회의

1. 당관이 국무부 및 재무부 관계관에 확인한바에 의하면, 표제 회의가 3.11(월) 예정대로 룩셈브르크에서 개최되며, 종전과 마찬가지로 KIMMITT 국무부 정무차관과 MULFORD 재무차관이 동 회의를 공동 주재하게된다함.

2. 동회의 초청 서한은 룩셈브르크 정부에서, 의제는 미 국무부에서 작성, 근일중 관계국에 송부 예정이라함.

3. RICHARDSON 한국과장은 당관 유참사관과 접촉 기회에 KIMMITT 차관의 동회의 참석 사실을 확인하면서 가능하면 아측에서도 고위급 관리가 참석하기를 희망한다는 의사를 전달하여왔음.

(대사 박동진-차관)

91.12.31 까지

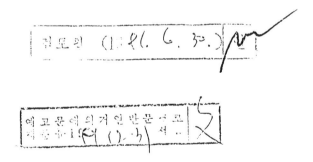

미주국	장관	차관	1차보	2차보	구주국	중아국	청와대	안기부

PAGE 1

91.02.28   10:21

외신 2과 통제관 BW

0012

원 본

외 무 부

종 별 : 지 급

번 호 : USW-0983　　　　　　　　　　일 시 : 91 0228 1610

수 신 : 장관(미북,재무부)

발 신 : 주 미 대 사

제 목 : 재정 지원 조정국 5차회의

　　연 WUS-0968

　　1. 연호, 국무성은 표제 회의 개최사실을 통보하는 키미트 차관및 멀포드 차관 공동 명의 서한을 의제와 함께 주한 대사관을 통하여 본부및 재무부에 전달예정이라함.

　　2. 국무부로부터 입수한 동 의제를 하기 보고함.

Ⅰ. WELCOMING REMARKS BY HOSTS

Ⅱ. INTRODUCTION BY CHAIR

Ⅲ. POLITICAL OVERVIEW

Ⅳ. PRESENTATION BY IMF AND WORLD BANK

Ⅴ. COMMITMENTS AND DISBURSEMENTS

-- REPORT OF WORKING COMMITTEE ON COMMITMENTS AND DISBURSEMENTS

-- ADDITIONAL COMMITMENTS FOR 1991

--TOUR DE TABLE ON COMMITMENTS, DISBURSEMENTS, AND TERMS AND CONDITIONS

Ⅵ. OTHER BUSTINESS AND CONCLUDING REMARKS BY CHAIR

Ⅶ. CLOSING REMARKS BY HOSTS

(대사 박동진-국장)예고: 91.12.31 까지

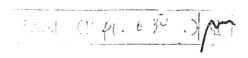

미주국　　2차보　　재무부

PAGE 1　　　　　　　　　　　　　　　　　　　　91.03.01　　10:46

AGENDA FOR FEBRUARY 5 MEETING OF GULF CRISIS
FINANCIAL COORDINATION GROUP

I.   INTRODUCTION BY CHAIR

II.   POLITICAL OVERVIEW

III. PRESENTATION BY IMF AND WORLD BANK

      A. IMF/WORLD BANK RESPONSES TO GULF CRISIS

      B. ECONOMIC DEVELOPMENTS IN AND STATUS OF DISCUSSIONS
          WITH EGYPT, TURKEY AND JORDAN.

IV.   STATUS OF COMMITMENTS AND DISBURSEMENTS

      A. REPORT OF WORKING COMMITTEE ON COMMITMENTS AND
          DISBURSEMENTS

      B. PROSPECTS FOR ACCELERATION OF DISBURSEMENTS

      C. ADDITIONAL COMMITMENTS FOR 1991.

V.   NEXT STEPS

0014

EMBASSY OF THE
UNITED STATES OF AMERICA

Feb. 28

Dear Director General Ban,

Attached is information on the Luxembourg Gulf Donors Meeting.

Regards,
Hank Hendrickson

0015

분류번호	보존기간

발 신 전 보

번 호 : WUS-0789　910301 1820 FD　종별 : 지 급

수 신 : 주　　미　　대사. 총영사

발 신 : 장 관 （미북）

제 목 : 제1차관보 방미

　　1. 정부는 걸프전 종전과 더불어 걸프지역에서의 평화와 질서회복 및 경제 부흥등에 관한 미국의 정책파악과 필요한 협의를 위해 이정빈 제1차관보를 3.6(수)-9(토)간 귀지에 파견 예정임.

　　2. 이와 관련, 귀관은 이 차관보 귀지 체재중 다음 인사와의 면담을 주선하고 결과보고 바람.

　　　　- 백악관 : Karl Jackson 동아.태 담당 선임 보좌관 및 기타 방미
　　　　　　　　목적에 적절한 인사 1인

　　　　- 국무부 : Kimmitt 정무차관

　　　　　　　　Solomon 동아.태 차관보

　　　　　　　　Kelly 중동 차관보

　　　　- 국방부 : Rowen 국제안보 차관보

　　　　- 학 계 : 중동 전문가 1-2명　　　　　끝

　3. 이차관보는 3.11 특별분2개최 재정지원공여국 조정회의 참석차 -
　　3.11에에 직접 특별분2향발 여정임.

（제1차관보 이 정 빈）

예 고 : 91.12.31.일반

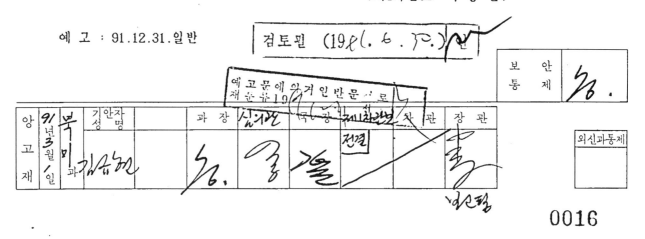

0016

보 도 자 료

외 무 부

제　　　호　　문의전화 : 720-2408~10　　보도일시 : ·91 · 3 ·2 : 시

제 목 :　걸프지역 전후문제에 관한 관계국과의 협의

o 정부는 걸프전이 종료됨에 따라 91. 3. 6(수) - 9(토)간 이정빈 외무부 제1차관보를 미국 워싱톤에 파견하여 걸프지역에서의 평화와 질서 회복, 그리고 경제 부흥등 전후의 제반 문제에 관해 미 정부 고위 관리들과의 협의를 가질 예정이다.

o 이정빈 차관보는 *상기 한·미 협의에* 이어 3. 11(월) 룩셈부르크에서 개최되는 걸프사태 재정지원 공여국 조정위원회 제5차 회의에 참석하여 전후 걸프지역 복구를 위한 관련국간의 공동노력 방안에 관해 협의할 예정이다.

끝.

공람 :

앙고제	복 · 년 · 비 · 1 · 인	담 당	과 장	심 의 관	국 장 · 차 관 보	차 관	장 관

0017

기 안 용 지

<table>
<tr><td>분류기호
문서번호</td><td colspan="2">미북 10200-</td><td colspan="3" rowspan="2" style="text-align:center">(전화 : 720-4648)</td><td>시 행 상
특 별 취 급</td><td></td></tr>
<tr><td rowspan="2">보존기간</td><td colspan="2" rowspan="2">영구. 준영구
10. 5. 3. 1.</td><td colspan="2">차 관</td><td>장 관</td></tr>
<tr><td colspan="3"></td><td></td></tr>
<tr><td>수 신 처
보존기간</td><td colspan="2">-</td><td colspan="3"></td><td rowspan="3"></td><td rowspan="3"></td></tr>
<tr><td>시행일자</td><td colspan="2">1991. 3. 2.</td><td colspan="3"></td></tr>
<tr><td rowspan="3">보조
기관</td><td>국 장</td><td></td><td rowspan="3">협조
기관</td><td colspan="2" rowspan="3">제1차관보

기획관리실장</td></tr>
<tr><td>심의관</td><td></td><td>문 서 통 제</td><td></td></tr>
<tr><td>과 장</td><td></td><td rowspan="2"></td><td rowspan="2"></td></tr>
<tr><td colspan="2">기안책임자</td><td>박호정</td><td rowspan="2"></td><td rowspan="2"></td><td>발 송 인</td></tr>
<tr><td rowspan="2">경
수
참</td><td>유신
신조</td><td rowspan="2">내 부 결 재</td><td rowspan="2">발
신
명
의</td><td rowspan="2"></td></tr>
<tr><td></td></tr>
</table>

제 목   걸프전 종전후 문제협의 및 제5차 조정위회의 대표단파견

걸프전 종전후 문제에 관한 대미협의 ~~대표단화~~ 91.3.11.

룩셈부르크에서 개최되는 제5차 걸프사태 재정지원 공여국 조정위회의

참석 대표단을 아래와 같이 파견코자 하오니 재가하여 주시기 바랍니다.

- 아   래 -

1. 대 표 단

    가. 걸프전 종전후 문제협의를 위한 방미 ~~대표단~~

대 표 : 이정빈 제1차관보   0018 /계속....

수행원 : 김규현 북미과 사무관

　나.　걸프 사태 재정지원 공여국 조정위 회의 대표단

수석대표 : 이정빈 외무부 제1차관보

수　행　원 : 이정보 재무부 경제협력국장

유명환 주미대사관 참사관

왕정중 경제기획원 행정예산 담당관

허덕행 외무부 중동2과 서기관

김규현 외무부 북미과 사무관

　2.　파견기간 :

　가.　방미 대표단 : 91.3.5-3.9(4박5일)

　나.　걸프 조정위 회의 : 91.3.9-3.13(4박5일)

　3.　대 상 국 : 미국, 룩셉부르크, 브랏셀　　　　끝.

예 고 : 91.12.31.일반　　검토필 (19P2.6 3ㄹ.)

예고문에 의거 일반문서로
재분류 19   서명

0019

제1차관보 방미시 중점 협의사항

91. 3.

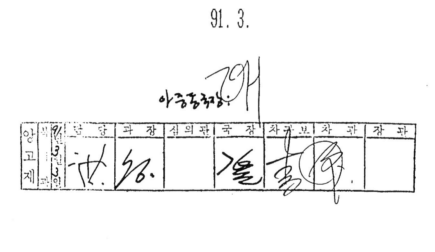

미 주 국

1. 걸프戰 終戰後 中東秩序 再編方案 把握 및 我國의 參與問題 協議

    ° 終戰以後 中東秩序 再編에 관한 美側의 構想을 問議
        - 中東地域 集團 安全保障 체제, 유엔 平和維持軍 또는 多國籍 平和維持軍 設置 방안
        - 향후 이라크의 域內 役割에 대한 構想
        - 中東地域 軍縮 推進方向(核 및 化學武器 등 대량 학살武器 減縮 및 미사일등 移動手段 技術 移轉 제한등)
        - 팔레스타인 問題等 아랍.이스라엘間 和解 摸索방향

    ° 상기 構想 및 方案에 대한 我國의 參與 및 役割 가능성에 대한 美國의 立場과 意見 타진

    ° 安保體制 構築에 있어서의 이집트, 시리아의 役割과 對韓 修交促進을 위한 美國의 居中 役割 요청

2. 戰後 中東建設 計劃 및 我國의 參與 *요청*

    ° 美側의 戰後 中東地域 經濟復興計劃을 問議
        - 가칭 中東 經濟開發復興銀行 設立 또는 IMF, IBRD 등 旣存 機構活用 방안 등
        - 쿠웨이트 및 이라크의 戰後 復舊 構想
        - 걸프戰 前線國 財政支援 供與國 調整會議의 향후 活動계획

0021

o 我國의 參與 및 役割에 대해 協議

  - 新設 또는 旣存 多者間 復興機構에의 參與 방안

  - 쿠웨이트 緊急復舊 計劃 및 이라크 再建 計劃

3. 新世界 秩序 宣言을 위한 頂上會談 開催 計劃 파악

o 美國이 構想中인 것으로 알려진 多國籍軍 派遣國과 기타 支援國 수뇌간

  頂上會談 開催 計劃과 UN의 향후 役割

  - 同 計劃이 事實일 경우, 我國의 參與 확인

o 3.6-16間 Baker 長官의 中東地域 巡訪時 中東 各國과의 協議 계획

4. 韓國 軍 醫療支援團 및 軍 輸送團 追加 活動問題

o 쿠웨이트內 緊急 醫療需要에 부응, 현재 사우디에서 활동중인 韓國軍

  醫療支援團의 쿠웨이트로의 移動問題 協議 ── 외국병, 대비 대니든지 ?출어

  - 당분간 活動 계속 意思를 表明하고 美側 反應 및 立場을 파악

  - 상기 活動地域 移動 및 活動期間 延長은 人道的 堅持에서도 적절

o UAE 알아인 機地에서 活動中인 軍 輸送支援團(C-130 5臺 및 運營要員 150名)

  活動 계속 協議 ── 라니부, 근혜 비3영12촘의 출어. 흔비라염

  - 中東地域 배치 美軍들에 대한 輸送支援 계속을 위해 당분간 계속 배치할

    計劃임을 통보하고 美側 反應을 파악

0022

5. 걸프事態 관련 我國의 2次 支援 約束額의 執行方案 協議(美側 擧論時 對應)

   ○ 1億1千万弗의 執行方案(現金 6千万弗, 輸送 5千万弗)에 대한 美側 立場

   ○ 1億7千万弗 규모 軍需物資 支援의 執行方案에 관한 美側 立場
      - 對英國 支援額 3千万弗 捻出 ~~~~~~~~~~~~~~~
      - 戰爭地域에 콜레라등 傳染病 만연 가능성에 대비한 支援
      - 食水, 醫藥品 등 緊急 人道的 支援
      - 環境汚染 防止對策 支援

⑥ 外務長官 訪美 日程 協議

   ○ 베이커 國務長官과의 會談可能 일정 協議

   ○ 부쉬 大統領, 퀘일 副統領, 체니 國防長官, Scowcroft 白堊館 安保補佐官
      등 行政府 高位人士 및 議會 指導者들과의 面談 可能性 파악

   ○ 戰後 中東秩序 再編 및 復舊計劃, 韓.美 頂上會談 問題, 韓半島 問題, 通商
      問題 및 亞.太 問題등을 協議하기 위한 韓.美 外相會談 早期 開催 필요성을
      提示하고 美側 反應을 타진

~~7. 其他 事項~~

7. ○ 我國의 UN 加入問題와 관련, 美 國務部 關係者들과의 協議   - 끝 -

0023

발 신 전 보

WUK-0400   910304 1817   FD

번   호 :   종별 :

수   신 : 주   영   대사.총영사

발   신 : 장 관   (미북)

제   목 : 제1차관보 경유

　　　　이정빈 제1차관보(김규현 북미과 사무관 수행)가 3.11(월) 룩셈부르크에서 개최되는 걸프사태 재정지원 공여국 조정위원회 제5차 회의 참석후 귀로에 다음과 같이 귀지 경유 예정임.

　　　　　3.12(화)　　　17:00　　　브랏셀 발 AE-131편 런던 도착(Gatwick 공항)
　　　　　　　　　　　　19:30　　　KE-908편 서울 향발(Gatwick 공항)　　끝.

　　　　　　　　　　　　　　　　　　　　(미주국장   반기문)

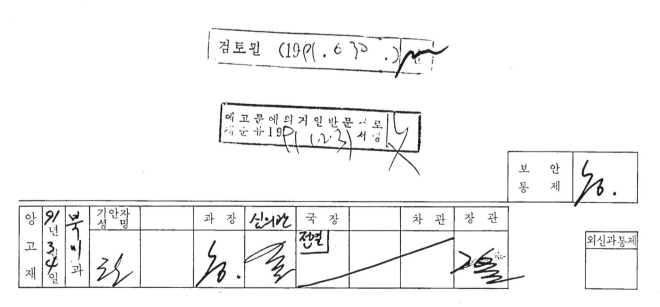

앙 고 재	91 년 3 4 일	북 미 과	기안자 성명		과 장	신의현		국 장	전결		차 관	장 관		외신과통제

보안통제

0024

	분류번호	보존기간

발 신 전 보

WLA-0308   910304 1816 FD

번 호 :

종별: 지 급

수 신 : 주   라성   대사.총영사

발 신 : 장 관   (미북)

제 목 : 제1차관보 방미

이정빈 제1차관보(김규현 북미과 사무관 수행)가 걸프전후 문제 등 협의를 위해 워싱톤 D.C. 출장도중 다음과 같이 귀지 경유 예정인 바, 환승간 편의 제공 바랍.

         3.5(화)   15:30   KE-018편 라성 향발

                     08:00   라성 도착

                     13:30   AA-036편 워싱톤 D.C. 향발.   끝.

검토필 (1991. 6. 30.)   (미주국장 반기문)

예고문에 의거 기일반문 (로)
재분류 19   (2.31) 서명

								보 안 통 제	

앙 고 재	91년 3월 4일	북미 과	기안자 성안명		과 장	심의관	국 장	전결	차 관	장 관		외신과통제

	분류번호	보존기간

발 신 전 보

번 호 : WUS-0824   910304 1817 FH   종별 : 긴급

수 신 : 주   미   대사. 총영사

발 신 : 장 관 (미북)

제 목 : 걸프사태 재정지원 공여국 조정위 회의

1. 정부는 3.11(월) 룩셈부르크에서 개최되는 표제회의에 이정빈 제1차관보를 수석대표로 파견 예정(단원:이정보 재무부 경제협력국장, 유명환 주미대사관 참사관, 왕정중 경기원 행정예산과장 및 김규현 사무관)인 바, 이를 재정지원 공여국 조정위 사무국에 통보바람. *허덕행중용2라세기만,*

2. 이와관련 유명환 참사관의 동 회의 참석을 위한 워싱턴 D.C.-뉴욕 - 브랏셀-워싱턴 D.C. 2등 항공요금을 지급 보고 바람.

3. 한편, 제1차관보 귀지 방문 및 조정회의 참석 일정이 다음과 같이 확정되었으니 3.5(화)-3.9(토)간 적절한 호텔에 Junior Suite 1실, Single 1실 예약바람.

3.5(화)	15:00	라성 향발(KE-018편)
	08:00	라성 도착
	13:30	워싱톤 향발(AA-036편)
	21:16	워싱톤 도착(델레스 공항)
3.9(토)	오 후	뉴욕 향발(서틀편)
	19:55	브랏셀 향발(PA-34편)

/ 계 속 /

		보 안 통 제	능.

	기안자 성명	과 장	국 장	차 관	장 관	
앙 고 재 91년3월4일 북미과	김유현과	능.	결	전결	기울	외신과통제

3.10(일)	09:15	브랏셀 도착
	오 후	룩셈부르크 도착(차량편)
3.11(월)	오 후	브랏셀 향발(차량편)
3.12(화)	17:00	브랏셀 출발(AE-131편)
	17:00	런던 도착(Gatwick 공항)
	19:30	서울 향발(KE-908편, Gatwick 공항)

    4. 상기 일정중 뉴욕-브랏셀 구간만은 유 참사관에 대해서도 서울에서
우선 예약 조치하였으니 귀지에서 재확인 바라며, 브랏셀-D.C. 구간은 상기
일정을 감안 귀지에서 예약 조치바람.   끝.

                                        (미주국장   반기문)

                        검토필 (1990. 6. 30.)

예 고 : 91.12.31.일반

                        예고문에의거일반문:로
                        재분유19   (2.3) 서 ㅇ

                                                    0027

분류번호	보존기간

발 신 전 보

번 호 : WBB-0090   910304 2127 BX   종별 :

WEC-0123

수 신 : 주 벨기에   대사. 총영사 (사본 : 주EC대사)

발 신 : 장 관 (미북)

제 목 : 제1차관보 방미일정

연 : WBB-0089

제1차관보는 귀지 방문전 걸프전후 문제 및 유엔가입문제 등 협의를 위해
다음 일정으로 방미 예정임을 참고바람.

3.5(화)	15:00	라성 향발 (KE-018편)
	08:00	라성 도착
	13:30	워싱톤 향발 (AA-036편)
	21:16	워싱톤 도착 (델레스 공항)
3.9(토)	오 후	뉴욕 향발 (셔틀편)
	19:55	브랏셀 향발 (PA-34편) - 끝 -

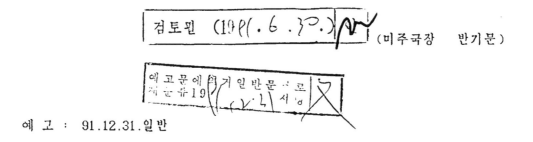

검토필 (1991. 6. 30.)   (미주국장   반기문)

예고문에 의거 일반문서로
재분류 19

예 고 : 91.12.31.일반

보 안 통 제		½.

앙고재	91년 3월 4일	북미 과	기안자 성 명	과 장 상의란	국 장 전 열	차 관	장 관	
			김유영	½.			거울	

외신과통제

0028

	분류번호	보존기간

발 신 전 보

번 호 : WBB-0089   910304 1821 FH   종별 : 지급

수 신 : 주 벨기에   대사. 총영사 (사본 : 주 EC 대사)

발 신 : 장 관 (미북)

제 목 : 제1차관보 방문

연 : WBB - 0082

1. 이정빈 제1차관보를 단장으로 한 아국 대표단(유명환 주미 참사관,
김규현 북미과 사무관 수행)이 3.11. 룩셈부르크에서 개최되는 걸프사태 재정지원
공여국 조정위 제5차 회의 참석차 다음 일정으로 귀지 및 룩셈부르크를 방문 예정임.
(기타 대표단원인 이정보 재무부 경협국장, 왕정중 경기원 행정예산 과장, 허덕행
중동2과 서기관은 3.10(일) 룩셈부르크에서 합류 예정)

3.10(일)	09:15	뉴욕발 PA-034편 브랏셀 도착
	오 후	룩셈부르크 도착(차량편)
3.11(월)	오 후	브랏셀 도착 (차량편)
3.12(화)	17:00	AE-131편 런던 향발

2. 이와관련 재정지원 공여국 조정위 참석 대표단을 위해 다음과 같이
숙소 예약 조치 바람.

가. 룩셈부르크 (3.10)

ㅇ Junior Suite 1실, Single 2실, Twin 2실(1박)

/ 계 속 /

	보 안 통 제	능.

앙 고 재	91 년 3 월 4 일	북 미 과	기안자 성 명	김규현	과 장	능.	심의관	국 장	전결	차 관	장 관		외신과통제

0029

나 . 브 랏 셀 (3.11)

　　　ㅇ 연호 2항 대신 Junior Suite 1실, Single 2실, Twin 1실(1박)

　　3.　아울러, 상기 대표단의 조정회의 참석 지원을 위하여 귀관직원
1명을 3.10(일)-11(월)간 룩셈부르크에 출장 조치바라며, 대표단을 위한 브랏셀
-룩셈부르크-브랏셀 차량편의 제공바람.

　　4.　한편, 상기 조정회의 참석후 이정보 국장과 허덕행 서기관은 제1차관보와
동행 예정이며(단, 이국장은 귀지 방문시 제1차관보 공식 행사에는 불참), 왕정중
과장은 룩셈부르크에서 파리향발 예정인 바, 이들의 룩셈부르크 도착 일정등 관련
상세사항은 추후 통보하겠음.　　끝.

　　　　　　　　　　　　　　　　　　　　(미주국장　　반기문)

예 고 : 91.12.31 일반

검토필 (1991 . 6 . 30 .)

예고문에의거일반문로
재분류19( ) 서

외 무 부

종 별 : 지급

번 호 : USW-1012

일 시 : 91 0304 1829

수 신 : 장관(미북)

발 신 : 주 미 대사

제 목 : 걸프 사태 조정위

대 WUS-0824

1. 대호, 금 3.4 표제 회의 준비 주관 부서인 재무부에 대표단 명단을 봉보하였음.

2. 동 관계관은 룩셈브르크 정부에도 대표단 명단을 봉보 하여 줄것을 요청하였는바, 조치 바람.

(대사 박동진-국장)

91.12.31 일반

검토필 (1'91. 0.30.)

예고문에 의거 일반문서로
재분류 1991.2.3 서영

미주국	장관	차관	1차보	2차보	청와대	안기부

'91.03.05 09:42
외신 2과 통제관 FE

원 본

외 무 부

종 별 : 지급

번 호 : USW-1024

일 시 : 91 0304 1935

수 신 : 장관(미북,경기,재무부)

발 신 : 주미 대사

제 목 : GULF CRISIS FINANCIAL COORDINATION GROUP MEETING

1. 91.3.4(월) 1400 미 재무성에서 개최된 걸프 사태 재정 지원 공여국 조정위 회의에 당관 허노중 재무관과 유명환 참사관이 참석하였는바, 회의 시작전 걸프 사태에 도와준 우방국에 대한 KUWAIT 대표의 감사의 표시가 있었고, 이어서회의 순서에 따라서 MR.DALLARA 미국무성 국제 담당 차관보의 사회로 진행되었음.

2. 미국측은 배경 설명을 통해 이제 군사적 조치는 끝난 상태이나, 경제적,외교적 조치로서 해결해야할 문제가 남아 있다고 전제하고, 경제적 정치적 안정이 이지역의 평화를 위하여 무척 중요함과 요르단을 포함한 FRONT-LINE 국가에대한 추가 지원약속및 지원 이행이 계속되어야한다는 입장을 표명하였음.

3. 당관 허노중 재무관은 발언을 봉하여 쿠웨이트 정부 수복에 대하여 축하의 뜻을 전하고, 이어서 아국의 재정 지원 약속의 조속 이행을 위한 다각적 노력에도 불구하고, 종전 회의시 자료에 변동이 없음과 계속해서 FRONT-LINE 국가와 양자간 협의를 계속할것임을 천명하였음.

4. MR.DALLARA 는 제출된 자료에 변동사항이 있으면 다음 1 일 LUXEMBURG 회의를 위하여 늦어도 3.7(목)까지는 UPDATED DATA 를 봉보해줄것을 요망하였음.

5. 회의후 미 재무성 부차관보인 MR.J.H. FALL, III 와 만나 미국의 중동 개발 은행 설립 추진 문제에 대하여 문의한바, 미국측은 재무성, 국무성의 협조하에 잘 운영되고 FULF CRISIS FINANCIAL COORDINATION GROUP MEETING 을 활용할계획이며, 새로운 개발 은행 설립을 생각하고 있지 않으며, 다음 LUXEMBURG 회의에서 타국이 설립 문제를 제기하면 각국의 의견을 들어 볼수도 있다는 입장 이었음.

6. 금일 회의 자료 는 별전 (USW(F)-0752) 로 FAX 송부함.

(공사 손명현-국장)

91.12.31 까지

미주국	장관	차관	1차보	2차보	중아국	경제국	청와대	재무부

오버!

ㄹ

GULF CRISIS FINANCIAL COORDINATION GROUP
WORKING COMMITTEE MEETING
March 4, 1991

AGENDA

I.   Introduction by Chair

II. Political Overview

III. Presentation by IMF and World Bank

    A.   Overview of Post-War Financing Requirements

IV. Tour de Table on Commitments and Disbursements

V.   Preparations for the Coordination Group Meeting in
    Luxembourg

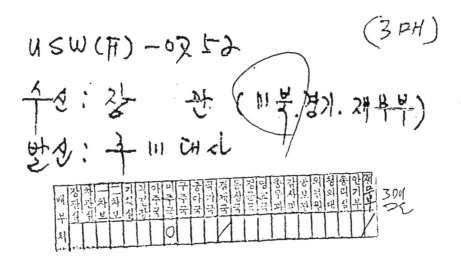

USW(주)-02 52   (3 PH)

수신: 장 관 (비부.경기.재무부)

발신: 주 미 대사

0033

TERMS AND CONDITIONS ON GULF CRISIS FINANCIAL ASSISTANCE FOR EGYPT, TURKEY AND JORDAN

(Millions of U.S. Dollars)

3/1/91

	GRANTS						LOANS					NOT SPEC.	TOTAL
	BOP	Human.	Project	In-Kind	Unspec.	Total	BOP	Project	Co-Fin.	Unspec.	Total		
GCC	3290	0	500	1270	250	5310	0	850	0	0	850	188	6348
Saudi Arabia	1000		500	1160		2660					0	188	2848
Kuwait	1540			110		1650		850			850	0	2500
UAE	750				250	1000					0	0	1000
EC	346	105	0	13	631	1095	67	517	7	288	879	550	2523
EC Budget		78			443	521				239	239	45	805
Bilateral:	346	27	0	13	188	574	67	517	7	49	640	505	1718
Belgium				7		7	26				26		33
Denmark					30	30					0		30
France						0					0	200	200
Germany	346	14				360	13	517			530	300	1190
Ireland				6		6					0		6
Italy					101	101				49	49		150
Luxembourg		4				4					0		4
Netherlands					56	56			7		7		63
Portugal					1	1					0		1
Spain		9				9	28				28		36
U.K.						0					0	5	5
OTHER	0	49	33	0	109	190	0				0	46	236
Australia						0					0	14	14
Austria			9		2	11							11
Finland		15				15							15
Iceland		3				3							3
Norway						0						32	32
Sweden		22	24		7	52							52
Switzerland		9			100	109							109
JAPAN	9				20	29	1636		350		1986	111	2126
CANADA	20	37			9	66							66
KOREA				33		33				50	50		83
TOTAL	3665	190	533	1316	1019	6723	1703	1367	357	318	3765	895	11382
% of Total						59.1					33.1	7.9	

GULF CRISIS FINANCIAL ASSISTANCE *
1990-91 COMMITMENTS AND DISBURSEMENTS

(Millions of U.S. Dollars)

	TOTAL			Egypt			Turkey			Jordan			Humanitarian/Unall. 1/			Other States			GRAND TOTAL		
	Commit.	Disb. to Date	Future Disb.	Commit.	Disb. to Date	Future Disb.	Commit.	Disb. to Date	Future Disb.	Commit.	Disb. to Date	Future Disb.	Commit.	Disb. to Date	Future Disb.	Commit.	Disb. to Date	Future Disb.	Commit.	Disb. to Date	Future Disb.
GCC STATES 2/	6348	3230	3118	3123	2363	760	2995	800	2195	0	0	0	230	67	163	3105	2384	721	9453	5614	3839
Saudi Arabia 3/	2848	1788	1060	1688	1388	300	1160	400	760	0	0	0	0	0	0	1503	1203	300	4351	2991	1360
Kuwait	2500	855	1645	1015	555	460	1485	300	1185	0	0	0	0	0	0	1184	763	421	3684	1618	2066
UAE 3/	1000	587	413	420	420	0	350	100	250	0	0	0	230	67	163	418	418	0	1418	1005	413
EC	2523	1097	1427	1222	398	824	530	277	253	561	360	200	211	62	149	183	0	183	2706	1097	1609
EC Budget	805	624	181	254	207	48	240	193	48	214	173	41	96	51	45	0	0	0	805	624	181
Bilateral:	1719	473	1246	968	191	777	290	84	206	346	187	159	115	11	104	183	0	183	1902	473	1429
Belgium	33	7	26	16	6	10	0	0	7	0	0	9	0	0	0	0	0	0	33	7	26
Denmark	30	10	20	20	4	16	0	0	0	10	6	4	0	0	0	0	0	0	30	10	20
France 4/	200	0	200	50	0	50	30	0	30	20	0	20	100	0	100	30	0	30	230	10	230
Germany	1190	360	830	770	153	617	173	73	100	247	134	113	0	0	0	144	0	144	1334	360	974
Ireland	6	0	6	0	0	0	0	0	0	6	0	6	0	0	0	0	0	0	6	0	6
Italy 5/	150	37	114	75	10	65	49	0	49	27	27	0	1	0	1	9	0	9	159	37	123
Luxembourg	4	1	3	0	0	0	4	1	3	0	0	0	0	0	0	0	0	0	4	1	3
Netherlands	63	45	18	18	18	0	18	11	7	18	11	7	9	5	4	0	0	0	63	45	18
Portugal	36	9	27	12	0	12	11	0	11	14	0	14	0	0	0	0	0	0	36	9	27
Spain	5	5	0	0	0	0	5	5	0	0	0	0	0	0	0	0	0	0	5	5	0
U.K.													3	5	0	0	0	0			
OTHER EUROPE/AUSTRALIA	235	62	172	38	2	35	34	2	32	65	21	44	97	37	60	21	21	0	255	83	172
Australia	14	3	11	1	0	1	0	0	0	0	0	0	13	3	10	0	0	0	14	3	11
Austria	11	1	10	1	0	0	0	0	0	0	0	9	2	3	1	0	0	0	11	3	10
Finland	15	13	2	0	0	0	0	0	0	3	3	0	12	10	2	0	0	0	15	13	2
Iceland	3	2	1	0	0	0	1	1	0	1	1	0	1	0	1	0	0	0	3	2	1
Norway	32	14	18	2	2	0	5	0	5	2	2	0	23	8	15	21	21	0	53	35	18
Sweden	52	21	31	10	2	10	4	0	4	26	16	10	12	5	7	0	0	0	52	21	31
Switzerland	109	9	100	25	0	25	25	0	25	25	0	25	34	9	25	0	0	0	109	9	100
JAPAN	2126	800	1326	629	336	293	720	218	502	717	186	531	60	60	0	0	0	0	2126	800	1326
CANADA	66	17	49	22	0	22	4	0	4	23	0	23	17	17	0	0	0	0	66	17	49
KOREA	83	5	78	23	0	23	20	5	15	15	0	15	25	0	25	17	2	15	100	7	93
(a) TOTAL COMMITMENTS	11381	5211	6170	5058	3099	1959	4303	1302	3002	1381	568	813	640	243	397	3326	2407	919	14707	7618	7089
(b) EST. EFFECT OF GULF CRISIS 6/	13580	13580	–	3375	3375	–	5910	5910	–	4295	4295	–	–	–	–	–	–	–	–	–	–
DIFFERENCE (a minus b)	-2199	-8369	–	1683	-276	–	-1607	-4608	–	-2914	-3727	–	–	–	–	–	–	–	–	–	–

* Does not include contributions to the multinational force. Totals may not equal sum of components due to rounding. 1/ Unallocated among Egypt, Jordan, and Turkey. Includes special humanitarian assistance. 2/ GCC financing for "Other States" is for Syria, Morocco, Lebanon, Somalia, and Djibouti. 3/ Grant aid to Turkey: $1160 million from Saudi Arabia and $250 million from the UAE. 4/ Protocols for $130 million of grant total were signed by end-November. Aid to "Other States" is for Morocco. 5/ Italian aid to "Other States" is for Somalia. 6/ IMF/World Bank estimates (oil at $31/barrel) circulated to Group shown for illustrative purposes. Not intended to represent precise figure of impact.

0035

외 무 부

종 별 : 지 급

번 호 : BBW-0156

일 시 : 91 0304 1730

수 신 : 장 관(미북)

발 신 : 주 벨기에 대사

제 목 : 제1차관보 방문

대:WBB-0089

1. 대호 걸프사태 재정지원 공여국 회의관련, 룩셈부르크 외무부에서는 당관앞 공한을 통해 동 회의가 룩셈부르크 국제 회의장에서 3.11.(월) 13:00 대표단 WORKING LUNCHEON 이후 전체 회의로 하룻동안 진행될 예정임을 통보해 오면서동 회의에 참가하게될 아국 대표의 직, 성명을 통보해 줄것을 요청해 옴.

2. 상기 회의 개시 시간과 부랏셀-룩셈부르크간 거리(약 200KM, 차량으로 2 시간 미만 소요) 감안, 아국 대표단은 3.10.(일) 당지에서 1 박하고 3.11(월) 오전중 차량편 룩셈부르크 향발함이 편리할 것으로 사료되는 바, 이에 대한 지침을회시바람.

3. 3.10.(일) 룩셈부르크 합류예정인 기타 대표단원의 경우도, 동일 부랏셀도착토록 일정 조정함이 좋을 것으로 사료됨.

4. 아국 대표단 명단은 대표에 의거, 룩셈부르크측에 적의 통보할 예정임.끝.

(대사 정우영-국장)

예고:1991. 12.31. 일반

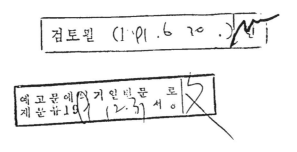

미주국   차관   1차보

PAGE 1

91.03.05   03:16

외신 2과   통제관 CW

0036

분류번호	보존기간

발 신 전 보

번 호 : WBB-0093   910305 1750 AO 종별 : 자 급

WEC -0127   WFK -0150

수 신 : 주 벨 기 에   대사.총영사 (사본 : 주EC 대표부)
주 프랑크푸르트총영사

발 신 : 장 관   (미북)

제 목 : 제1차관보 방문

대 : BBW-0156

연 : WBB-0089

1. 대호 2항 귀건의대로 조치바라며 연호 2항 대신 3.10-3.12간 귀지에
Junior Suite 1실, Single 2실, Twin 1실 2박 예약 바람.

2. 연호 이정빈 제1차관보 일행 귀지 도착 일정이 다음과 같이 변경되었음.

3.9(토)		프랑크푸르트 향발(워싱톤발 LH-419편)
3.10(일)	07:50	프랑크푸르트 도착
	09:05	브랏셀 향발(LH-1714편)
	10:05	브랏셀 도착

끝.

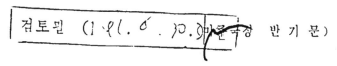
검토필 (1.91. 6. 30.에 준국정 반 기 문)

예 고 : 91.12.31.일반

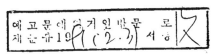
예고문에 의거 기인발문 로
채.. 유 19 (2.7) 서 명

보 안 통 제	88.

앙 고 재	91 년 3 월 5 일	기안자 성명 김승연	과 장 88.	국 장 전결	차 관	장 관

외신과통제

0037

91. 3. 5.

주 미 대 사 관

정 무 과

0038

```
┌─────────────────────────────────────────────┐
│   * 숙소  :  Park Hyatt Hotel(202-789-1234)   │
│        . 이 차관보님 : 915호                  │
│        . 김규현 사무관 : 911호                │
└─────────────────────────────────────────────┘
```

o 3. 5. (화)

        21:16   덜레스 공항 도착 (AA - 036편)

o 3. 6. (수)

        09:30   NSC Sandra Charles 중동담당 보좌관 및 Douglas Paal
                  아시아담당 보좌관 면담

        11:00   국무부 David Mack 근동담당 부차관보 면담

        16:30-   국무부 Robert Kimmitt 정무차관 면담
        16:50

o 3. 7. (목)

        14:30   국방부 Carl Ford 국제안보담당 부차관보 면담

        15:30   국무부 Richard Solomon 동아태 차관보 면담

        18:00   대사님 이임 리셉션 (장소 : Willard Hotel 내
                  Crystal Ballroom)

        20:00   대사님 주최 만찬 (장소 : Hisago)

o 3. 9. (토)

        10:51   운동 (장소 : TPC)

        17:50   덜레스 공항 출발(LH - 419편)

0033

걸프사태 재정지원 공여국 조정위원회 회의, 1990-91. 전6권 (V.4 제5차. Luxemburg, 1991.3.11 : 기본문서)   45
```
```

관리번호	91-65

외 무 부

종 별 :

번 호 : USW-1093   일 시 : 91 0307 1825

수 신 : 장관(미북,중근동,미안,기정)

발 신 : 주 미 대사

제 목 : 제 1차관보 방미

　　당지를 방문중인 이정빈 제 1 차관보는 금 3.7(목) WILLIAM QUANDT 브리킹스 연구소 선임 연구관을 면담하고 걸프 사태 이후 중동지역 정치, 경제 문제에 대하여 의견을 교환한바, 주요 내용 하기 보고함.

　　1. 제 1 차관보는 걸프전의 성공적 종료에 대해 축하하면서, 미 행정부가 BUSH 대통령의 3.6. 대의회 연설등을 통해 걸프전 이후의 대중동 청사진을 밝히고 있으나, CAMP DAVID 회담에 직접 참여하기도 하는등 중동 문제를 오랫동안 연구해온 QUANDT 연구관의 걸프전후 중동 정세에 대한 의견을 문의함.

　　2. 이에 대해 QUANDT 연구관은 걸프전의 성공적 종료로 중동의 정치, 군사적 환경이 많이 개선된것으로 본다고 전제하면서 주요 문제에 대한 본인의 견해를 아래와 같이 밝힘.

　　가. 지역 안보체제 수립

　　O 당분간은 아랍, UN, 미국의 3 자가 모두 참여하는 평화 유지군의 구성이 필요할것으로 봄.. 이경우 아랍군은 주로 이집트 및 시리아군으로 구성될 것이고,UN 평화유지군은 상징적인 역할을 하게 될것이며, 미국은 어제 BUSH 대통령이 밝힌바와 같이 주로 해.공군력에 의한 지원을 하게될것으로 봄.

　　O 중동에서 가장 분쟁 발생 가능성 높은곳이 걸프지역인바, 금번 걸프전을 통해 이락의 군사력이 제거되었고, 이란은 금번 사태를 통해서도 상당한 자제력을 보여주어 전반적으로 중동의 안보 환경이 많이 개선된것으로 봄.

　　O 그러나 이란이 이락내의 시아파를 사주하여 이락내의 분규를 조성하여 역내의 영향력 행사를 기도할 가능성등 분쟁의 요인은 상존함.

　　나. 군비 통제

　　O 중동 평화 유지를 위해 군비 통제가 이루어져야 한다는 의견의 자주 제시되고

미주국 안기부	장관	차관	1차보	2차보	미주국	중아국	청와대	총리실

외신 2과 통제관 CH

0040

있으나, 걸프전을 통해 최신에 무기(PRECISION BOMB, ANTI- MISSILE MISSILE등) 의 효능이 증명되었으므로 역내 국가들이 최신에 무기를 구입하는등 오히려 군비경쟁이 재연될 가능성도 크다고 봄.

다. 이스라엘. 아랍 문제

0 이스라엘의 안보 위협은 이집트, 시리아, 이락 3 국으로 부터의 위협이 가장 심각한 것이었는바, 이집트는 CAMPD DAVID 를 통하여 이스라엘과 화평하였고, 이락은 걸프전을 통해 그 군사력이 제거 되었으므로, 이제 현실적인 군사 위협은 사실상 시리아 1 국에서만 가능한것으로 보임.

0 시리아는 종래 서방과의 대결적 입장에서 탈피하여 서방과의 관계를 증진시키려는 의지를 보이고 있으므로 , 이스라엘이 골란고원 문제, WEST BANK 문제등을 양보하면 시리아와의 관계 개선도 가능하다고 봄.

0 문제는 이스라엘의 현 집권층이 매우 비 타협적 성격이라 이스라엘 로 부터 안보리 결의안 242 에 기초한 타협을 기대하기가 어렵다는 것임.

0 미국이 이스라엘로 하여금 타협을 하도록 영향력을 행사하여야 하는데, 문제는 미국내의 친이스라엘 로비가 아직도 매우 강하다는데 있음.

(QUANDT 연구관은 그 예로 최근 대이스라엘 원조를 둘러싼 미 행정부.이스라엘간의 알력을 듦) 한가지 다행한것은 BUSH 대통령의 높은 인기도를 기반으로 이스라엘 문제에 대해서도 강력한 리더쉽을 발휘할수 있다는 점임.

0 본인의 예상으로는 수주안에 중동평화 및 팔레스타인 문제토의를 위한 다자간 회의 소집이 가능하다고 보나, 이스라엘이 계속 팔레스타인 문제에 비타협적 자세를 고집하게 되면 모처럼만의 기회가 무산될것임.

라. 경제 복구 문제

0 쿠웨이트 재건에 관심이 쏠리는 것이 당연하나, 이란도 서방과의 경협을 강화해 나갈것으로 전망됨.

0 이락은 걸프전 이전에도 이미 1 천억불의 대외부채를 짊어지고 있었고, 대이란, 쿠웨이트 배상금이 1 천억불 이상으로 이야기되고 있는데, 이는 이락의 제일 큰 수입원인 원유 판매대금 약 10 년분에 해당 되므로 이락의 배상금 지불은 사실상 매우 어려운 문제로 보이며, 경제 복구도 자금 부족으로 어려움을 겪을 것임.

0 아랍 개발 은행 설립이 자주 논의되고 있는바, 자금 규모가 수입억불만 되어도 충분히 소기의 효과를 기대할수 있을것으로 생각됨. 걸프전에 약 5 백억이 소요된것과

PAGE 2

0041

비교하면 아랍 개발은행 설립은 크게 어려운일이 아니라고 봄.

3. 제 1 차관보는 상기 설명에 대해 사의를 표하면서 소련이 중동지역문제에 깊이 관여하여 왔음에 비추어 향후 중동정치, 안보, 경제 구조 정착에 있어 소련이 어떤 역할을 해나가리라고 보는지 문의한바, QUANDT 연구관은 언론에서는미국이 소련의 대걸프전 역할에 대해 불만일것으로 보도하기도 하나 <u>미 행정부는 소련의 역할에 대해 대체적으로 만족하고 있는것으로 본다</u>고 하면서, 소련은 개혁 정책을 추진함에 있어 서방과의 협조가 긴요한 상황이므로 중동문제에 있어서도 서방과 협조해 나갈것으로 본다는 낙관적 견해를 표시함.

(대사 박동진- 장관)

예고:91.12.31. 일반

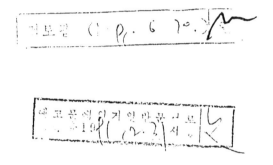

외 무 부

종 별 : 지 급

번 호 : USW-1105

일 시 : 91 0307 1949

수 신 : 장관(미북,중동일, 미안,국연, 아일,아이)

발 신 : 주 미 대사

제 목 : 제1차관보 방미 활동 보고(ANDERSON 부차관보 면담)

당지 방문중인 이정빈 차관보는 금 3.7. 국무부 ANDERSON 동아태 부차관보를 면담하였는바, 동 면담 요지 하기 보고함(미측 RICHARDSON 한국과장, 아측 유명환 참사관 및 김규현, 임성남 서기관 배석)

1. 걸프전 관련 지원 문제

가. 이차관보는 우선 걸프전의 성공적 종료에 대한 축하를 전달하고, 전후 복구과정등에 있어서 한미간의 긴밀한 협조관계가 계속 유지되기를 희망한다고 언급한바, ANDERSON 부차관보는 한국이 그 간 보여준 강력한 정치적 지원과 대미,대전선국 지원에 크게 감사한다고 답변함.

나. 이어서, ANDERSON 부차관보는 의회 및 언론등에서 금번 전쟁관련 각국의 지원 내용 및 약속이행 실적으로 본격적으로 평가할 예정인 점등을 감안, 한국측이 기 천명한 지원 내용은 가능한한 조속히 실행하는것이 바람직할것으로 보인다고 강조함

2. 부쉬 대통령의 아주 순방 문제

가. 이 차관보가 부쉬 대통령의 아주순방 추진동향을 문의한데 대해, ANDERSON 부차관보는 금년가을에 동 순방을 추진할예정이기는 하나 더 이상의 구체적사항은 현재 정해지지 않았다고 (NOT PINNED ANY MORE) 답변함.

나. 또한 ANDERSON 부차관보는 동 순방 관련 한국측의 입장을 잘알고 있다고 하고, 구체적인 진전동향이 있는대로 아측에 이를 통보하겠다고 언급함.

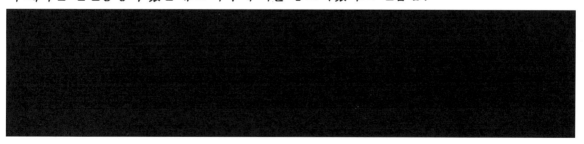

미주국	장관	차관	2차보	아주국	아주국	미주국	중아국	국기국

4. 한-베트남 관계 개선

가. 이차관보는 베트남측이 4 월초 아국개최 예정인 ESCAP 총회 참석등을 계기로 대한국 관계 개선을 강력히 희망하고 있다는 점을 언급하고, 한-베트남 관계 개선 문제에 대한 미측 입장을 타진함.

나. 이에 대해 , ANDERSON 부차관보는 캄푸치아 문제 해결을 위한 대 베트남 교섭이 현재 가장 중요한 시점(CRUNCH POINT) 에 도달했다는 점을 언급하고, 현재와 같이 각 관련국이 협조해 나가는가운데 대 베트남 압력이 계속 가중되어 나간다면 2-3 개월내로 동 교섭이 타결될수 있을것으로 본다고 설명함.

다. 이어서 아측이 단계적 방식의 대 베트남 관계 개선을 추진함으로써 일종의 DUAL-TRACK 정책을 채택하는 방안도 가능하지 않겠느냐고 언급한데 대해, ADNERSON 부차관보는 미 의회 일각에서도 여사한 구상이 제기되고 있고, 베트남측도 구라파 및 호주, 일본과의 교역 및 부자관계 확대에 큰 관심을 갖고 있다고하면서 , 여사한

PAGE 2

0044

대베트남 경제관계 확대는 현 상황 하에서 캄푸치아 문제 관련 교섭 타결의 가능성을 감소 시키는 결과를 초래할 가능성이 큰 만큼, 한국측도 대 베트남 관계 개선을 자제(HOLD OFF)해 줄것을 분명한 어조로 요청함.

(대사 박동진- 장관)

예고:91.12.31. 일반

검토필 (1 9(6 7)

예고문에의거인박문 로 재 는 하 1 (2 3)서

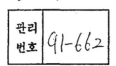

외 무 부

종 별 : 지 급

번 호 : USW-1108   일 시 : 91 0307 2004

수 신 : 장관(친전)사본:경제기획원장관, 국방부 장관, 대통령 외교안보 보좌관

발 신 : 주 미 대사

제 목 : 제1차관보 방미(걸프 사태관련 지원 문제)

　　　당지를 방문중인 이정빈 제 1 차관보는 금 3.7(목)오후 CARL FORD 미국방부국제안보 부차관보를 면담하고 걸프사태와 관련하여 우리의 지원 집행문제에 관하여 협의 하였는바, 주요 내용 하기 보고함(유명환 참사관, 박세헌 주미해군 무관, 김규현 사무관 배석)

　　　1. 한국의 지원에 대한 평가

　　　-제 1 차관보는 먼저 미국이 부쉬 대통령의 영도하에 걸프전쟁을 승리로 마무리 지은데 대해 축하를 표하였음.

　　　-이에 대해 FORD 부차관보는 미국이 우방국의 도움을 절실히 필요로했던 걸프사태에서 한국이 제때에 지원을 아끼지 않았던데 사의를 표하고 미국은 이를 오래 기억할것이라고 언급 하였음.

　　　2. 추가 지원중 1 억 1 천만불의 구성문제

　　　-FORD 부차관보는 한국측이 제안한 현금 6 천만불, 수송 지원 5 천만불의 지원에 이견이 없다고 하였음(다만 상부로 부터 다른 의견이 있으면 알려주겠다고 부언)

　　　3.1.7 억불 상당의 군수물자 지원문제

　　　-FORD 부차관보는 미국정부는 대이락 무력사용 개시이후 미국에 대한 지원은 물자(IN-KIND) 형태로는 받지 않는다는 방침을 확정하였다고 하면서 한국이 지원을 약소한 1.7 억불 상당의 군수물자 지원을 현금으로 전환하여 줄것을 요청하고, 이와 같은 미국 정부의 공식입장을 체니 국방장관 명의 서한을 통하여 아국정부에 곧 통보하게 될것이라고 말함.

　　　-이에 대해 제 1 차관보는 한국이 추가 지원을 고려할 당시 우리로서는 1.1 억불의 현금 및 수송지원이 우리의 경제 여건등을 고려할때 최대의 지원 가능한 규모 였으나, 주한 미군측이 군수물자 지원을 요청해 옴에 따라 당장의 재원 확보 없이 미국에 대한

장관　미국총　참차대　외경기정　통제안보

PAGE 1   91.03.08   15:25

지원을 극대화 하기 위해 한국군이 사용 중이거나 비축용인군수물자 까지도 포함하여 추가지원 규모를 2 억 8 천만불로 책정한 배경을 설명하고 금년들어 1,2 월 2 개월만에 33 억 8500 만불의 무역적자를 기록하는등 경제적으로 매우 어려운 상태에있기 때문에서 동 군수물자를 현금으로 하여 지원하는것은 어려울것으로 본다고 답변하였음.

-이어 동 부차관보는 미국의 요청이 생일 선물 상자를 개봉한후 동 선물을 다른것으로 바꾸어 달라는것과 같아 어색(AWKWARD) 하기는 하지만 한국정부가 군수물자 지원을 현금으로 전환하여 지원하지 못하는 경우 미 행정부로서는 1.1 억불의 현금 및 수송지원만을 미국에 대한 추가지원으로 계상할것이라고 언급하였음.

(동 부차관보는 한국이 1.1 억불만을 지원할 경우 최소한 일본의 1/15 규모는 지원해야 한다는 미정부내 비공식 입장에 비추어 미 의회나 여론으로 부터 한국에 대한 비난이 대두될 가능성이 있음을 시사)

-FORD 부차관보 의 발언에 대해 제 1 차관보는 지원규모 의 다과도 중요하겠으나 그보다는 우방국으로서 적시에 능력 범위내에서 최대한의 지원을 기꺼이 제공해온 우리정부와 국민의 자세가 보다 높이 평가되어야 한다고 강조하고 여하간 미국 정부의 요청 내용을 본국에 보고하겠다고 말함.

4. 영국 전비 지원문제

-제 1 차관보는 영국의 전비 요청내용을 자세히 설명하고 우리정부로서는 걸프전에서의 영국의 기여도등을 감안하여 가능한한 영국에 대해 서도 지원할 방침이라고 전제하고, 그러나 이미 약속한 5 억불 이상의 추가 재원 마련이 현실적으로 거의 불가능한 만큼 대미군사지원 군수물자 1.7 억불중에서 2,000 만불 내지 3,000 만불을 영국에 대한 전비 지원으로 전환하는 방안에 대한 미측의 의견을 구하였음.

-이에 대해 FORD 부차관보는 동 문제는 전적으로 한국정부가 결정할 문제라고 하면서 다만 1.7 억불중 일부를 영국에 대한 지원으로 전환할 경우 미국에 대한 지원은 그만큼 감소되는것이며 따라서 공평하지 않다는 감을 줄수도 있다는점을 유의해 달라고 하였음.

5. 의료 지원단 및 군수송단 활동문제

-제 1 차관보는 걸프지역에서 전쟁이 종결되었으므로 우리의 의료지원단 및공군 수송단의 활동 지속문제에 대한 미측의 의견을 문의하였음.

-이에 대해 FORD 부차관보는 동 문제는 한국정부의 결정사항이나 미국으로서는

전부행위는 정지되었으나 전후 처리 문제를 고려할때 당분간 활동을 계속하는것이 바람직할것으로 본다고 언급하였음.

(동인은 의료지원단의 경우 쿠웨이트내 병원들이 수용능력 부족으로 어려움을 겪고 있는바 한국군 의료단이 쿠웨이트내에서 진료활동을 하는것도 바람직할것이라고 부연함)

-이어 동부차관보는 사실 군 의료단과 수송단의 활동을 당분간 더 계속함이좋겠다는 이유는 차후 미 의회나 여론에서 한국의 지원이 미흡하다는 비판이 대두될 경우 한국 의료단이나 수송단이 현지에서 활동을 계속하고 있는점을 부각시켜 이러한 비판을 어느정도 무마시킬수 있는 효과를 거둘수 있을것으로 기대되기 때문이라고 하였음.

또한 수송단은 현지에 도착한지 불과 얼마되지 않은점도 고려해야 될것이라고 말함.

6. 관찰 및 평가

- 미국은 걸프전이 종결됨에 따라 금번 걸프 전쟁에서 사용한 미군의 장비 및 물자를 가능한한 사우디, 쿠웨이트등 국가에 판매하고자 하는 구상을 갖고 있으며 더욱이 전부행위가 종결된 현시점에서는 미국에 대한 현금이나 수송지원 이외의 현물(IN-KIND) 지원은 불필요하다는 최종 입장을 확정한것으로 감지됨.

-이에 따라 미측으로서는 우리정부의 대미 추가 지원중 1 억 7 천만불 상당의 군수물자를 현금으로 지원해 줄것을 요청하고 있으며 만약 아국의 형편상 현금 지원으로의 전환이 안될 경우 이를 대미지원액수 총액에서 삭제하겠다는 방침을 갖고 있는 것으로 보임.

- 대영국 지원을 위한 전용 문제는 기본적으로 아국 정부가 결정할 문제이지 미국 정부가 이를 수락 또는 거부할 성질이 아니라는관점에서 미측도 명확한 답변을 계속 유보할것으로 보이는바 본부에서 최종 입장 결정후 미측에 통보하는형식을 취하는것이 좋을것으로 사료됨.

(대사 박동진- 장관) 예고: 91.12.31. 일반

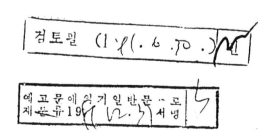

PAGE 3

0048

분류번호	보존기간

발 신 전 보

번 호 : WBB-0100   910308 1957 CT   종별 : _____
                                              WEC -0134
수 신 : 주   벨기에   대사 . 총영사   (사본 : 주 EC 대사)

발 신 : 장 관   (미북)

제 목 : 제5차 걸프사태 재정지원 공여국 조정회의

     연 :

     연호 표제 대표단 일원인 이정보 재무부 경협국장, 왕정중 기획원

행정예산 담당관은 3.10(일) 09:55 SN-952편 귀지 도착 예정이며, 허서기관은

3.8(금) 21:10 SN 220편 도착 예정임.   끝.

                                              (미주국장 반기문)

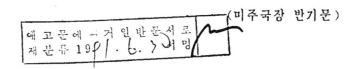

예고문에 의거 일반문서로
재분류 1991. 6. 5   여명

앙 고 재	91 년 3 월 10 일	북 미 과	기안자 성명		과 장	심의관	국 장		차 관	장 관		보 안 통 제	50.
						전결						외신과통제	

                                              0049

외 무 부

종 별 : 지 급

번 호 : BBW-0180

일 시 : 91 0311 1700

수 신 : 장관(미북,사본:주영대사-직송필)

발 신 : 주 벨기에 대사

제 목 : 제1차관보 항공일정 변경

대:WBB-0103

대호, 이정빈 차관보 일행(4 명: 차관보, 이정보국장, 허덕행, 김규현)의 3.12 부랏셀-런던구간 항공편은, 이차관보의 당지 일정(3.12. ERIC SUY 외무장관고문과의 오찬)으로 인해 16:20 당지발,16:25 런던착(히드로) BA 397 편으로 결정, 관련 조치 필하였음.

(대사 정우영-국장)

예고:91.12.31 일반

검 토 필 (1991.6.30)

예고문에의거일반문서로
재분류 19 (. .) 서명

미주국

PAGE 1

Mr. Rhee Soo Hyu
Vice Minister of Finance
Ministry of Finance

Mr. Yoo Chong Ha
Vice Minister of Foreign Affairs
Ministry of Foreign Affairs

Dear Colleague:

    You will recall that we agreed during the last meeting of
the Gulf Crisis Financial Coordination Group on February 5 in
Washington to hold our next meeting some time around
mid-March. Since then, the Luxembourg authorities have offered
to host the March meeting in their capacity as current
President of the European Council, and have suggested a date of
March 11.

    As was the case with our November 5 meeting in Rome, our
hosts will issue the formal invitations and have kindly agreed
to make all logistical arrangements. We have attached an
agenda for the meeting and will separately distribute
background materials for your use. We look forward to seeing
you ·in Luxembourg.

Sincerely,

David C. Mulford   Robert M. Kimmitt
Undersecretary of the   Undersecretary of
Treasury for   State for
International Affairs   Political Affairs

Attachment: as stated

0051

O   THE UNITED STATES VIEWS THE MARCH 11 MEETING OF THE GULF
CRISIS FINANCIAL COORDINATION GROUP AS ANOTHER IMPORTANT
OPPORTUNITY TO DEMONSTRATE OUR CONTINUING SOLIDARITY IN
CONFRONTING IRAQ AND TO MOBILIZE BROAD-BASED AND EFFECTIVE
SHARING OF THE ACCOMPANYING RESPONSIBILITIES.

O   IT IS CRUCIAL THAT WE CONTINUE TO SUPPORT THOSE COUNTRIES
WHICH ARE BEARING THE ECONOMIC BRUNT OF THE CRISIS. THEIR
NEEDS ARE REAL AND IMMEDIATE AND REQUIRE PROMPT
DISBURSEMENT OF ECONOMIC ASSISTANCE. EXPEDITED
DISBURSEMENT OF EXISTING COMMITMENTS IS NECESSARY AND
SHOULD BE ACCOMPANIED BY NEW COMMITMENTS.

O   WE WOULD HOPE YOUR REPRESENTATIVES WILL COME TO THE MEETING
PREPARED TO ANNOUNCE THAT SUBSTANTIAL PROGRESS HAS BEEN
MADE IN EACH OF THESE AREAS.

O   THE IMPORTANCE THAT THE USG ATTACHES TO THE MEETING IS
ATTESTED TO BY THE LEVEL OF OUR OWN REPRESENTATION -- AT
THE LEVEL OF UNDER SECRETARY. WE HOPE THAT YOUR GOVERNMENT
WILL BE REPRESENTED BY OFFICIALS OF COMPARABLE RANK.

0052

MEETING OF THE GULF CRISIS FINANCIAL COORDINATION GROUP
Luxembourg
March 11, 1991

AGENDA

I.   Welcoming remarks by hosts

II.   Introduction by chair

III.   Political overview

IV.   Presentation by IMF and World Bank

V.   Commitments and disbursements

--   Report of working committee on commitments and
       disbursements

--   Additional commitments for 1991

--   Tour de table on commitments, disbursements, and terms
       and conditions

VI.   Other business and concluding remarks by chair

VII.   Closing remarks by hosts

0053

MEETING OF THE
GULF CRISIS FINANCIAL COORDINATION GROUP

Luxembourg; March 11, 1991

INFORMAL PRESS GUIDANCE

At the invitation of the Government of Luxembourg, in its
capacity as European Council President, the Gulf Crisis Financial
Coordination Group held its fifth meeting in Luxembourg on March
11, 1991, under U.S. chairmanship. Participants included senior
officials from 26 countries, the European Commission, and the
Gulf Cooperation Council. Representatives from the International
Monetary Fund and the World Bank also attended.

Participants welcomed the liberation of Kuwait by coalition
forces and look forward to the cessation of hostilities after
Iraq's full implementation of all relevant U.N. resolutions.
Nonetheless, they noted that a number of countries continue to be
seriously affected by economic disruptions arising directly from
the crisis and reiterated their commitment to provide exceptional
economic assistance to address these disruptions.

In this connection, participants confirmed $15.7 billion in
financing commitments for the August 1990 – December 1991 period
for Egypt, Turkey and Jordan, and numerous other countries
contributing to the international coalition. Disbursement of
approximately $8.3 billion has occurred to date, the bulk of
which has been provided in grant form. Substantial additional
disbursements will be made in the coming months.

The Group's contributions on the economic front have been an
important element in the coalition strategy to achieve a
satisfactory resolution to the crisis. Participants agreed that
the Group would continue its work to address financing needs.
Consideration will also be given to means of fostering longer
term development and growth in the region, working closely with
existing regional and multilateral institutions.

0054

원 본

외 무 부

종   별 : 지 급

번   호 : BBW-0182   일   시 : 91 0312 1000

수   신 : 장관(미북,중동2,사본:경제기획원장관,재무부장관,주미대사-중계필)

발   신 : 주 벨기에 대사

제   목 : 걸프사태 재정공여국 조정위 제 5차회의

표제 회의는 예정대로 3.11(월)13:00-18:00 간 룩셈부르크 시내 유럽 센타 회의실에서 26 개 공여국 대표 및 EC, GCC, IMF, 세계은행 대표의 참석하에 종전과같이 미국대표의 사회(MULFORD 재무차관, KIMMITT 국무차관의 공동주재)로 개최되었음. 아국에서는 이정빈 제 1 차관보를 단장으로 이정보 재무부 경협국장, 유명환 주미 대사관 참사관, 왕정중 경기원 행정예산 과장등이 참석했는바, 동 회의 결과를 요지 아래와같이 보고함.

1. 업무 오찬 형식으로 개최된 회의에서 MULFORD 재무차관 및 KIMMITT 국무차관은 하기 요지의 발언을 하였음.

가. MULFORD 차관

0 걸프사태를 성공적으로 해결하게된데에는 군사적, 외교적, 경제적 세가지뒷바침이 주효했기 때문이며 재정공여국 회의는 경제적 측면에서 중요한 역할을 수행했는바 총 148 억불의 공여약속액중 약 77 억불이 이미 집행됨.(회의 종료후 발표된 기자브리핑 자료는 91.3.8 현재 총 157 억불의 약속액중 약 83 억불이 집행된것으로 집계됨)

0 걸프사태의 해결을 위한 수단으로 조정위 회의가 지금까지 추진되어왔으나 분쟁이 종결된 이후에는 전후복구와 평화정착이라는 새로운 사태에 대처할수 있도록 조정위의 기능이 재검토되어야 할것임.

0 전후 중동질서의 대폭적 개편과 더불어 걸프지원 조정위는 복잡한 정치, 경제적 상황에 융통성있게 효율적으로 적응할수 있어야 하지만 이를 제도화, 기구화 해야할 필요성은 없다고 봄.

나. KIMMITT 차관

0 공여국 조정위는 승전으로 확보된 걸프지역에서의 평화를 항구적으로

미주국 재무부	장관	차관	1차보	2차보	중아국	청와대	안기부	경기원

정착하기위한 임무를 앞으로도 당분간 계속 수행해야 될것임.

0 중동에서 항구적 안보장치를 구축하기 위해서는 군사적 장치만으로는 불가능하며, 평화 정착을위한 경제적, 정치적 장치가 필요한바, 필요시 재정 지원 대상국은 북부아프리카 마그레브 지역까지 확대되어야 할것임.

0 현 GCC 기구를중심으로 역외국가까지 포함된 다자적 공동노력으로 중동지역의 평화보장을 위해 현 조정위의 정치, 경제적 기능을 더욱 강화해야 함.

2. 이어 IMF, 세계은행 대표는 전선 3 개국의 경제 상황을 설명하고 전후 긴급복구, 역내 정치 안정을위한 경제개발문제, 원조자금의 효율적 사용문제등에대한 분석 보고를 했으며, 동 지역 국가의 경제개발을 위한 보다 장기적인 계획을 문서로 작성, 조정위에 제출하기로함.

3. 이어서 각국대표로부터 자국의 집행 실적에대한 발표가 있었으며, 이정빈 제 1 차관보는 하기와같이 아국입장을 설명했음.

0 한국의 총 지원액은 115 백만불이며, 현재까지 EDCF 차관 1,000 만불의 대 요르단 공여 및 전선국에대한 물자지원등으로 약 2,000 만불이 집행되었으나 조만간 집행될 예정임. 또한 잔여분에대한 집행도 수원국가와 긴밀히 협의 조속히 추진할것임.

0 원조의 조속한 집행을위해 정부는 두번째의 고위대표단을 이집트, 요르단에 2.24-3.9 간 파견하였으며 수원국들과 잔여 미집행액의 신속, 효과적인 집행방안에 대해 진지하게 토의를 한바있음.

0 조기집행을 위해 직업훈련원 건립, 의료기자재 공급, EDCF 차관 공여조건완화등 대책을 강구하고 있음.

0 현 조정위의 기능이 효율적인 재정지원을 위한 발전적인 장치로 전환되길희망함.

이하 BBW-0183 으로 계속됨.

PAGE 2

기2(30) | 원 본 |

외 무 부

종 별 : 지 급

번 호 : BBW-0183   일 시 : 91 0312 1000

수 신 : 장관(<u>미북</u>,중동2,사본:경제기획원장관,재무부장관,주미대사-중계필)

발 신 : 주 벨기에 대사

제 목 : BBW-0182 의 계속분

4. O MULFORD 차관은 일본 및 EC 의 원조 집행이 가속화된데 만족을 표명하고 지원 사업의 추진을위한 <u>공여 조건완화 필요성을 강조했으며</u>, GCC 대표는 <u>총 150 억불의</u> <u>자금을 동원</u> 향후 10 년간 아랍권 개발을위한 <u>걸프계획을 실시할 예정임을 발표한바</u> 이는 걸프조정위의 기능을 금후에도 계속 유지 GCC 를 중심으로한 역내 경제개발, 협력 사업추진을 측면 지원케할 의사를 표명한것임.

O 회의 참석자들은 중동지역 평화정착을위한 군사적 장치로서 아랍 평화유지군 창설과 GCC 를 중심으로한 경제협력을 통하여 중동지역내 평화정착을 위한 정치적, 경제적 결속을 강화해야한다는 필요성에 대해서는 공감을 표시함.

O 또한 주요 공여국인 <u>일본 및 독일은 미국주도의 조정위 기능강화에는 소극적인</u> <u>자세를 보였으며</u> 특히 일본은 공여국 통계자료에 자국만이 별도로 분류(여타국의 경우는 EC, GCC, 기타국으로 분류) 된것을 언론보도시에는 <u>기타국으로 분류하여</u> 발표하도록 요청하는등 회의진행 방법 및 자료작성등에 있어 민감한 반응을 보였음.

O 한편 동 조정위가 전후에도 계속 능동적으로 기능하기 위해서는 앞으로 더욱 IMF 등 <u>기존 국제기구의 기능 활용등 운영방식의 개선이 시급하다</u>는 데 대해서도 대체로 <u>의견이 모아졌음.</u>

5. 차기회의 장소관련 GCC 대표는 조정위 운영 및 역내 경제개발에 있어 GCC 가 주도적 역할을 해야한다는 취지에서 차기 회의를 GCC 역내에서 개최할것을제안했으며 이에따라 차기회의는 <u>5 월중순경 쿠웨이트 또는 주변 GCC 국가에서개최될것으로 보임.</u>

6. 평가 및 건의

O 금번 재정공여국 조정위는 전쟁종식후 처음열린 회의로서 각국이 약속한 원조액의 조속한 집행을 촉구하기 위한것뿐만 아니라 걸프역내 국가의 항구적 경제 발전이 지역 평화유지에 긴요하다는 취지에서 단기적 원조를 포함, 장기적인 경제원조

미주국 재무부	장관	차관	1차보	2차보	중아국	청와대	안기부	경기원

계획이 필요하다는 분위기가 크게나타났으며 이를위해서는 GCC 국가를 중심으로한 역내 국가의 이니시아티브가 중요하다는데 의견의 일치를 보이고 있음.

　0 또한 금후 조정국 회의의 성격과 관련 이를 제도화하는것 보다는 회의운영상 유연성을 확보하기위해 앞으로 1-2 회 정도는 현재와 같은 형태로 지속할것으로 보임.

　0 회의시 발표된 집행실적표에 의하면 아국의 원조 집행실적이 여타 국가에비해 가장 저조한것으로 나타났으며, 한편 수원국의 국내사정을 이유로 집행 실적이 저조하다는 설명에는 설득력이 없으며 따라서 차기 회의시까지는 아국도 집행 실적을 어느정도의 수준까지는 높여야 할것으로 사료됨. 끝.

　　(대사 정우영-장관)

　　예고:91.12.31 까지

외 무 부

종 별 :

번 호 : BBW-0185   일   시 : 91 0312 1700

수 신 : 장관(미북)

발 신 : 주 벨기에 대사

제 목 : 제 1차관보 방문

제 1 차관보 일행은 예정대로 당지 방문 일정을 마치고 귀국차 금 3.12(화)16:20 런던 향발함. 끝.

(대사정우영-국장)

미주국

대 언론 설명 자료

91. 3. 13.

1. 출장개요

o 본인은 지난 3.5. (화) 부터 3.9(토) 간 미국 워싱톤을 방문하여 미 행정부 인사들과 걸프사태 이후의 중동질서개편 구상등에 관해 의견을 교환하였음.

o 미국방문을 마친후 3. 11 (화) 룩셈부르크에서 개최된 걸프사태 재정 지원 공여국 조정 위원회 제 5차 회의에 정식대표로 참석 하여 아국의 전선국가및 주변국가등에 대한 지원 내용을 발표하였음.

2. 방미시 주요 협의 내용

o 워싱톤 방문시 면담인사는 Karl Jackson 부통령 안보보좌관, Douglas Paal NSC 아시아담당 선임 보좌관 비경자, Sandra Charles NSC 중근동담당 보좌관, David Mack 국무부 중근동 부차관보, Desaix Anderson 국무부 동아태 부차관보, 그리고 Carl Ford 국방부 국제안보 부차관보 등이 있었으며 이외는 별도로 중동문제전문가인 William Quandt 브루킹스 연구소 선임 연구원도 만나보았음.

0060

o 방미시 이들 미정부 인사들과 걸프사태 이후
중동에서의 질서 개편 문제, 경제 복구 문제등에
의견을 교환하고 한미 양국의 공동 참여 방안에
관해서도 협의를 바랐음.
(중동문제 이외의 사항에 대한 협의는 없었음을 강조함)

o 한편, 미 정부 인사들은 한걸 같이 걸프사태의
조속한 해결을 위해 우리정부와 국민이 보내준 지원과
협조에 사의를 표하고 향후 중동지역에서
항구적인 평화와 안정을 정착시키는 과정에
우리가 적극적으로 참여해 줄 것을 기대하였음.

3. 걸프사태 재정지원 공여국 조정위원회 제5차회의 참석결과

o 금번 회의는 걸프사태가 종료된후 처음
개최된 회의로서 EC 의장국인 룩셈북르크 가
동회의를 초치하여 3.11(화) 동국의 유럽센타
(European Center)에서 미국, 영국, 프랑스, 독일, 일본등
아국을 비롯하여
26개국 대표와 EC, GCC, IMF 및 IBRD 의
대표들이 참석한 가운데 개최되었음.

o 합의회의에서 각각 대표들은 여구동성으로

후웨이트가 다국적군의 희생과 노력으로 여사호복귀
~~그~~ 해방원 데 대해 환영을 표하고

걸프사태가 국제적인 노력으로 성공적인
마무리를 짓게 된 데는 연합군의 진선국가등
주변국가에 대한 경제지원이 커다란 기여를 했다는
점을 ~~평가~~ 평가 하였음.

o 합의회의에서는 1990.8 ~1991.12.12 총 157억불의
진선국가에 대한 지원약속액중 3.11. 현재 약
83억불상당이 집행되었음을 확인하고
중동지역의 경제복구 촉진을 위하여 각국이 기 약속한
지원을 보다 신속히 집행할 필요가 있다는데
의견이 모아졌음.

o 금반 걸프사태가 성공적으로 종결된 만큼
~~전쟁 지원 능력급 회의는~~ 진선국가등 국면피해경제에
대한 보다 장기적인 지원방안등에 관하여서도
IMF, LBRD등 기존의 국제기구와 보다 긴밀히
협의하에 논의를 해나갈 필요가 있다는 점을
확인하였음.

o ~~다음 조정위 회의 개최시기는 상호 협의하에~~

0062

2. 英文

Thank you, Mr. Chairman, for giving me the floor.

I would like to express my sincere appreciation to the Government of
Luxemburg for hosting the Fifth Meeting of the Gulf Crisis Financial
Coordination Group in this beautiful city of Luxemburg.

It is with great sense of relief that the Government and people of the
Republic of Korea welcome the victory of the coalition forces in the Gulf
War and the onset of a peace process through the adoption of the peace
resolution by the U.N. Security Council. I wish to extend once again our
deep appreciation to ~~the peoples and the valiant soldiers of~~ the coalition
forces/ ~~countries~~ for their devout efforts for international justice and the
implementation of the U.N. Security Council resolutions. *And Taking*
this opportunity, I would like to congratulate the
Kuwaiti representatives on their liberation ~~of Kuwait~~

Let me first brief you on the disbursement status of Korea's financial
support to the front-line states, *that is $115 million*
pledge for 1990-91.
$115 million

To expedite the disbursement of the financial support Korea has

promised to render to the front-line states, a second Government delegation visited

Egypt and Jordan from Feb. 24 to March 9. The delegation had earnest

discussions with those governments on the ways to make effective and speedy

disbursement of Korea's outstanding pledge, ~~for the year 1990, which is~~ =1991

~~40 million U.S. dollars in EDCF(Economic Development Cooperation Fund) and~~ 60 to 115 million U.S. dollars

~~20 million dollars in kind~~. Among the ways discussed were establishment

of vocational training centers, supply of medical equipments, and easing

the terms and conditions of EDCF loan. ~~Also being discussed are ways to~~ 추가 복지

~~expedite the disbursement of the 25 million U.S. dollars pledged as financial~~

~~support to the front-line states for 1991.~~

" Economic Development and Cooperation Fund "

Chairman Mulford, Chairman Kimmitt, Distinguished Delegates,

I sincerely hope that our Contribution to the front-line states will

be helpful to their efforts to recover from the economic losses. Now that

the War is over, it is my view that the time has come for us to examine

the possibility of modifying the Meetings of this Coordination Group so

that they could meet the task of making effective support to the front-line

states and of mapping out a balanced long-term plan to assist the economic

0064

At present, ~~$3~~ about 20 million U.S. dollars out of 115 million U.S. dollars has been ~~disbursed~~ or about to be disbursed. And we expect the rest of our commitment will soon be disbursed. ~~as~~ I wish to confirm that ~~the Republic of~~ Korean Government is ready to disburse ~~if and when~~ as soon as recipient countries come up with items and projects they want in close consultation with the recipient countries.

③

rehabilitation of the entire Middle East region. When the current series of Meetings, which already is a good forum of debate and exchange of information, develops into a more efficient and suitable apparatus with active participation of Member Countries, Korea will be more than willing to join in their efforts.

Now let me mention the measures the Korean Government has taken for the Kuwaiti people after the liberation.

Considering the urgent need of medical service in Kuwait, we have decided, after consultation with the Governments of Saudi Arabia and the United States, to relocate the Korean Military Medical Supporting Group, now in service in Saudi Arabia, to Kuwait to provide medical support there.

To help clear away the massive discharge of Kuwaiti crude oil by Iraq and prevent further contamination of the Gulf, we have decided to provide Saudi Arabia, Bahrain and Qatar with equipments and materials to fight maritime contamination. We also decided to provide emergency supplies of clothing and the like to Kuwait.

Taking this opportunity, I wish to reiterate the earnest wish of the Government and people of the Republic of Korea that the scars of the War will be healed and peace and order restored in the Gulf region in the earliest possible future. Our special concern and heartfelt consolation is extended to the people of Kuwait, who underwent all kinds of sufferings before and during the War. We sincerely hope that they soon rehabilitate their war-torn economy and lead secure and prosperous life as before.

Korea will not spare any effort within its capacity to help the maintenance of peace and order and the post-war economic reconstruction of the Gulf region.

Thank you.

0067

기조 발언

(손글씨: 걸프지역에 대한 노동력 수출 아시아3가에 대한 경제지원)

1. 국 문

발언권을 주신 의장께 감사드립니다.

우선 아름다운 룩셈부르크시에서 금번 제5차 조정위 회의를 주최한 룩셈부르크 정부의 노고에 치하의 말씀을 드립니다.

대한민국 정부와 국민은, 걸프전이 다국적군의 최종 승리와 유엔 안보리의 평화 결의안 채택으로 걸프지역에 평화정착 과정이 개시된 것을 매우 다행스럽게 생각하며 이를 충심으로 환영하는 바입니다.

본인은 국제정의와 UN 결의의 이행을 위해 온갖 노력과 희생을 아끼지 않은 연합국 여러나라 국민들과 특히 연합국 장병들의 노고에 대한 대한민국 정부의 깊은 감사의 뜻을 다시한번 전하고자 합니다.

먼저 걸프사태로 인한 주변 피해국들에 대한 한국의 지원 집행상황을 보고 드리겠읍니다.

대한민국 정부는 전선국가들에 지원키로한 약속 금액의 집행 가속화를 위해 지난 2월24일부터 3월9일까지 한국 정부의 고위실무 대표단이 이집트, 요르단등 전선국을 순방하였읍니다. 동 대표단은 이들 국가들과 90년도분 잔여 집행액의

0068

효과적이고 신속한 지원방법에 대해 진지한 토의를 가졌으며, 이러한 협의결과를 토대로 대외협력기금(EDCF) 4,000만불 지원과 생필품 등 물자지원을 위한 3,900만불의 조기 집행을 위한 구체적 절차를 가속화 해 나갈수 있을 것으로 전망됩니다. 이러한 방법에는 직업훈련소 설립, 의료 기자재 공급, EDCF 자금의 조건 완화등도 포함되어 있읍니다. 또한 91년도 주변국 경제 지원액으로 약속한 2,500만불의 조기 집행계획도 동시에 협의중입니다.

펄포드 의장, 키미트 의장, 그리고 우방국 대표 여러분 !

본인은 이러한 한국 정부의 지원이 이들 국가의 경제적 피해를 극복하는 데 다소 도움이 되기를 희망하면서 걸프전 종전에 따라 주변 피해국에 대한 보다 효과적인 지원과 장기적으로 중동지역 전체의 경제부흥과 균형있는 경제발전을 위해 지난 5차에 걸친 조정위회의를 보다 발전적인 장치로 전환하는 방안을 검토할 시점이 도래했음을 지적코자 합니다.

이 회의가 단순한 정보 교환과 토론장으로서의 성격에서 한걸음 더 나아가 여러 관련국들의 주도에 따라 실효적인 재정지원 장치로 발전될 경우 한국 정부도 이에 적극 참여할 예정입니다.

아울러 쿠웨이트 해방직후 쿠웨이트 국민들을 위해 한국 정부가 취한 몇가지 조치를 말씀드리고자 합니다.

0069

한국 정부는 사우디와 미국 정부와 협의하여 쿠웨이트 탈환직후 쿠웨이트내
긴급 의료수요를 감안, 현재 사우디에서 활동중인 한국군 의료지원단을
쿠웨이트로 이동시켜 쿠웨이트 주민들에 대한 의료지원 활동을 개시키로
하였습니다.

또한 이라크측의 쿠웨이트 원유 방류로 인한 걸프지역 해상 오염방지를 지원키
위해 사우디, 바레인, 카타르등에 필요한 물자를 지원키로 하였으며, 쿠웨이트에
대해 의류등 긴급 물자를 지원키로 결정하였습니다.

이 기회를 빌어 본인은 걸프전이 종료함에 따라 걸프지역에 하루속히 전쟁의
상처가 치유되고 평화와 안정이 회복되기를 바라며, 특히 불의의 침략을 받아
한때 나라를 잃고 온갖 고초를 겪어온 쿠웨이트 국민들이 조속히 나라를 재건
하여 안정된 생활을 되찾게 되기를 기원합니다.

또한 대한민국 정부는 종전후 걸프지역의 평화와 질서유지 및 경제재건을 위해
가능한 지원을 아끼지 않을 것임을 다짐하는 바입니다.

감사합니다. 의장

0070

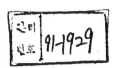

외무부 제1차관보 출장결과 보고서

(91. 3. 5 ~ 3. 13)

┌──────── 출 장 목 적 ────────┐

- 걸프전후 중동질서 개편 및 경제 복구에 대한
  미측 구상 파악

- 룩셈부르크 개최 걸프사태 재정지원국 조정회의
  참석

└────────────────────────┘

91. 3. 14.

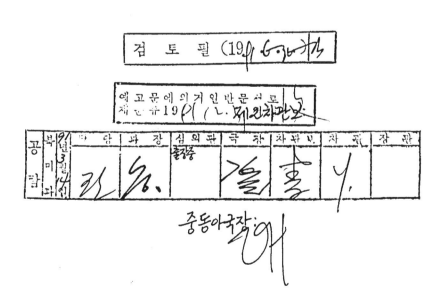

0071

- 목 차 -

0072

I. 출장 개요

1. 출장 기간 : 91. 3. 5 (화) ~ 3. 13 (수)

2. 출장 목적 :

   - 걸프사태 이후 미국의 중동질서 재편 및 경제복구계획 파악

   - 걸프사태 재정지원 공여국 조정위 제5차회의 참석

   - 외무장관 방미문제등 협의

3. 출 장 자 :

   가. 미 국 (91. 3. 5-9) : 이정빈 외무부 제1차관보
                          김규현 외무부 북미과 사무관

   나. 룩셈부르크 (3. 11. 걸프사태 재정지원 공여국 조정위원회 제5차 회의참석)

      - 단 장 : 이정빈 제1차관보

      - 단 원 : 이정보 재무부 경제협력국장
                유명환 주미대사관 참사관
                왕정중 경기원 행정예산과장
                허덕행 외무부 중동과 서기관
                김규현 외무부 북미과 사무관

0073

4. 주요 일정

3.5 (화)	15:00	서울 출발
	08:00	L.A. 도착
	21:16	워싱톤 D.C. 도착
3.6 (수)	09:30	Sandra Charles NSC 중근동 담당 보좌관, Karl Jackson 퀘일 부통령 안보보좌관, Duglas Paal NSC 아시아 담당 보좌관 면담
	11:00	David Mack 국무부 중근동 부차관보 면담
3.7 (목)	10:30	William Quandt 브루킹스 선임 연구원 면담
	14:30	Carl Ford 국방부 국제안보 부차관보 면담
	15:30	Desaix Anderson 국무부 동아.태 부차관보 면담
3.9 (토)	17:50	워싱톤 D.C. 출발
3.10 (일)	10:05	브랏셀(벨기에) 도착
3.11 (월)	13:00 -18:10	룩셈부르크 조정위원회 회의참석
3.12 (화)	12:30	오찬(Eric Suy 벨기에 외무성 고문)
3.13 (수)	17:40	서울 도착

2

5. 주요 면담인사

   가. 미 국

   (백악관) . Karl Jackson   퀘일 부통령 안보보좌관
            . Charles Sandra   NSC 중근동 보좌관
            . Douglas Paal   NSC 아시아 보좌관

   (국무부) . Desaix Anderson   동아. 태 부차관보
            . David Mack   중근동 부차관보

   (국방부) . Carl Ford   국제안보 부차관보

   (학 계) . William Quandt   Brookings 연구소 중근동선임연구원

   나. 벨 기 에

            Eric Suy   벨기에 외무성 고문

3

0075

Ⅱ. 주요 협의내용

1. 걸프전 전후 처리문제 및 아국의 지원문제

  가. Sandra Charles 미 NSC 중근동 보좌관 면담

   1) 이정빈 차관보는 미국 주도하의 다국적 노력으로 인해 금번 걸프
      전쟁이 성공적으로 종료된 것을 축하하고, 아측으로서도 여사한
      다국적 노력에 동참할 수 있었던 것을 기쁘게 생각하고 있다고
      언급함.

   2) Sandra Charles 보좌관은 다국적 협력이 가능했기 때문에 금번
      전쟁을 승리로 이끌수 있었다고 설명하고, 아측의 지원에 대해
      사의를 표명하고 전후 처리문제에 대해 다음과 같이 언급함.

    가) 전후 처리문제의 대강

     o 기본적으로 전후 처리문제는 현재의 정전 상태를 공식화하는
       문제 및 걸프지역 전후 질서 재편문제의 두가지로 대별됨.
       전쟁을 승리로 이끄는 일은 끝났지만 앞으로 외교적으로
       중동지역에 평화를 정착시키는 일이 더욱 어려운 일임.

    나) 정전상태의 공식화 문제

     o 우선, 이라크측이 억류하고 있는 다국적군 포로 및 쿠웨이트
       민간인들이 석방되어야 함. 다국적군측도 이라크군 포로를
       송환하여야 하는 입장인 바, 수송수단을 마련해야 하는 등
       이 문제 자체만도 매우 복잡한 사안임.

4

o 이라크의 쿠웨이트 합병선언은 당초 이라크 국회에 대해 채택된 반면, 합병 무효선언은 이라크 혁명 평의회(RCC)에 의해 채택 되었는 바, 이라크측의 여사한 무효조치에 법적하자가 없는지를 현재 검토중임.

o 이라크측이 대쿠웨이트 배상 용의 및 이라크로 약탈해 간 쿠웨이트 재산의 반환 용의를 표명하는등 정전상태를 공식화 하기 위해 적극적인 자세를 보이고 있는 바, 이라크측은 정전 상태의 조기 공식화를 통해 대이라크 경제제재조치가 가능한한 신속히 해제되기를 희망하고 있는 것으로 보임. 현재 일부 국가들이 쿠웨이트 재산 동결 조치등을 해제하고 있기는 하나, 미측으로서는 가까운 장래에 대이라크 경제제재조치를 해제할 의사가 없음.

o 정전 공식화의 마무리 단계가 되면, 다국적군이 이라크 남부로 부터 철수하는 동시에 정전 협정이 서명될 것으로 보며, 그간 미결 상태였던 쿠웨이트와 이라크간의 국경선도 분명히 확정될 것으로 봄. 또한 유엔평화 유지군도 창설되어 쿠웨이트-이라크 국경지대에 주둔할 것인 바, 구성을 어떻게 할 것이며 구체적 으로 어디에 배치할지 등이 논의되어야 함.

다) 걸프지역 전후 질서재편 문제

o 안보 문제

- 다국적군이 금명간 철수 예정인 점을 감안할 때, 쿠웨이트를 포함하는 걸프역내의 안전보장 장치를 가능한한 빠른 시일 내에 수립하는 것이 긴요함.

- 미측으로서는 군사장비의 쿠웨이트내 계속 배치, 해군력의 걸프역내 계속 주둔 및 평시 공군훈련 강화등을 통해 미국과 걸프제국간에 일정수준의 군사훈련(constant level of military exercise)을 지속적으로 유지할 생각이기는 하나 지상군을 주둔시킬 계획은 없음.(지상군 주둔은 주둔국내 일부 세력의 반대를 유발함으로써 오히려 destabilizing factor로 작용할 가능성이 크기 때문임.)

- 쿠웨이트와는 이란-이라크 전쟁시 쿠웨이트 국적선 호위등을 통해 사실상의 안보협력 관계를 발전시켜 왔으며, 사우디, 바레인과도 상호 방위조약을 체결하고 있지는 않으나 오랫동안 안보 협력관계를 유지해 왔음. 특히, 오만에서는 미 공군이 그동안 각종 훈련을 실시해 왔는 바, 앞으로는 온건 아랍국들이 보다 더 적극적으로 미국 주도의 각종 합동 군사훈련에 참여할 것으로 봄.

o 정치 문제

- 금번 베이커 국무장관 중동 순방시 중동지역 peace process 추진을 위한 방안에 관해 관련제국의 견해를 청취 예정인 바, 구체적으로는 금번 걸프사태를 계기로 구축되기 시작한 이스라엘과 온건 아랍국간의 상호신뢰와 우호관계를 바탕으로 신뢰구축조치(CBM)를 실시하는 방안 및 이스라엘과 팔레스타인간의 대화를 재개시키는 방안등 2원적 차원에서의 평화구축 방안을 추진할 예정임.

- 한편, 금번 걸프사태 기간중 PLO측은 친이라크 입장을 고수함으로써 온건 아랍국으로 부터의 신뢰도가 실추된 (discredited) 상황임. 종전후 무바락 대통령의 연설에서 PLO에 대한 언급이 전혀 없는 것이 이를 반영하고 있음.

0078

o 경제 문제

  - 이라크가 쿠웨이트 침공을 정당화 하기 위해 아랍권내
    빈부국간 격차해소를 내세운 점등을 감안, 금번 베이커
    국무장관 중동 순방시 동 문제에 대해서도 협의 예정임.
    주변국에 대한 경제원조는 계속되어야 할 것으로 보며
    통상증진, 투자도 적극 추진되기를 기대함.

  - 다만 과거 아랍권내 국가간 원조가 현금지원 위주로
    이루어짐으로써 별다른 경제개발 효과를 거두지 못했던
    점을 고려, 앞으로는 경제개발 프로젝트와 연관된
    형태의 원조가 이루어져야 할 것으로 보는 바, GCC 내부
    에서도 이 문제에 대해 진지하게 고려하고 있는 것으로
    알고 있으며, Fund 설립을 희망하고 있는 것으로 알려짐.

o 미, 소 협력문제

  - 소련과는 걸프사태 초기부터 긴밀한 협력을 하여 왔으며,
    이는 전후처리에 있어서도 계속 유지될 것으로 생각하는
    바, 특히 소련의 참여는 건설적인 것이 되어야 할 것임을
    강조함.

다) 기타 질의 응답시, Charles 보좌관의 주요 언급 요지

o 이락 국내정세

  - 현재 이라크내 약 15개 도시에서 시아파가 주동하는 반정부
    시위가 진행되고 있는 바, 바스라에서는 정부군이 동
    시위를 진압중임. 현재의 상황에서 이라크가 전투행위를
    재개할 가능성은 거의 없는 것으로 봄.

7

0079

- 이라크 북부에 배치되어 있던 공화국 수비대가 시위 진압에 동원되고 있고, 이라크내 반정부 세력이 쿠르드족, 시아파 등 각 종족별로 분파되어 있는 상황이기 때문에 반정부 시위가 후세인 정권의 붕괴로까지 연결될 수 있을지를 속단키 어려움.

- 다만, 이라크 주변국들에서 이라크내 반체제 세력에 대한 각종 지원을 계속하고 있으므로, 이라크 국내 정국의 불안정 양상이 당분간 계속될 가능성이 있음.

o 전후 정상회담 개최문제

- 부쉬 대통령이 3.13-14. 간 오타와를 방문, 멀루니 수상과 회담 예정이고, 3.14. 은 마티니크에서 미테랑 대통령과 미불 정상회담 예정이기는 하나, 일본 언론에 보도된 것과 같은 대규모 정상회담 개최 구상에 대해서는 아는 바 없음. (메이저 수상과의 미.영 정상회담 시기, 장소는 상금 미정)

- 미테랑 대통령은 5개 안보리 상임이사국 정상회담을 제의한 바 있으나 의견차이로 소집하지 않기로 한 바 있음.

8

0080

나. Douglas Paal NSC 아시아 선임보좌관 내정자 면담

- 이정빈 차관보는 중동 각국에서 건설 프로젝트 참여를 통해 많은
  경험을 쌓은 아국 건설 업체들이 쿠웨이트 복구 사업에도 참여함
  으로써 아국 나름의 협조를 제공할 준비가 되어 있음을 설명하고,
  동건 관련 미측의 적극적인 협조를 요청함.

- 이에 대해 Paal 보좌관은 한국도 전후 복구사업에 적극 참여하기를
  희망한다고 말하고, 자신이 알기로는 쿠웨이트 정부가 다국적군
  참여국등 걸프전쟁 관련 지원국의 은혜를 잊지 않겠다는 입장을
  표명하면서 이에따라 복구사업 참여 가능국과 불가국을 구분하는
  일종의 리스트를 작성하였던 바, 한국은 당연히 복구 참여 가능국에
  포함된 것으로 알고 있다고 언급함.

- 한편, 동 보좌관은 아직도 유엔의 각종 대이락 경제제재조치 등이
  유효한 만큼 이라크내 복구사업 참여문제는 추후 적절한 시점에
  신중히 검토하여야 할 것이라 첨언함.

다. Carl Ford 미 국방부 국제안보 부차관보 면담

1) 한국의 지원에 대한 평가

- 제1차관보는 먼저 미국이 부쉬 대통령의 영도하에 걸프전쟁을
  승리로 마무리 지운데 대해 축하를 표하였음.

- 이에 대해 Ford 부차관보는 미국이 우방국의 도움을 절실히
  필요로 했던 걸프사태에서 한국이 제때에 지원을 아끼지
  않았던데 대해 사의를 표하고 미국은 이를 오래 기억할
  것이라고 언급하였음.

9

0081

2) 추가지원중 1억1천만불의 구성문제

　o Ford 부차관보는 한국측이 제안한 현금 6천만불, 수송지원
　　5천만불의 지원에 이견이 없다고 하였음. (다만 상부로부터 다른
　　의견이 있으면 알려 주겠다고 부언)

3) 1.7억불 상당의 군수물자 지원문제

　o Ford 부차관보는 미국 정부는 대이라크 무력사용 개시이후 미국에
　　대한 지원은 물자(in-kind) 형태로는 받지 않는다는 방침을 확정
　　하였다고 하면서 한국이 지원을 약속한 1.7억불 상당의 군수물자
　　지원을 현금으로 전환하여 줄 것을 요청하고 이와 같은 미국
　　정부의 공식 입장을 체니 국방장관 명의 서한을 통하여 아국
　　정부에 곧 통보하게 될 것이라고 언급함.

　　- 이에대해 제1차관보는 한국이 추가지원을 고려할 당시 우리
　　　로서는 1.1억불의 현금 및 수송지원이 우리의 경제여건 등을
　　　고려할 때 최대의 지원 가능한 규모였으나, 주한 미군측이
　　　군수물자 지원을 요청해 옴에 따라 당장의 재원 확보없이
　　　미국에 대한 지원을 극대화하기 위해 한국군이 사용중이거나
　　　비축용인 군수물자까지도 포함하여 추가지원 규모를 2억
　　　8천만불로 책정한 배경을 설명하고 금년 들어 아국은 1, 2월
　　　2개월 동안에 33억 8,500만불의 무역적자를 기록하는 등
　　　경제적으로 매우 어려운 상태에 있기 때문에 동 군수물자를
　　　현금으로 지원하는 것은 어려울 것으로 본다고 답변하였음.

10

- 이어 동 부차관보는 미국의 요청이 생일선물 상자를 개봉한 후
  맘에 안든다고 동 선물을 다른 것으로 바꾸어 달라는 것과같아
  어색(awkward)하기는 하지만 한국 정부가 군수물자 지원을
  현금으로 전환하여 지원하지 못하는 경우 미 행정부로서는
  1.1억불의 현금 및 수송지원만을 미국에 대한 추가지원으로
  계상할 것이라고 언급하였음. (동 부차관보는 한국이
  1.1억불만을 지원할 경우 최소한 일본의 1/15 규모는 지원
  해야 한다는 미 정부내 비공식 입장에 비추어 미 의회나
  여론으로 부터 한국에 대한 비난이 대두될 가능성이 있음을
  시사)

- 이에 대해 제1차관보는 지원규모의 다과도 중요하겠으나 그
  보다는 우방국으로서 적시에 능력 범위내에서 최대한의 지원을
  기꺼이 제공해 온 우리 정부와 국민의 자세가 보다 높이 평가
  되어야 한다고 강조하고 여하간 미국 정부의 요청 내용을
  본국에 보고하겠다고 말함.

4) 영국 전비지원 문제

- 제1차관보는 영국의 전비 요청내용을 자세히 설명하고 우리
  정부로서는 걸프전에서의 영국의 기여도등을 감안하여
  가능한한 영국에 대해서도 지원할 방침이라고 전제하고,
  그러나 이미 약속한 5억불 이상의 추가재원 마련이 현실적
  으로 거의 불가능한 만큼 대미 지원 군수물자 1.7억불중에서
  2,000만불 내지 3,000만불을 영국에 대한 전비지원으로 전환
  하는 방안에 대한 미측의 의견을 구하였음.

11

0083

- 이에 대해 Ford 부차관보는 동 문제는 전적으로 한국 정부가
  결정할 문제라고 하면서, 다만 1.7억불중 일부를 영국에 대한
  지원으로 전환할 경우 미국에 대한 지원은 그만큼 감소되는
  것이며, 따라서 공평하지 않다는 감을 줄수도 있다는 점을
  유의해 달라고 하였음.

5) 의료지원단 및 군 수송단 활동문제

- 제1차관보는 걸프지역에서 전쟁이 종결되었으므로 우리의
  의료지원단 및 공군 수송단의 활동지속 문제에 대한 미측의
  의견을 문의하였음.

- 이에대해 Ford 부차관보는 동 문제는 한국정부의 결정사항이나
  미국으로서는 전투행위는 정지되었으나 전후처리 문제를 고려
  할때 당분간 활동을 계속하는 것이 바람직할 것으로 본다고
  언급하였음. (동인은 의료지원단의 경우, 쿠웨이트내 병원들이
  수용능력 부족으로 어려움을 겪고 있는 바, 한국군 의료단이
  쿠웨이트에서 진료활동을 하는 것도 바람직할 것이라고
  부연함.)

- 이어 동 부차관보는 사실 군 의료단과 수송단의 활동을 당분간
  더 계속함이 좋겠다는 이유는 차후 미 의회나 여론에서 한국의
  지원이 미흡하다는 비판이 대두될 경우 한국 의료단이나
  수송단이 현지에서 활동을 계속하고 있는 점을 부각시켜 이러한
  비판을 어느정도 무마시킬 수 있는 효과를 거둘수 있을 것으로
  기대되기 때문이라고 하였음. 또한 수송단은 현지에 도착한지
  불과 얼마되지 않은점도 고려해야 될 것이라고 말함.

12

0084

라. David Mack 국무부 중근동 부차관보 면담
 (John Kelly 차관보는 명일부터 시작되는 Baker 장관의 중동순방 대책
 회의 등으로 인해 면담이 이뤄지지 못함.)

1) 제1차관보는 우선 미측이 커다란 인명피해 없이 걸프전을 승리로
 종결짓고 동 지역에서 평화와 안정을 회복하기 위한 발판을 마련한
 데 대해 축하를 하고 걸프전 이후 중동지역의 안정과 평화유지를
 위해 미국의 구상을 문의하였음.

2) 이에대해 Mack 차관보는 미국이 비록 대부분의 군을 파견하고
 주도적인 역할을 했지만 어디까지나 연합군(coalition forces)의
 일원이었으며 여타 연합국들의 협조없이는 금번 사태를 이처럼
 성공적으로 마무리 지을수는 없었을 것이라고 하고 한국이 재정
 및 수송지원을 해준데 대해 감사를 표하였음. (동 부차관보는 특히
 한국의 수송지원은 걸프사태 해결에 있어 결정적인 순간에 커다란
 도움이 되었으며 한국등 우방국인 이집트, 요르단, 터어키등에 대해
 재정지원을 함으로써 다국적군의 연합전선에 균열이 가지 않도록
 하는데 기여한 것으로 평가한다고 언급)

3) 이어 동 부차관보는 전후 중동지역의 안보 및 경제복구 등을 위한
 지역 안보체제 수립, 이스라엘-아랍문제 특히 팔레스타인 문제,
 레바논 문제, 경제부흥 문제, 군비통제 등과 관련한 미측의 입장
 및 구상을 다음과 같이 밝히면서 이러한 문제는 앞으로 역시
 국제적인 협력하에서 추진해야 할 것이라고 말함.

가) 지역안보 체제 수립

- 미국이 현재 지역안보 문제에 관한 확실한 청사진 등을 갖고
 있지는 않으나 중동의 현실이 유럽과는 다르므로 NATO 또는
 CSCE 같은 유럽의 경험이 중동에 그대로 적용될 수 없으며,

13

0085

동 지역 국가들이 스스로 지역안보에 대한 계획을 창안해내야
한다는 것이 미국의 기본 입장임.   이 문제와 관련, GCC 국가
외무장관들이 3. 3. 리야드에서 회동한 바, 좋은 구상이 나올
것을 미국은 기대하고 있음. (금일 리야드에서 재차 회동)
한편, 미국은 부쉬 대통령 누차 천명한 바와 같이 지상군을
주둔시키지는 않을 것이며 동 지역에 오래전부터 배치된
미국의 해군력 및 공군력이 있기 때문에 온건 아랍국가가
군사적으로 지원하고 GCC 국가가 중심이 된 지역 안보체제가
긴밀한 협조를 하게되면, 장래에 대비하는데 충분하다고 봄.

- 베이커 장관은 금번 중동 순방중에 리야드에서 GCC 국가대표
  들과 면담하고 타이푸에서 쿠웨이트 정부 인사들과도 만날
  예정이며, 또한 시리아, 이집트, 이스라엘, 터어키도 방문,
  지역안보 문제에 대한 아랍 국가들의 의향을 타진하고 미국이
  할수 있는 역할에 대한 모색을 하게될 것임.

나) 이스라엘-아랍 문제(팔레스타인 문제)

- 미국으로서도 어떤 구체적 해결책을 갖고 있지는 않으나 아랍
  국가들이 금번 걸프사태를 계기로 보다 현실적인 인식을 하게
  되었으므로 단계적으로 이 문제를 풀어 나갈수 있을 것으로
  기대함.

다) 군비 통제

- 미국으로서는 최근 무바락 이집트 대통령이 제안한 바 있는
  중동지역에서의 장거리 미사일등 비재래식 무기 금지 제안
  등을 환영하며 중동지역 정세불안요인 제거 차원에서 군비
  통제를 적극 추진 예정임.

14

0086

라) 경제복구 문제

- 현재 GCC 국가와 이집트등이 중심이 되어 세계은행(IBRD)과
  유사한 아랍개발은행(Arab Development Bank) 설립을 추진
  하고 있는 바, 일본, 독일, 한국 및 서구 국가들의 역할이
  기대되고 있음.

- 한국의 경우 과거 중동지역 건설시장 진출등의 경험이 축적
  되어 있는만큼 걸프지역 복구에 중요한 역할을 할수 있을
  것으로 봄.

4) 제1차관보는 상기 설명에 대해 사의를 표한 후 우리나라가 걸프
   지역의 안정 회복과 경제복구에 지원을 할 용의가 있음을 표명하고
   전후 쿠웨이트 복구사업에 아국의 참여문제에 관해 미측의 협조를
   요청하였음. 이에대해 동 부차관보는 쿠웨이트 정부가 전후
   쿠웨이트 복구사업을 위해 임시로 워싱턴 D.C.에 설치하여 운영해
   오고 있는 쿠웨이트 경제복구위원회(Council on Economic
   Reconstruction of Kuwait)는 지금까지 담당하던 업무를 쿠웨이트
   정부내 기관으로 이관하고 있는 중이며, 쿠웨이트 복구와 관련,
   전기, 상.하수도 및 쓰레기 처리시설등 긴급히 복구가 요청되는
   분야에 있어서는 단기적으로 미국정부가 커다란 역할을 하게될
   것이나 도로, 항만, 정부건물, 주택등 사회 간접자본 복구는
   전적으로 쿠웨이트 정부가 계획을 수립 시행하게 될 것이라고
   언급함.

5) 한편, 중동질서 개편에 관한 소련의 역할에 관한 질문에 대해 동
   부차관보는 걸프사태 발생이래 미국은 소련과 긴밀한 협의를 통해
   유엔을 중심으로 국제적 평화회복 노력을 전개해 왔는 바, 미국
   으로서는 앞으로도 중동지역 문제 해결에 있어 소련의 건설적 참여
   (constructive participation)를 기대하고 있다고 언급함.

15

0087

마. Desaix Anderson 국무부 동아.태 부차관보 면담

1) 이 차관보는 우선 걸프전의 성공적 종료에 대한 축하를 전달하고, 전후복구 과정등에 있어서 한.미간의 긴밀한 협조관계가 계속 유지되기를 희망한다고 언급한 바, Anderson 부차관보는 한국이 그간 보여준 강력한 정치적 지원과 대미, 대전선국 지원에 크게 감사한다고 답변함.

2) 이어서, Anderson 부차관보는 의회 및 언론등에서 금번 전쟁관련 각국의 지원내용 및 약속이행 실적을 본격적으로 평가할 예정인 접등을 감안, 한국측이 기 천명한 지원내용은 가능한한 조속히 실행하는 것이 바람직할 것으로 보인다고 강조함.

바. William Quandt 브루킹스 연구소 선임연구관 면담

1) 제1차관보는 걸프전의 성공적 종료에 대해 축하하면서, 미 행정부가 Bush 대통령의 3.6. 대화의 연설등을 통해 걸프전 이후의 대중동 청사진을 밝히고 있으나, Camp David 회담에 직접 참여하기도 하는 등 중동문제를 오랫동안 연구해온 Quandt 연구관의 걸프전후 중동 정세에 대한 의견을 문의함.

2) 이에대해 Quandt 연구관은 걸프전의 성공적 종료로 중동의 정치, 군사적 환경이 많이 개선된 것으로 본다고 전제하면서 주요문제에 대한 본인의 견해를 아래와 같이 밝힘.

가) 지역안보체제 수립

- 당분간은 아랍, UN, 미국의 3자가 모두 참여하는 평화유지군의 구성이 필요할 것으로 봄. 이 경우 아랍군은 주로 이집트 및 시리아군으로 구성될 것이고, UN 평화유지군은 상징적인 역할을 하게될 것이며, 미국은 어제 Bush 대통령이 밝힌바와 같이 주로 해.공군력에 의한 지원을 하게될 것으로 봄.

'6   0088

- 중동에서 가장 분쟁발생 가능성이 높은 곳이 걸프지역인 바,
  금번 걸프전을 통해 이라크의 군사력이 제거되었고, 이라크는
  금번 사태를 통해서도 상당한 자제력을 보여주어 전반적으로
  중동의 안보환경이 많이 개선된 것으로 봄.

- 그러나 이란이 이라크내의 시아파를 사주하여 이라크내의
  분규를 조성하여 역내의 영향력 행사를 기도할 가능성등
  분쟁의 요인은 상존함.

나) 군비 통제

- 중동평화 유지를 위해 군비통제가 이루어져야 한다는 의견이
  자주 제시되고 있으나, 걸프전을 통해 최신예 무기(precision
  bomb, anti-missile missile등)의 효능이 증명되었으므로
  역내 국가들이 최신예 무기를 구입하는등 오히려 군비경쟁이
  재연될 가능성도 크다고 봄.

다) 이스라엘, 아랍 문제

- 이스라엘의 안보위협은 이집트, 시리아, 이라크 3국으로부터의
  위협이 가장 심각한 것이었는 바, 이집트는 Camp David를
  통하여 이스라엘과 화평하였고, 이라크는 걸프전을 통해
  그 군사력이 제거되었으므로, 이제 현실적인 군사위협은
  사실상 시리아 1국에서만 가능한 것으로 보임.

- 시리아는 종래 서방과의 대결적 입장에서 탈피하여 서방과의
  관계를 증진시키려는 의지를 보이고 있으므로, 이스라엘이
  골란고원 문제, West Bank 문제등을 양보하면 시리아와의
  관계개선도 가능하다고 봄.

17

- 문제는 이스라엘의 현 집권층이 매우 비타협적 성격이라
  이스라엘로부터 안보리 결의안 242에 기초한 타협을 기대
  하기가 어렵다는 것임.

- 미국이 이스라엘로 하여금 타협을 하도록 영향력을 행사하여야
  하는데, 문제는 미국내의 친이스라엘 로비가 아직도 매우
  강하다는데 있음. (Quandt 연구관은 그 예로 최근 대이스라엘
  원조를 둘러싼 미 행정부, 이스랑엘간의 알력을 듬) 한가지
  다행한 것은 Bush 대통령이 높은 인기도를 기반으로 이스라엘
  문제에 대해서도 강력한 리더쉽을 발휘할 수 있다는 점임.

- 본인의 예상으로는 수주안에 중동평화 및 팔레스타인 문제
  토의를 위한 다자간 회의 소집이 가능하다고 보나, 이스라엘이
  계속 팔레스타인 문제에 비타협적 자세를 고집하게 되면
  모처럼만의 기회가 무산될 것임.

라) 경제복구 문제

- 쿠웨이트 재건에 관심이 쏠리는 것이 당연하나, 이란도 서방과의
  경협을 강화해 나갈 것으로 전망됨.

- 이라크는 걸프전 이전에도 이미 1천억불의 대외부채를 짊어지고
  있었고, 대이란, 쿠웨이트 배상금이 1천억불 이상으로 이야기
  되고 있는데, 이는 이라크의 제일 큰 수입원인 원유 판매대금
  약 10년분에 해당되므로 이라크의 배상금 지불은 사실상 매우
  어려운 문제로 보이며, 경제 복구도 자금부족으로 어려움을
  겪을 것임.

- 아랍개발은행 설립이 자주 논의되고 있는 바, 자금규모가 수십억불만 되어도 충분히 소기의 효과를 기대할 수 있을 것으로 생각됨. 걸프전에 약 5백억불이 소요된 것과 비교하면 아랍개발은행 설립은 크게 어려운 일이 아니라고 봄.

3) 제1차관보는 상기 설명에 대해 사의를 표하면서 소련이 중동지역 문제에 깊이 관여하여 왔음에 비추어 향후 중동정치, 안보, 경제구조 정착에 있어 소련이 어떤 역할을 해 나가리라고 보는지 문의한 바, Quandt 연구관은 언론에서는 미국이 소련의 대걸프전 역할에 대해 불만인 것을 보도하기도 하나, 미 행정부는 소련의 역할에 대해 대체적으로 만족하고 있는 것으로 본다고 하면서, 소련은 개혁정책을 추진함에 있어 서방과의 협조가 긴요한 상황이므로 중동문제에 있어서도 서방과 협조해 나갈 것으로 본다는 낙관적 견해를 표시함.

2. 부쉬 대통령 아주순방 및 외무장관 방미

가. 부쉬 대통령 아주순방 문제

(Douglas Paal NSC 아시아 보좌관 면담)

o Duglas Paal NSC 아시아 선임 보좌관 내정자는 일본 언론 보도와는 달리 부쉬 대통령의 일정상 일본 방문은 금년 9월 또는 10월경이 될 가능성이 높다고 언급함.

o 제1차관보는 부쉬 대통령이 일본 방문 기회에 한국도 반드시 방문 하도록 협조를 당부하였으며, Paal 보좌관은 한국의 입장은 재차 반복하지 않아도 잘 알고 있다고 하고 최선을 다하겠다고 답변함.

19

0091

(Desaix Anderson 국무부 동아. 태 부차관보 면담)

o 이 차관보가 부쉬 대통령의 아주순방 추진 동향을 문의한데 대해,
Anderson 부차관보는 금년 가을에 동 순방을 추진할 예정이기는
하나 더이상의 구체적 사항은 현재 정해지지 않았다고(not pinned
any more) 답변함.

o 또한 Anderson 부차관보는 동 순방 관련 한국측의 입장을 잘 알고
있다고 하고, 구체적인 진전 동향이 있는대로 아측에 이를 통보
하겠다고 언급함.

나. 한.미 외상회담 추진

o 제1차관보는 Desaix Anderson 동아.태 부차관보를 면담, 아국
외무장관이 취임이래 지금까지 베이커 국무장관과 회동의 기회가
없었다는 점을 상기시키고, 아측으로서는 4. 25-5. 3. 기간중 한.미
외무장관 회담을 추진할 계획이라고 언급하고 국무부측의 적극
협조를 요청함. (당초 이 차관보는 Solomon 동아. 태 차관보를 면담
토록 예정되어 있었으나, Solomon 차관보의 의회 증언 일정이
금일 오후 늦게까지도 계속됨에 따라 부득이 Anderson 부차관보와
면담케 되었음.)

o 이에대해, Anderson 부차관보는 기본적으로 아국 외무장관의 방미를
크게 환영한다고 언급하고, 동 방미 구상이 실현된다면 한.미 양국
관계 긴밀화에 크게 도움이 될 것으로 본다고 부연함.
이어서 Anderson 부차관보는 전후처리 문제등과 관련 베이커 장관의
해외출장이 매우 잦은 관계로 일정이 매우 유동적(in flux)이지마는
최선의 노력을 경주하도록 하겠다고 말함.

20

0092

3. 제5차 조정국 회의 결과

    가. 일시 및 장소 :

        1991. 3. 11(월)   13:00-18:10   룩셈부르크 European Center

    나. 참석국(30개국)

        o GCC 국가 :   사우디 아라비아, 쿠웨이트, UAE, 카타르 등

        o EC 국가 :   벨지움, 덴마크, 프랑스, 독일, 아일랜드, 이태리,
                          룩셈부르크, 화란, 포루갈, 스페인, 영국

        o 기타 구주국가 :   오스트리아, 핀랜드, 아이슬란드, 노르웨이,
                              스웨덴, 스위스

        o 일본, 한국, 미국, 카나다

        o 기타 IMF, IBRD, EC, GCC 대표 참석

    다. 회의 진행

        o Mulford 재무부차관, Kimmitt 국무부 정무차관 공동 주재로
          쿠웨이트 해방 축하 및 전선국 등 피해국가에 대한 지원 계속
          필요성 강조

        o IBRD, IMF 대표의 이집트, 터어키, 요르단 경제상황 및 피해규모
          평가 설명

        o 기존 약속금액의 집행상황 및 추가약속 문제에 대한 각국 대표의
          발표

_ 21

0093.

라. 오찬 회의시 Mulford 재무차관 및 Kimmitt 국무차관 발언요지

(Mulford 차관)

o 걸프사태를 성공적으로 해결하게 된데에는 군사적, 외교적, 경제적
측면에서의 뒷바침이 주효했기 때문이며, 재정공여국 회의는 경제적
측면에서 중요한 역할을 수행했는 바, 총 148억불의 재정지원
약속액중 약 77억불이 이미 집행됨. (회의 종료후 발표된 기자
브리핑 자료는 91.3.8. 현재 총 157억불의 약속액중 약 83억불이
집행된 것으로 집계됨)

o 걸프사태의 해결을 위한 수단으로 조정위 회의가 지금까지 효율적
으로 운영되어 왔으나 분쟁이 종결된 이후에는 전후복구와 평화정착
이라는 새로운 사태에 대처할 수 있도록 조정위의 기능이 재검토
되어야 할 것임.

- 전후 중동질서의 대폭적 개편과 더불어 걸프지원 조정위는 복잡한
정치, 경제적 상황에 융통성 있게 효율적으로 적응할 수 있어야
하지만 이를 제도화, 기구화 해야할 필요성은 없다고 봄.

(Kimmitt 차관)

- 공여국 조정위는 승전으로 확보된 걸프지역에서의 평화를 항구적
으로 정착시키기 위한 임무를 앞으로도 당분간 계속 수행(keep
its momentum)해야 될 것임.

. 조정국 회의는 현재 임무를 완수하지 못했으며(unfinished
business), 걸프사태로 인한 경제적 파괴가 심한데다(economic
dislocation) 향후 상당한 기간동안 이라크에 대한 경제제제
조치 및 이라크 재무장 방지를 위한 무기 금수조치를 계속할
필요성이 있음에 비추어 조정위는 계속 임무를 수행해야 함.

22

0094

- 중동에서 항구적 안보장치를 구축하기 위해서는 군사적 요소만
  으로는 불가능하며 평화 정착을 위한 경제적, 외교적 요소가
  필요함.

- 현재 중동을 순방중인 Baker 장관은 중동지역의 안보, 미사일
  비확산 등 군축문제, peace process 및 경제복구 등에 관해
  사우디, 시리아, 이스라엘, 쿠웨이트 당국과 협의를 하고 있음.

- 중동지역 경제복구와 관련, 필요시 재정지원 대상국은 북부
  아프리카 마그레브 지역까지 확대되어야 할 것임.

- 현 GCC 기구를 중심으로 역외국까지 포함된 다자적 공동 노력으로
  중동지역의 평화보장을 위해 현 조정위의 adaptability 와
  flexibility를 계속 유지해야 함.

마. 이정빈 제1차관보 발언요지

○ 한국의 총 지원액은 115백만불이며, 현재까지 EDCF 차관 1,000만불의
  대요르단 공여 및 전선국에 대한 물자지원등으로 약 2,000만불이
  집행되었거나 조만간 집행될 예정임. 또한 잔여분에 대한 집행도
  수원국가와 긴밀히 협의, 조속히 추진할 것임.

○ 원조의 조속한 집행을 위해 정부는 두번째의 고위대표단을 이집트,
  요르단에 2.24-3.9.간 파견하였으며, 수원국들과 잔여 미집행액의
  신속, 효과적인 집행 방안에 대해 진지하게 토의를 한바 있음.

○ 조기 집행을 위해 직업훈련원 건립, 의료기자재 공급, EDCF 차관
  공여조건 완화 등 대책을 강구하고 있음.

23

0095

바. 주요 발언내용

o Mulford 차관은 터키와 요르단에 대한 지원약속이 필요에 크게 못
   미치고 있다고 하고 터키가 Operation Desert Storm에 크게 기여한
   점을 감안 각국이 특별 고려해 줄 것을 요청하고 요르단에 대해서
   일본과 유럽이 특별 관심을 촉구함. 동 차관은 이어 일본 및 EC의
   원조 집행이 가속화된데 만족을 표명하고 지원사업의 추진을 위한
   공여 조건완화 필요성을 강조했음.

o GCC 대표는 향후 10년간 아랍권 개발을 위한 총 150억불 상당의
   아랍 프로그램을 실시할 계획임을 발표한 바, 동 아랍 프로그램은
   중동지역에 있어 민간부문의 발전을 도모 하기 위한 것이며, 현재
   기술적인 측면에 대한 검토가 진행중이라 합. 또한 GCC 대표는
   조정위가 Arab Programme을 지원할 수 있을 것이라고 언급함.

o 미측은 91년도 1/4분기내 각국의 지원약속이 모두 이행될 수 있도록
   지원집행 가속화를 촉구함. 특히 Kimmitt 차관은 요르단의 정치적
   정향(orientation)에 실망하고 있으나 요르단이 대이라크 경제제재
   조치의 실효성 확보에 기여하고 있는 점 및 중동정세 안정에 중요점
   등을 감안, 계속적인 지원이 필요하다고 언급함.
   또한 미측은 워싱톤에서 걸프사태 재정지원 공여국 조정위 실무
   회의을 보다 효율적으로 활용할 것을 제의함.

o 사우디 대표는 사우디 정부가 파키스탄에 대해 3개월간 매일 5만
   배럴의 원유를 무상으로 제공(약 7천만불 상당)키로 결정하였으며,
   모로코에 대해서도 2억불의 지원을 기완료한 바, 여타 지원 약속도
   모두 정해진 시간표에 따라 차질없이 집행될 것이라고 발표함.
   또한 인도적 차원의 지원은 대부분 이집트와 시리아에 제공될
   것이라고 발언함.

24

0096

o 일본 대표는 제4차 조정국 회의 결과에 따라 일본 정부가 요르단에
   대해 450백만불의 새로운 지원을 하기로 결정하였으며, 기존의
   대요르단 지원약속도 그대로 이행할 예정임을 언급함. 또한 일본
   대표는 일본이 중동지역의 정세안정에 시리아가 차지하는 비중을
   감안 동국에 대해 110백만불의 untied loan을 제공키로 한 사실을
   강조함.

o 독일 대표는 370백만 DM의 추가지원을 발표하면서 시리아의 중요성을
   감안, 이중 110백만 DM을 동국에 지원키로 하였다고 함. 한편,
   독일은 동 추가지원의 90%를 grant 형태로 하여 수원국에 다음주에
   통보 예정이며, 단기간에 집행이 될 것임을 밝힘.

o 주요 공여국인 일본 및 독일은 미국 주도의 조정위 기능 강화에는
   소극적인 자세를 보이며 IMF, IBRD 등을 활용할 것을 주장하였음.
   특히 일본은 공여국 통계자료에 자국만이 별도로 분류(여타국의
   경우는 EC, GCC, 기타국으로 분류) 된 것을 보도자료에 기타국으로
   분류하여 발표하도록 요청하는 등 회의진행 방법 및 자료작성 등에
   있어 민감한 반응을 보였음.

사. 금번 회의시 합의내용

o 회의 참석자들은 중동지역 평화정착을 위한 군사적 장치로서 아랍
   평화유지군 창설과 GCC를 중심으로한 경제협력을 통하여 중동지역내
   평화정착을 위한 정치적, 경제적 결속을 강화해야 한다는 필요성에
   대해서는 공감을 표시함.

o 전선국가에 대한 지원은 timing이 중요한 바, 가능한 신속히 지원을
   집행키로 노력할 필요가 있다는데 의견이 모아짐.

25

0097

o IMF, 세계은행은 걸프지역 국가의 경제개발을 위한 보다 장기적인 계획을 문서로 작성, 조정위에 제출하기로 함.

o 한편, 동 조정위가 전후에도 계속 능동적으로 기능하기 위해서는 앞으로 더욱 IMF등 기존 국제기구의 기능활용등 운영방식의 개선이 시급하다는데 대해서도 대체로 의견이 모아졌으며, 차기 조정위 회의시 조정위 재편 문제도 논의하기로 하였음.

아. 차기 회의

o GCC 대표는 조정위 운영 및 역내 경제개발에 있어 GCC가 주도적 역할을 해야 한다는 취지에서 차기 회의를 GCC 역내에서 개최할 것을 제안했으며, 이에따라 차기 회의는 5월 중순경(early middle May) GCC 국가에서 개최키로 잠정 합의함.

4. 유엔 가입문제

26

0098

나. Eric Suy 벨기에 외무성 고문 오찬면담

(제1차관보 발언요지)

ㅇ 북한이 유엔가입을 원할 경우, 북한과 함께 북한이 원하지 않거나
   준비가 되어 있지 않다면 우리로서는 먼저 유엔가입 조치를 취하고
   북한의 추후 가입을 기다리겠으며, 이러한 일련의 가입조치는
   금년 유엔총회중에 마무리 지었으면 좋겠다는 우리의 입장을 설명
   하고, 금년 4월중 안보리 의장국을 맡게 될 벨지움의 각별한 배려로
   40년 이상 오랜 현안문제로 되어 있는 우리의 유엔가입 문제가
   타결되도록 특별한 협조를 요청함.

27

0099

o 최근 유엔가입 문제와 관련한 소련과 중국 및 북한의 입장을 상세히
   설명하고 금년중 남.북한의 유엔가입 문제를 타결하는 방안으로서
   안보리 상임이사국들이 남.북한의 유엔가입이 통일전까지의 잠정적
   조치라는 양해하에 비공식 콘센서스로 남.북한의 유엔가입을 권유
   하고 남.북한은 동 권유에 따라 상기 양해사항을 공개적으로 밝힌후
   유엔가입 조치를 취할수 있도록 4월중 안보리 의장국인 벨지움이
   중국을 포함한 여타 상임이사국들과 협의해 줄 것을 비공식적으로
   제시하였음.

o 상기 협의결과가 4월중 실효를 거두지 못할 경우 우리 정부로서는
   북한과 함께 유엔에 가입하는 노력을 부득이 포기하고 우리의
   단독 유엔가입을 추진할 수 밖에 없음을 밝히고 그간 우리가 중국의
   입장을 고려하여 취하여온 제반조치를 감안해서 중국이 거부권
   행사를 자제하도록 요청하여 줄 것도 아울러 당부하였음.

o 한편, 가입추진에 따른 구체적인 절차문제는 우방국 전문가들과
   긴밀한 협의하에 추후 대처해 나가고자 하며 지난번부터 core
   group의 일원으로 참여하기 시작한 벨지움에 대한 우리의 기대가
   큼을 강조해 두고 4월중 벨지움의 노력으로 유엔 가입문제에 대한
   안보리의 권고 결의가 매듭지어지면 5월초로 예정된 벨지움 외상의
   방한시 좋은 외교적인 선물이 될 것이라고 언급하였음.

(Suy 고문 발언요지)

o 4월중 남.북한의 유엔 가입문제가 상임이사국간의 콘센서스에 의해
   처리될 수 있도록 벨지움이 최대한 노력하겠다고 하고 중국측으로서도
   남.북한의 유엔가입을 실현시킬 경우 외교적으로도 잃을 것이 없을
   것이라는 점을 지적하면서 벨지움 외무성 실무진과 정우영 대사간의
   긴밀한 협의하에 이 문제를 추진해 보겠다고 하였음.

28

0100

o 유엔 가입문제와 관련된 점은 절차문제로서 한가지를 상기시키고저
   한다고 하면서 남.북한이 별도 문서 또는 단일 문서로 각기 가입
   신청을 하고 안보리가 이를 단일 결의안으로 처리하는 문제는
   신중을 기해야 한다고 하였음.   그 근거로 상임이사국중 어느 일국이
   반대입장을 교묘하게 취하고 그 결과가 단일 결의안 형태로 반영될
   경우, 한국의 유엔 가입은 자동적으로 봉쇄되는 결과가 될 것임을
   지적하였음.

5. 한-베트남 관계개선

가. 이 차관보는 Anderson 미 국무부 동아.태 부차관보 면담시 베트남측이
    4월초 아국개최 예정인 ESCAP 총회 참석등을 계기로 대한국 관계개선을
    강력히 희망하고 있다는 점을 언급하고, 한-베트남 관계개선 문제에
    대한 미측 입장을 타진함.

나. 이에대해, Anderson 부차관보는 캄푸치아 문제 해결을 위한 대베트남
    교섭이 현재 가장 중요한 시점(crucial point)에 도달했다는 점을
    언급하고, 현재와 같이 각 관련국이 협조해 나가는 가운데 대베트남
    압력이 계속 가중되어 나간다면 2-3개월내로 동 교섭이 타결될 수
    있을 것으로 본다고 설명함.

다. 이어서 아측이 단계적 방식의 대베트남 관계개선을 추진함으로써
    일종의 dual-track 정책을 채택하는 방안도 가능하지 않겠느냐고
    언급한데 대해, Anderson 부차관보는 미 의회 일각에서도 여사한
    구상이 제기되고 있고, 베트남측도 구라파 및 호주, 일본과의 교역
    및 투자관계 확대에 큰 관심을 갖고 있다고 하면서, 여사한 대베트남
    경제관계 확대는 현 상황하에서 캄푸치아 문제관련 교섭 타결의
    가능성을 감소시키는 결과를 초래할 가능성이 큰 만큼, 한국측도
    대베트남 관계개선을 자제(hold off)해 줄 것을 분명한 어조로 요청함.

29

0101

Ⅲ. 관찰 및 건의

1. 걸프전후 처리문제

  o 중동지역 안보문제와 관련 미국으로서는 아랍세계 및 소련등의 반발을
    의식하여 지상군을 주둔시키지는 않되, 친미 온건 아랍국가들을 주축
    으로 한 지역 안보체제 수립을 유도하는 한편, 동 지역에 있어 미국의
    해.공군력을 강화하여 동 지역안보 체제에 대한 후견인 역할을 통해
    중동지역의 정세안정을 도모하는 구상을 추진중인 것으로 보임.

  o 쿠웨이트 복구사업과 관련 단기적 긴급 복구계획에 관해서는 미국정부가
    주도 및 지원하고 있는 것으로 보이며, 그외 중.장기적인 복구사업은
    쿠웨이트 정부가 자체 판단에 따라 계약을 체결하여 시행하게 될 전망임.

  o 중동지역 질서 개편 및 복구관련 미국은 소련이 냉전적 사고에 입각,
    중동지역 정세에 개입하는 것을 수용하지 않으나 중동국가들과 상호
    경제적 이익을 공유(mutually shared economic interests)하는 건설적인
    관계를 발전시켜 나가기를 바라고 있는 것으로 관찰됨.

2. 아국의 지원문제

  (대미 지원문제)

  o 미국은 걸프전이 종결됨에 따라 금번 걸프전쟁에서 사용한 미군의 장비
    및 물자를 가능한한 사우디, 쿠웨이트등 국가에 판매하고자 하는 구상을
    갖고 있으며, 더욱이 전투행위가 종료된 현 시점에서는 미국에 대한
    현금이나 수송지원 이외의 현물(in-kind) 지원은 불필요하다는 최종
    입장을 확정한 것으로 감지됨.

30

0102

o 이에따라 미측으로서는 우리정부의 대미 추가지원중 1억7천만불 상당의 군수물자를 현금으로 지원해 줄 것을 요청하고 있으며, 만약 아국의 형편상 현금지원으로의 저환이 안될 경우 이를 대미지원 액수 총액에서 삭제하겠다는 방침을 같고 있는 것으로 보임.

o 대영국 지원을 위한 전용문제는 기본적을 아국 정부가 결정할 문제이지 미국 정부가 이를 수락 또는 거부할 성질이 아니라는 관점에서 미측은 명확한 답변을 계속 유보할 것으로 보이는 바, 본부에서 최종 입장 결정후 미측에 통보하는 형식을 취하는 것이 좋을 것으로 사료됨.

(전선국 및 주변국 지원)

o 금번 재정공여국 조정위는 전쟁 종식후 처음 열린 회의로서 각국이 약속한 원조액의 조속한 집행을 촉구하기 위한것 뿐만아니라 걸프역내 국가의 항구적 경제발전이 지역 평화유지에 긴요하다는 취지에서 단기적 원조를 포합, 장기적인 경제원조 계획이 필요하다는 분위기가 크게 나타났으며, 이를 위해서는 GCC 국가를 중심으로한 역내 국가의 이니시아티브가 중요하다는데 의견의 일치를 보이고 있음.

o 또한 금후 조정국 회의의 성격과 관련 이를 제도화하는 것보다는 회의 운영상 유연성을 확보하기 위해 앞으로 1-2회 정도는 현재와 같은 형태로 지속할 것으로 보임.

o 회의시 발표된 집행 실적표에 의하면 아국의 원조 집행 실적이 여타 국가에 비해 가장 저조한 것으로 나타났는 바, 수원국의 국내사정을 이유로 집행 실적이 저조하다는 설명은 더이상 설득력을 가질수 없음. 따라서 차기 회의시까지는 아국도 집행 실적을 어느정도의 수준 까지는 높여야 할 것으로 사료됨.

첨 부 : 걸프사태 재정지원 현황.   끝.

예 고 : 91. 12. 31. 일반

31

0103

Table 1

GULF CRISIS FINANCIAL ASSISTANCE *
COMMITMENTS FOR 1990-91
DISBURSEMENTS THROUGH 3/11/91
(US$ Millions)

Donor/Creditor	Egypt/Turkey/Jordan		Other States 1/		TOTAL	
	Commitments	Disbursements	Commitments	Disbursements	Commitments	Disbursements
GCC STATES	6348	3230	3180	2384	9528	5614
Saudi Arabia	2848	1788	1578	1203	4426	2991
Kuwait	2500	855	1184	763	3684	1618
UAE	1000	587	418	418	1418	1005
EC	2531	1109	184	1	2715	1110
EC Budget	805	624	0	0	805	624
Bilateral:	1726	485	184	1	1910	486
France	200	0	30	0	230	0
Germany	1190	360	144	0	1334	360
Italy	150	37	9	0	159	37
Other EC 2/	186	88	1	1	187	89
JAPAN	2126	800	0	0	2126	800
OTHERS	398	96	99	62	497	158
Korea	83	5	17	2	100	7
Norway	24	7	82	60	106	67
Switzerland	120	17	0	0	120	17
Other 3/	171	67	0	0	171	67
TOTAL COMMITMENTS	11403	5235	3463	2447	14866	7682

* All commitments and disbursements are bilateral economic assistance and do not include contributions to the multinational force.
  Totals may not equal sum of components due to rounding. Based on data submitted to the Gulf Crisis Financial Coordination Group.

1/ For Bangladesh, Djibouti, Lebanon, Morocco, Pakistan, Somalia, and Syria.

2/ Other EC includes Belgium, Denmark, Ireland, Luxembourg, Netherlands, Portuagal, Spain, and the U.K.

3/ Austalia, Austria, Canada, Finland, Iceland, and Sweden.

0104

Table 2

GULF CRISIS FINANCIAL ASSISTANCE *
COMMITMENTS FOR 1990–91
DISBURSEMENTS THROUGH 3/11/91
(Millions of U.S. Dollars)

Donor/Creditor	Egypt		Turkey		Jordan		Humanitarian/ Unallocated 1/		TOTAL		Other States 2/		GRAND TOTAL	
	Commit	Disb. to Date	Commit	Disb. to Date	Commit	Disb. to Date	Commit	Disb. to Date	Commit	Disb. to Date	Commit	Disb. to Date	Commit	Disb. to Date
GCC STATES 3/	3123	2363	2995	800	0	0	230	67	6348	3230	3180	2384	9528	5614
EC	1222	398	533	287	559	362	217	62	2531	1109	184	1	2715	1110
EC Budget	254	207	240	193	214	173	96	51	804	624	0	0	804	624
Bilateral 4/	968	191	293	94	345	189	121	11	1727	485	184	1	1911	486
JAPAN	629	336	720	218	717	186	60	60	2126	800	0	0	2126	800
ALL OTHERS 5/	100	3	55	7	105	23	138	63	398	96	99	62	497	158
TOTAL COMMITMENTS	5074	3100	4303	1312	1381	571	645	252	11403	5235	3463	2447	14866	7682

* All commitments and disbursements are bilateral economic assistance and do not include contributions to the multinational force.
Totals may not equal sum of components due to rounding. Based on data submitted to the Gulf Crisis Financial Coordination Group.
1/ Humanitarian and unallocated commitments to Egypt, Turkey, and Jordan.
2/ For Bangladesh, Djibouti, Lebanon, Morocco, Pakistan, Somalia, and Syria.
3/ Saudi Arabia, Kuwait, and the UAE.
4/ Belgium, Denmark, France, Germany, Ireland, Italy, Luxembourg, Netherlands, Portugal, Spain, and the U.K.
5/ Australia, Austria, Canada, Finland, Iceland, Korea, Norway, Sweden, and Switzerland.

TABLE A

GULF CRISIS FINANCIAL ASSISTANCE *

($ Billions – as of 3/11/91)

Donor/Creditor	Commitments
GULF STATES	9.5
EUROPEAN COMMUNITY	2.7
JAPAN	2.1
OTHER	0.6
TOTAL	14.9

* Includes all commitments to date for extraordinary economic assistance in 1990 and 1991. Does not include contributions to the multinational force, existing bilateral assistance, or funds made available by the IMF and World Bank.

<u>TABLE B</u>

GULF CRISIS FINANCIAL ASSISTANCE *

($ Billions – as of 3/11/91)

Donor/Creditor	Total Commitments	<u>1990–91 Commitments</u>		Other States
		Egypt/Turkey/Jordan	Humanitarian**	
GULF STATES	9.5	6.1	0.2	3.2
EUROPEAN COMMUNITY	2.7	2.4	0.1	0.2
JAPAN	2.1	2.0	0.1	0.0
OTHER	0.6	0.3	0.2	0.1
TOTAL	14.9	10.8	0.6	3.5

* Includes all commitments to date for extraordinary economic assistance in 1990 and 1991.
Does not include contributions to the multinational force, existing bilateral
assistance, or funds made available by the IMF and World Bank.
Includes both unallocated commitments and multilateral humanitarian assistance.

TABLE C

GULF CRISIS FINANCIAL ASSISTANCE *
($ Billions – as of 3/11/91)

Donor/Creditor	Commitments	Disbursements
GULF STATES	9.5	5.6
EUROPEAN COMMUNITY	2.7	1.1
JAPAN	2.1	0.8
OTHER	0.6	0.2
TOTAL	14.9	7.7

* Includes all commitments to date for extraordinary economic assistance in 1990 and 1991. Does not include contributions to the multinational force, existing bilateral assistance, or funds made available by the IMF and World Bank.

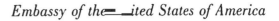

Embassy of the United States of America

Seoul, Korea

March 19, 1991

Mr. Ban Ki Moon
Director General
American Affairs Bureau
Ministry of Foreign Affairs
Seoul

Dear Director General Ban:

I have the honor to transmit the text of a letter to
Assistant Minister Lee Joung Binn from Under Secretary of
State Robert M. Kimmitt which the Embassy received
telegraphically.

I would be grateful for your assistance in passing on the
letter to the Assistant Minister.

Sincerely,

E. Mason Hendrickson
Minister-Counselor for
Political Affairs

Enclosure:
  as stated

0109

His Excellency
Lee Joung Binn
Assistant Minister for Political Affairs
Ministry of Foreign Affairs
Republic of Korea

Dear Assistant Minister Lee:

I want to express my personal appreciation for your
participation in the March 11 meeting in Luxembourg of the
Gulf Crisis Financial Coordination Group. Your presence
at the meeting sent an important political signal about
the importance of the GCFCG effort.

As you know, I had to depart the meeting before its
conclusion, so I was not able to thank you personally for
your presence and contribution to the meeting. I hope we
will soon have the chance to meet again, at which time I
would welcome the opportunity to discuss GCFCG or other
issues with you.

Thank you again for your participation and support.

Sincerely,

Robert M. Kimmitt

0110

주 벨 기 에 대 사 관

벨정 20501-9*9*   1991. 3. 20.

수신 : 외무부장관

참조 : 미주국장

제목 : 제 5차 걸프사태 재정지원 공여국 조정회의

　　　91.3.11(월) 룩셈부르크에서 개최된 표제회의 참석자 명단을 별첨
송부하오니, 참고하시기 바랍니다.

첨부 : 동 명단 (룩셈부르크측 작성) 1부. 끝.

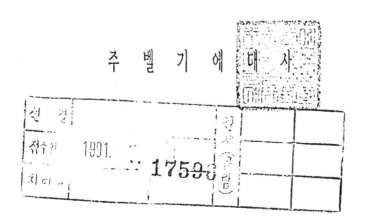

0111

ETAT		NOM et PRENOM	QUALITE
Arabie Saoudite	4	AL SORIASRY Jabbarah Dr. ZEDAN Faysal Dr. AL-JASSER Muhammed Sulaiman IBRAHIMEL Abdullah	Deputy Minister FIN Chargé d'Affaires, Ambassade d'Arabie Saoudite en Belgique
Australie	2	CURTIS P.C.J. FRENCH S.	Ambassador of Australia to Belgium, Luxembourg and the EC Counsellor (financial), Australian Mission to the OECD
Autriche	2	JANKOWITSCH Peter Dr. GEBETSROITHNER Judith Dr.	Staatssekretãr Conseiller
Banque Mondiale	2	QURESHI Moeen BOCK David	Senior Vice-President of Operations Director of Operations Staff
Belgique	2	WILLEMARCK Luc VAN ORMELINGEN	Ministre Conseiller, Ambassade de Belgique à Luxembourg Ministère des Finances
Canada	2	DE KERCKOVE Ferry HALEY J.	Directeur des Relations économiques avec les PVD MAE Division des finances et du développement international FIN
C.E.	4	GHIMERS Christian PRAT Juan VAN DER LINDEN Eric INNOCENTI	Administrateur DG II Commission Directeur Général chargédes Relations Nord-Sud DG I Commission Administrateur principal DG I Commission Conseil
Corée	8	LEE Joung Binn LEE Joung Bo YU Myung Hwan WANG Jeong Jung HUR Duck Haeng KIM Kyou Hyun KIM Kwang Dong YOO Jung Hee	Assistant Minister for Political Affairs MAE Director General Economic Cooperation Bureau FIN Counsellor Embassy of the Republic of Korea in Washington Director, Division of Administration Budget Economic Planing Board Deputy Director, Division II of Middle East Affairs MAE Deputy Director, Division of North America Affairs MAE Counsellor, Korean Mission to EEC First Secretary, Korean Embassy to Belgium
Danemark	2	RUBOW Suzanne KRISTENSEN Jens Pagter	Chargé d'Affaires a.i., Luxembourg Head of Division, Ministry of Economics
E.A.U.	2	AL-AGROOBI Salem AL-AWADHI Nariman	Ambassadeur Directeur adj.de l'Aministration des Investissements FIN
Espagne	2	CASANOVA Luis Javier REIG Arturo	Ambassadeur d'Espagne à Luxembourg Conseiller de l'Ambassade d'Espagne à Luxembourg
Etats-Unis	14	MULFORD David DALLARA Charles FALL James EICHENBERGER Joseph KLINE Dean KIMMITT Robert McALLISTER Eugene WOLFF Alejandro BASS Peter DANAHER Scott DAWSON Thomas DLOUHY David B. DAVIS Kenneth B. GALLAGHER Michael	Under Secretary for International Affairs, Department of Treasury Assistant Secretary for International Affairs, Department of Treasur Deputy Assistant Secretary for Developing Nations, Department of Tre International Economist, Department of Treasury International Economist, Department of Treasury Under Secretary for Political Affairs, Department of State Assistant Secretary for Economic and Business Affairs, Department of Special Assistant to Under Secretary KIMMITT, Department of State Office of the Legal Advisor Department of State Economic Bureau, Department of State Executive Director, IMS, Department of Treasury Counselor of Embassy First Secretary of the US Embassy in Luxembourg Financial Attaché, US Mission to the EC
F.M.I.	1	BOORMAN John T.	Director of Exchange & Trade Relation Department
Finlande	1	KAUPILLA Seppo HJERPPE Reino	Ambassadeur Directeur Politique du Ministère des Affaires Etrangères Conseiller financier de la mission finlandaise auprès des CE
France	2	SAMUEL-LAJEUNESSE Denis BERACHA Pascale	Chef de service des Aff.Int.à la Direction du Trésor Ministère de l' Sous-Directeur chargé des questions financières internationales au M
Grèce	1	TERZIS Georges PROTOPAPAS	Expert de 1er rang MAE Représentation Permanente de Grèce auprès des CE
Irlande	1	RIGNEY Liam	Ambassadeur d'Irlande à Luxembourg
Islande	1	GUNNARSSON Gunnar Snorri	Chargé d'Affaires a.i. à l'Ambassade d'Islande à Bruxelles
Italie	3	ZUCCONI Gaetano PARISI Stefano DRAGHI	Directeur des Affaires Economiques MAE Secrétariat technique du Ministre des Affaires Etrangères Directeur Général du Ministère du Trésor
Japon	4	WATANABE Kōji UTSUMI Makoto KANEKO Yoshiaki HOBO Nobuhito	Deputy Minister for Foreign Affairs Vice Minister of Finance for International Affairs Minister, Embassy of Japan in the USA Deputy Director, Loan Aid Division, Economic Cooperation Bureau MAE
Koweit	1	AL-SAMMAK Ali	Conseiller
Luxembourg	4	MERSCH Yves BERNS Alphonse HEINEN Georges BICHLER Marc	Directeur des Finances FIN Directeur des Relations Economiques Internationales et de la Coopéra Chargé de Mission FIN Chargé de Mission MAE

GULF CRISIS FINANCIAL COORDINATION GROUP

0112

Norvège	4	HERNES Helga	Secrétaire d'Etat au Ministère des Affaires Etrangères
		RAEDER Peter	Chef de Division au Ministère des Affaires Etrangères
		ELLEFSEN Vegard	Conseiller au Ministère des Affaires Etrangères
		KARLSEN Prode	Directeur adjoint au Ministère des Finances
Pays-Bas	2	DE NEREE TOT BABERICH F.J.F.M.	Conseiller financier, Ambassade des Pays-Bas à Washington FIN
		LE POOLE J.P.	Chef, Bureau des Affaires Economiques MAE
Portugal	2	TOSCANO José Inacio	Chef de Cabinet de S.E. le Secrétaire d'Etat du Trésor
		SA MARTHA Francisco	Secrétaire d'Ambassade
Qatar	1	KAMAL Yousuf Hussain	Director of Financial Affairs
R.F.A.	3	KÖHLER Horst	Staatssekrtär FIN
		JUNCKER Ulrich	Chef de service Auswärtiges Amt
		LIPTAU G. Dr.	Conseiller, Bundesministerium für Zusammenarbeit
Royaume Uni	2	BONE Roger	Head of Economic Relations Department MAE
		WICKS Nigel	Ministry of Treasury
Suède	2	LUND Gunnar	Under-Secretary of State FIN
		JOHANSSON Sven-Olof	Assistant Under-Secretary FIN
Suisse	3	GYGI Ulrich	Directeur de l'Administration fédérale des finances
		KAESER Daniel	Sous-directeur de l'Administration fédérale des finances
		LAUTENBERG Alexis P.	Ministre Département fédéral des Affaires Etrangères

TOTAL :   84

GULF CRISIS FINANCIAL COORDINATION GROUP

0113

정 리 보 존 문 서 목 록					
기록물종류	일반공문서철	등록번호	15252	등록일자	1999-10-26
분류번호	772	국가코드	XF	보존기간	영구
명 칭	걸프사태 재정지원 공여국 조정위원회 회의, 1990-91. 전6권				
생 산 과	북미1과/경제협력2과/중동2과	생산년도	1990~1991	담당그룹	
권 차 명	V.5 제5차. Luxemburg, 1991.3.11 : 자료				
내용목차	★ 수석대표 : 이정빈 외무부 제1차관보 ★ 1991.3.6-9 이정빈 외무부 제1차관보 미국 방문 ★ 협의사항, 참고자료 등				

第 1 次官補 訪美時
重點 協議 事項

1991. 3

美 洲 局

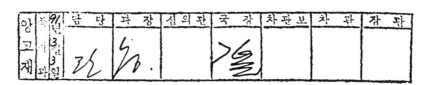

目　　　次

0003

添附 :　1. 主要人士 人的事項

　　　　2. 걸프事態 關聯 支援 推進 現況

　　　　3. 걸프戰 終戰에 따른 中東地域 秩序 再編 構想

0004

1. 人事 말씀

ㅇ 美軍을 비롯한 聯合軍이 걸프戰에서 가히 奇蹟이라 할 만한 최소한의
   人命 被害를 내면서 迅速한 勝利를 거둠으로써 그간 世界 平和와 安定을
   威脅하던 걸프事態가 終決되게 된 것을 祝賀함.

ㅇ 今番 걸프事態는 지난 40여년간 東.西間 冷戰이 崩壞되고 새로운 國際
   秩序가 形成되는 過程에서 發生하여 全 世界에 衝擊을 던져 주었음.

ㅇ 그러나 부쉬 大統領의 迅速하고 結緣한 指導力을 바탕으로 한 美國의
   主導下에 國際社會가 유엔 決議에 따라 一致 團結하여 地域 覇權을
   追求하는 이라크의 侵略을 擊退하고 걸프地域에서 平和와 安定을 回復
   하므로써 앞으로의 世界에 있어 集團 安全保障 措置를 통해 地域紛爭을
   解決하는 좋은 先例를 確立하였다고 봄.

ㅇ 한편, 우리로서는 아직도 武力赤化統一 路線을 固守하고 있는 北韓이
   걸프戰爭에서 敎訓을 얻어 非現實的인 政策을 하루속히 버리고 和解와
   協力의 길로 나와 韓半島에서 冷戰의 殘滓를 말끔히 씻어낼 수 있는
   契機가 마련되기를 期待함.

-1-   0005

1. Greetings

o I congratulate you that the gulf crisis which posed a serious
threat to the peace and stability of the world has come to
the end with an early and clear-cut victory by the U.S.-led
coalition forces and with miraculouslys mall number of casualties
on them.

o The Gulf crisis was a shock to the entire world. It was all
the more so because it took place when the world is undergoing
a transition from the collapse of the Cold War to a new
international order.

o However, the international community, in an unprecedented unity
led by President Bush's firm and resolute leadership and under
the auspices of the United Nations, succeded in repelling Iraqi
aggression aimed at regional hegemony and restoring peace and
stability in the Gulf region. We believe this sets another
good example of resolving regional conflict through collective
security measures.

o We in Korea hope that North Korea learns a lesson from the Gulf
crisis and gives up its unrealistic policy of military unification
so that new era of conciliation and cooperation prevails over
the Cold War con frontation on the Korean Peninsula as well.

0006

2. 中東秩序 再編 方案 및 我國의 參與

가. 美國의 中東秩序 改編 構想

○ 베이커 國務長官은 지난 2.6. 및 2.7. 上.下院 外交委에서 戰後
   걸프地域에 대한 美國의 構想을 發表한 것으로 알고 있음.
   당시 베이커 國務長官은 걸프地域의 安全保障 裝置는 걸프協力 會議
   (GCC) 等과 같이 域内 國家 全體의 參與를 基盤으로 해야 하며, 戰後
   걸프協力 會議나 UN 傘下의 地上軍 維持 可能性을 밝히고, 國境 保障을
   위해서 美國이 걸프地域에 海.空軍力을 駐屯시킬 수 있음을 暗示한
   것으로 알고 있는바, 이에 관한 美國의 보다 具體的인 構想은 ?

   * 베이커 國務長官이 밝힌 戰後 걸프 構想
     - 걸프地域 勢力均衡과 相互 侵略 防止를 위한 安全保障 裝置 마련
     - 化生放 武器의 供給 遮斷을 包含한 軍縮 協商
     - 域内國間의 貧富格差 解消를 위한 經濟 再建 計劃
     - 팔레스타인 問題 및 아랍-이스라엘 紛爭 解決 努力
     - 美國의 中東石油 依存度를 낮추는 政策 追求

○ 또한 유럽에서의 NATO 와 같은 安保機構 創設 論議에 대한 評價는 ?
   * 同 構想에 대한 批判者들은 NATO 와 같은 機構 創設을 위해서는
     美國과 유럽 諸國間에 民主主義. 自由라는 共同의 價値와 蘇聯
     이라는 共同의 적의 存在가 必要하다고 主張

-2-

0007

o 또한 최근 言論報道에 의하면 Robert Gates NSC 安保 副補佐官을
中心으로 戰後 中東秩序 改編에 관한 構想이 거의 完成되었다는 바,
美國이 構想하고 있는 中東地域 集團 安全保障 體制와 유엔 平和
維持軍 設置 計劃等에 관해 說明을 듣고자 함.

o 금번에 이라크가 敗退하므로써 過去 急進的 아랍 民族主義가 衰退하고
걸프地域에서는 사우디를 中心으로 弱化된 勢力均衡(a healthy
balance of weakness)이 形成될 것이라는 展望도 있는데 이에 대한
美側의 評價는 ?

나. 中東地域 軍縮 推進 方向

o 금번 걸프事態의 經驗을 통하여 核 및 化學武器 等 大量 殺傷 武器와
미사일 減縮, 그리고 미사일 運搬 體系에 관한 技術移轉 制限等의
必要性이 더욱 切實해졌는바, 向後 中東地域에서의 非在來式 武器
減縮은 어떻게 推進할 것인지 ?(특히, 이스라엘의 軍備나 核武器
保有와 關聯 美側의 構想)

다. 팔레스타인 問題等 아랍-이스라엘間 和解 問題

ㅇ 今番 걸프戰으로 아랍-이스라엘 問題, 특히 팔레스타인 問題는
이 地域의 安定을 위해서는 반드시 解決되어야 한다는 點이 크게
浮刻되었음.

ㅇ 그러나, 걸프戰을 契機로 팔레스타인 특히 PLO 가 이라크 支持로
立志가 弱化된 반면, 이스라엘은 美國과의 關係 緊密化 等 外交的으로
立志가 強化되므로써 解決이 더욱 어려워질 可能性도 대두되고 있는
바, 이 問題에 대한 美側의 解決 方案은 ?

라. 中東秩序 再編 過程에의 我國 參與問題

ㅇ 우리 政府는 걸프事態 發生以來 5億弗의 財政支援과 醫療團 및
輸送團을 派遣하는 等 同 地域에서의 平和와 安定回復을 위한 國際的
努力에 積極 參與하여 왔음.

ㅇ 우리는 앞으로 걸프地域에서 戰爭이 終決됨에 따라 이 地域의 安定을
하루속히 回復하기 위하여 우리의 能力 範圍內에서 할 수 있는 일이
무엇인가를 積極 檢討하고 있음. 이와관련 美側의 좋은 意見이
있으면 알려주기 바람.

- 4 -

0009

2. Restructuring Order in the Middle East and ROK Partinipation

A. US Plan to Restructure Order in the Middle East

o In early February Secretary Baker mentioned some aspects of
the U.S. plan for post-war Gulf region at Foreign Affairs
Committees of the Senate and the House of Representatives.
At that time, Secretary, while emphasizing that new security
arrangements should be based on a broad participation from
the nations in the region including the GCC countries and
implied the possibility of maintaining ground fores under
the auspices of the GCC or the United Nations and of
stationing U.S. naval and air fores in the region. Could
you elaborate this idea a bit further?
And, I want to invite your opinion on the much talked-about
idea of a NATO of Middle East version.

o It was reported that an NSC special team headed by Robert
Gates has almost completed a plan on restructuring post-war
Gulf politics.

o It was also suggested that, with the defeat of Iraq, radical
Arab nationalism would recede and a healthy balance of weakness
centered around Saudi Arabia would emerge. What is your
assessment?

B. The Gulf War made it all the more compelling to prohibit
proliferation of mass destruction weapons and to restrict transfer
of technology on their delivery system. How is the United States
planning to deal with this non-conventional arms reduction issue
in the Middle East?
(In particular, the U.S. view on the Israeli capabilities)

0010

C. Arab-Isreali Conflicts

o The Gulf War seems to have pointed out with greater emphasis
   that the resolution of Arab-Israeli conflicts including the
   Palestinian issue is imperative for lasting stability in the
   region.

o However, with the PLO whose position is weakened by its support
   for Iraq and Israel far strengthened by its close cooperation
   with the United States during the War, the chance of resolving
   of these compelling issues does not look better. What is your
   view on this matter?

D. ROK Participation.

o The ROK Government has made its maximum possible contribution
   to international efforts to restore peace and stability in the
   region, which includer 500 million dollar financial support and
   dispatches of a 154-member medical team and 5 C-130 cargo
   aircrafts.

o Now as the War is over, the ROK Government is considering what
   it can do within its capability to help restore stability in
   the region. In this regard, we will welcome any advice or
   suggestions from the United States.

0011

3. 戰後 中東建設 計劃 및 我國의 參與 問題

가. 美國의 中東地域 經濟 復興計劃

   ○ 世界經濟에 있어 막대한 重要性을 갖고 있는 中東地域에서 恒久的인
     平和와 安定 維持를 위해서는 이 地域의 國家間 貧富의 差를 解消하고
     經濟復興을 이룩하여야 한다는 主張이 강한바, 이를 위하여 美國이
     2次大戰後 유럽에 대해 實施했던 Marshall Plan 과 같은 構想을 갖고
     있는지 ?

   ○ 이와관련 現在 美國은 戰後 中東地域 經濟 復興計劃을 뒷받침하기
     위해 가칭 中東經濟開發 復興銀行 設立을 推進한다는 說이 있는데
     이에 대한 美側의 說明을 要請함. 또한 이에 대한 우리의 役割 및
     參與 方案에 관한 美側의 意見은 ?

   ○ 또한 中東地域 經濟 復舊에 대한 IMF 나 IBRD 등 旣存의 機構의
     役割과 關聯 美國의 構想은 ?

나. 戰後 復舊事業 參與 問題

   ○ 쿠웨이트 再建은 政治, 經濟, 社會等 廣範한 領域에 걸쳐 이루어질
     것으로 展望되며, 向後 5年間 500-5,000億弗의 復舊費가 所要될 것으로
     推定된다함.

-5-   0012

o 美國 企業들은 지금까지 締結된 약 200건의 復舊事業 契約中 약 70%를 獨占한 것으로 報道되고 있음. 이와 關聯한 建設 輸出等 多樣한 經驗을 가진 우리 企業들도 쿠웨이트 復舊事業에 積極的으로 參與하기를 원하고 있는바, 美側의 支援이 있기를 期待함.

o 이라크의 復舊問題에 대해서도 美側의 構想이 있으면 알려주기 바람.

다. 걸프事態 財政支援 供與國 調整委員會(GCFCG)의 向後 運營 및 活動 計劃

o GCFCG 는 걸프事態로 被害를 입고 있는 前線國家에 대한 經濟支援을 效果的으로 執行하는 동시에 이를 加速化시키는데 크게 寄與해 온 것으로 評價함.

o 美側은 걸프戰이 終決됨에 따라 GCFCG 의 役割 및 活動을 再調整할 計劃이 있는지 ? 앞으로 同 機構가 中東 經濟復舊를 위한 機構로 institutionalize 될 가능성은 ?

3. Post-War Reconstruction Plan and ROK Participation

A. US Plan for Middle East Economic Reconstruction

o It has been reported that the United States is moving toward
  establishing a Middle East Development Bank as a way of
  supporting Post-War reconstruction and relabilitation. We
  would like to be provided with some explanation on this.
  We also want to have any opinion the United States has on
  the role and the way of ROK participation.

o I would like to further invite your views on this in relation
  with the role of such existing mechanism as IMF and IBRD.

B. ROK Participation in Post-War Reconstruction

o 50-500 billion dollar reconstruction projects in Kuwait will
  soon go underway.

o Reportedly the US corporations have taken around 70 percent
  of thus far concluded contracts of reconstruction projects.
  Korean companies with strong background in construction in
  the Middle East are eager to make some contribution. We
  expect that the United States render support for them.

o Any opinion on reconstruction in Iraq would also be appreciated.

0014

C. GCFCG's Future Management and Action Plan

o We evaluate that GCFCG has effectively carried out and
   accelerated economic assistance to the front-line states.

o Does the United States consider any readjustment of the role
   and function of the GCFCG, or does it have any intention to
   further institutionalize it?

0015

4. 新世界 秩序 宣言을 위한 頂上會談 開催 問題

　○ 最近 言論 報道에 의하면 美國은 多國籍軍 派遣國과 其他 支援 供與國
　　首腦들이 參與하는 頂上會談을 開催할 計劃이라는 바, 이의 事實 與否는 ?
　　또한, 同 報道內容이 事實일 경우 開催時期, 參與國家 등 計劃은 ?

　○ 한편, 베이커 長官은 걸프地域의 平和構造 樹立等 協議를 위하여 3.6-16 間
　　中東地域을 巡訪하고 있는 것으로 알고 있는바, 이에 관한 자세한 說明을
　　구함.

　○ 고르바쵸프 大統領은 얼마전 美.蘇 關係가 아직도 깨어지기 쉬운(fragile)
　　關係라는 發言을 했는바, 걸프事態 이후 美.蘇 關係에 대한 美側의 立場 및
　　對蘇政策을 알려주기 바람.

4. Issue of Holding a Summit Meeting for the Declaration of New
   International Order

   o It was recently reported that the United States is planning to
      hold an international conference at the summit level with
      participants from coalition partners and other donor countries.
      Could you confirm this report and, if true, could you elaborate
      it further?

   o With regard to Secretary Baker's tour of the Middle East, Could
      you give some more detailed information?

   o President Gorbachev some time ago said that the U.S.-Soviet
      relations is still in a fragile state. I would like to invite
      your views on the post-war US-Soviet relations and US policy
      toward the Soviet Union.

0017

5. 韓國軍의 醫療支援團 및 軍輸送團 追加 活動問題

가. 醫療支援團 쿠웨이트 移動 問題

　　o 現在 사우디 알 누아이리아에서 活動中인 我國軍 醫療支援團은 任務
　　　開始後 걸프戰이 終了될때까지 784名(사우디軍 524名, 이라크軍 47名,
　　　其他 多國籍軍 213名)을 治療하였음.

　　o 同 醫療團은 戰爭이 終決되었음에도 人道的 見地에서 診療 活動을
　　　繼續하고 있으며, 앞으로도 당분간 活動 豫定인바, 이와 關聯 美側의
　　　特別한 意見이 있는지 ?

　　o 한편, 우리 政府는 쿠웨이트內 緊急 醫療 需要에 副應키 위해 同
　　　醫療團을 쿠웨이트로 移動시키는 方案도 考慮하고 있는바, 이에대한
　　　美側의 立場은 ?

나. 空軍輸送團 活動 繼續 問題

　　o 우리 政府는 지난 2.21. UAE 알아인 基地에 派遣되어 지금까지
　　　多國籍軍에 대한 後方輸送 支援 業務를 擔當하고 있는 我國의 軍
　　　輸送團을 걸프 配置 美軍에 대한 輸送支援 業務를 繼續하기 위해
　　　당분간 Al Ain 에 繼續 配置할 생각인바, 輸送支援 活動 繼續 必要性에
　　　대한 美側의 立場은 ?

-8-

0018

5. Medical Support Group and Military Transport Team

    A. Relocating Medical Support Group to Kuwait

        o Korean Military Medical Support Group treated 784 Soldiers
           (524 Saudis, 47 Iraqis, 213 others) during the Gulf War.

        o We are going to continue to provide medical service from
           humanitarian viewpoint for some period after the War.
           Does the United States have any special comment on this
           matter?

    B. Continuing Military Transport Service

        o The Korean Government plans to have our Military Transport
           Team in Al Ain continue to provide transportation service
           to the U.S. forces.
           What is the U.S. position toward this plan?

0019

6. 걸프事態 關聯 我國의 支援

가. 第1次 支援 執行 現況

　o 90年度 對美 支援分으로 策定된 現金 5千萬弗과 輸送支援 3千萬弗은
　　全額 執行이 되었으며, 91년도 多國籍軍에 대한 支援으로 配定되었던
　　2,500萬弗도 1.23. Baker 長官의 要請에 따라 現在 美國에 대한 輸送
　　支援으로 配定, 現在 약 500萬弗을 執行하였으며, 輸送 支援等 現在도
　　繼續하고 있음.

　o 기타 多國籍軍에 대한 支援 및 前線國家에 대한 支援은 早期 執行을
　　위해 關聯國과 協議를 繼續하고 있음.

　　　* 90.10.27 ~ 11.8 간 정부 조사단 1차 파견
　　　　91. 2.24 ~ 3.9 간 정부 조사단 2차 파견(UAE, 이집트, 사우디,
　　　　요르단)

　　　* 前線國家 執行上 問題點
　　　　- 걸프事態 被害國에 대한 支援事業 協議次 我國은 政府調査團을
　　　　　90.10.27-11.8 및 91.2.24-3.9 간 派遣, 支援計劃을 協議
　　　　　하였으며, 駐在公館을 통해 早期支援을 希望하는 立場을 전하고
　　　　　早速한 支援事業 및 品目 選定을 督促해온 결과 터키, 요르단,
　　　　　모로코에 대한 支援은 比較的 순조로이 執行되고 있음.
　　　　- 그러나 이집트의 경우, 3차에 걸쳐 品目選定 및 借款利用計劃書
　　　　　提出을 督促하였으나 이집트 政府內 部處間 協議 지체로 인해
　　　　　상금 進陟이 없음.

-9-

0020

- 未修交國인 시리아의 경우 國防長官으로 부터 支援希望品目
提示가 있었으나 外交채널을 통한 시리아 政府의 公式立場
表明은 없음.

  · 我國은 駐日, 요르단 및 이란 公館을 통해 시리아 政府와
協議 推進中

ㅇ 한편 우리 政府는 91년도에 支援하기로 한 5千萬弗中 2,500萬弗은
對美 輸送支援으로 配定하였으며, 나머지 2,500萬弗은 前線國家에
대한 執行計劃을 樹立中에 있음.

나. 我國의 2次 支援 執行 方案 (美側 擧論時 對應)

ㅇ 우리 政府는 지난 2.20. 對美 追加支援 280百万弗中 現金 및 輸送
支援 110百万弗을 現金 60百万弗, 輸送支援 50百万弗로 支援할 것을
提示하였는 바, 이에 대한 美側의 立場은 ?

ㅇ 또한 170百万弗의 軍需物資 支援의 執行方案에 대한 美側의 立場은 ?

ㅇ 한편, 英國은 지난 2.13. John Weston 外務部 政務擔當 副次官을
我國에 派遣, 30百萬 내지 40百万弗의 戰費支援을 要請해 왔음.
우리 政府로서는 걸프戰에서의 英國의 寄與度等을 감안 英國에 대한
戰費 支援을 積極 檢討하고 있으나, 우리의 經濟與件上 旣約束한
500百万弗 以外의 追加 支援은 現實的으로 不可能한 實情임.

- 10 -   0021

ㅇ 우리는 美國이 이러한 우리의 立場을 充分히 理解하여 美國에 대한
軍需物資 支援 約束인 170百万弗에서 一部를 英國에 대한 戰費
支援으로 轉用하는 我側 提議를 受諾할 것을 要望함.

다. 美側의 追加支援 要請에 대한 우리 立場 (美側 擧論時 對應)

ㅇ 막대한 戰爭 所要 經費에 비추어 볼때, 韓國의 支援金이 相對的으로
크다도 볼 수는 없으나, 아래와 같이 韓國이 처한 事情下에서는
最大限의 金額이며, 이 規模를 上廻하는 어떤 金額도 韓國內에서 매우
深刻한 政治的, 財政的 問題를 야기하지 않고는 推進될 수 없으므로
美國이 韓國의 支援金 增額을 무리하게 시도하지 않는 것이 切實히
要望됨.

1) 日本과의 단순 GNP 對比만으로 韓國의 支援 能力을 計算하는 것은
現實的이지 못하며, 貿易收支, 對外資産, 政府 財政 狀態等을
考慮해야 함. (89년 基準 貿易黑字 日本/韓國 = 641億弗/46億弗,
對外純資産 日本/韓國 = 2,930億弗/-31億弗等)

2) 韓國은 美國의 同盟國中 가장 높은 GNP 對比 防衛費 負擔을 안고
있을뿐 아니라, 韓.美 兩者間 安保協力을 위한 防衛費 分擔이 매년
急增하고 있음.

3) 작년말 豫算 編成 당시 政治, 社會的으로 극히 重要한 秋穀 收買價도
약 3億弗 정도의 豫算 부족으로 인해 農民의 期待에 副應치 못함
으로서 人口의 15%에 해당되는 農村 人口로부터 심각한 反撥을

- 11 -

0022

야기시켰으며, 國會에서 野黨으로부터 殺人的 農政이라는 非難을 받고, 國會가 停會되는 事態까지 發生했음.

4) 우리나라는 今年들어 1月달에 17億 8千 4百万弗의 赤字에 이어 2月에도 16.1億弗의 赤字를 記錄, 總 33億 8千 5百万弗의 赤字를 記錄하는 等 매우 어려운 狀況임.

o 한편, 我國의 최근 對蘇 經協은 原則的으로 商業 베이스에서 이루어진 것이며, 政府 財政 支出이 아닌바, 消費財 輸出用 戰貸借款 15億弗, 資本財 輸出用 延拂輸出 5億弗, Libo 金利에 따른 銀行間 借款 10億弗로 構成되어 있음.

o 이러한 經濟協力은 韓國뿐만 아니라, 各國이 商業的 次元에서 施行하는 協力 形態이며, 蘇聯 極東 地域의 原木, 天然가스, 석탄 등 韓國으로 搬入 可能한 資源을 考慮하면, 借款 償還에 있어 큰 어려움이 없을 것으로 볼 뿐만 아니라, 韓.蘇間 協力은 蘇聯의 對北韓 軍事 援助 抑制, 北韓의 核安全 協定 締結 誘導等 政治的으로 肯定的인 影響도 期待됨.

o 韓國의 걸프事態 解決 支援 努力은 단순히 石油 供給의 安定이라는 經濟的 次元을 넘어 中東事態의 安定이 가져오는 國際 政治的 效果, 韓.美 同盟關係等을 考慮한 措置이며, 可能한 最大限의 支援을 한다는 點에 대하여 與野를 막론하고 異意가 없음을 다시한번 强調코자 함.

6. Contribution to the Multinational Efforts

A. Disbursement of First Pledge

o Our pledge to the United States for 1990, that is, 50 million
   dollars in cash and 30 million in transportation service, has
   been completely disbursed. At the request on Jan. 23 of
   Secretary Baker, we also reallocated 25 million dollars from
   the amount earmarked for support to multi-national forces in
   1991 to transportation support to the United States. Until
   now, about 5 million has been used, and we are continuing our
   transportation service.

o For speedy disbursement of our pledge to other coalition
   countries and the front-line states, we are consulting with
   the countries concerned.

o Among the pledge of 50 million dollars for 1991, 25 million is
   earmarked for transportation service for the United States.
   As to the remaining 25 million dollars, we are reviewing plans
   of our support to the front-line states.

B. Disbursement of Second Pledge

o On Feb. 20, we presented our proposal regarding the composition
   of the 110 million dollars, which is the portion for cash and
   transportation service among our total pledge of 280 million
   made to the United States. What is the U.S. reaction to our
   proposal of providing 60 million in cash and 50 million in
   transportation service?

0024

o   What is the U.S. position on the form of disbursement of the
    178 million dollars we promised to provide in military materiel?

o   The United Kingdom requested on Feb. 13 that Korea contribute
    32 to 40 million dollars to the U.K. Although we have positively
    examined the possibility of accommodating the U.K. request, we
    finally came to the conclusion that our difficult economic
    situation does not allow us to promise extra contribution.

o   I would like to request the United States to understand our
    position and agree to diverting some of the 178 million dollars
    earmarked as military materiel for the United States to support
    to the United Kingdom.

C. Korea's Position toward U.S. Request for Additional Contribution

    o   Although Korea's contribution is a small amount compared to
        the immense war expenditures, it is the maximum we can affort
        under current situations. It is necessary that the United
        States does not try to push us into making more contrbution
        so as not to cause serious political and financial problems
        in Korea.

    o   Our loan program for the Soviet Union was made on commercial
        base, and does not require government expenditure. The package
        is composed of 1.5 billion dollars of tied loan for export of
        consumer goods, 500 million dollars of deferred payment for
        export of capitial goods, and 1 billion dollars of bank loan
        at Libo rate.

0025

o We do not expect much problem in the repayment, considering
   the vast amount of timber, natural gas, coal and other
   resources we can import from the Soviet Union. In addition,
   we think that the economic cooperation with the Soviet Union
   may produce positive effect on the political side like the
   Soviet restaint of military assistance to North Korea and
   inducing North Korea to sign the safegurad agreement with
   the IAEA.

o Our decision to provide support to the coalition efforts in
   the Gulf was made in consideration not only of the need for
   a stable supply of crude oil but also of Korea-U.S. alliance
   and the positive impact a quick restabilization of the
   Middle East would probably have on international politics.
   I would like to emphasize once again that Korea has done
   its utmost best, and that everyone in Korea, Government
   or opposition, is in agreement on that point.

7. 外務長官 訪美 問題

ㅇ 新任 李相玉 外務長官이 조기에 美國을 訪問 韓.美 外務長官 會談을 조속
開催하여 戰後 中東秩序 再編 및 復舊計劃, 韓.美 頂上會談 問題, 韓半島
問題, 通商問題 및 亞.太 問題에 대해 率直한 意見을 交換하고 韓.美
兩國關係 强化 方案에 관해서도 協議를 할 必要가 있음.

ㅇ 韓.美 外務長官 會談 開催에 편리한 時期를 協議하기를 원하며, 李相玉
長官 訪美時 부쉬 大統領, 퀘일 副統領, 체니 國防長官, Scowcroft 白堊館
安保補佐官 等 行政府 高位人士 및 議會 指導者들의 面談이 可能하도록
美側의 積極的인 協調가 있기를 期待함.

- 13 -

0027

7. Foreign Minister's Visit to the U.S.

    o   It is desirable that new Foreign Minister Lee Sang-Ock have
        a meeting with Secretary Baker as soon as possible and
        exchange opinions on the reestabilishment of order and
        post-war rehabilitation of the Middle East, a possible summit
        meeting, and other issues related to R.O.K-U.S. relations.

    o   We hope to discuss a mutually convenient time to hold the
        ministerial meeting, and expect the U.S. cooperation in
        arranging Minister Lee's calls on President Bush, Vice
        President Quayle, Secretary Cheney, Mr. Scowcroft, and other
        high-ranking officials in the Executive Branch, as well as
        leading lawmakers.

0028

공   란

공   란

공   란

공   란

공   란

添附 : 1. 主要人士 人的事項

2. 걸프事態 關聯 支援 推進 現況

3. 걸프戰 終戰에 따른 中東地域 秩序 再編 構想

0034

1. 主要人士 人的事項

0035

Karl Jackson NSC 아시아 擔當 補佐官

ㅇ 姓　　名 : Karl JACKSON

ㅇ 職　　責 : 白堊館 國家安保會의 아시아 擔當 補佐官

ㅇ 生年月日 : 1942. 10. 30.

ㅇ 學　　歷 :

　　1965　　　프린스톤大 碩士

　　1971　　　MIT 大 博士

ㅇ 經　　歷 :

　　71-72　　　東西 交流 研究所 수습 研究員

　　72　　　　東西 交流 研究所 研究員

　　72-80　　　버클리大 政治學課 助教授

0036

77-78   태국 所在 UN 아시아.太平洋 開發 研究所 客員 研究員

80-82   버클리大 政治學課 副教授

82-83   國防省 東亞.太 擔當 副次官補 特別補佐官

83-84   國防省 政策企劃副室長

86-89.1   國防省 東亞.太 擔當 副次官補

89.2-   國家安保會議 아시아 擔當 補佐官

o 家族事項 : 기혼, 1男2女

0037

Kimmitt 정무차관

o 성   명 : Robert M. KIMMITT

o 직   책 : 정무차관

o 생년월일 : 1947.12.19

o 출 생 지 : Logan, Utah

o 학   력

  1969   미 육사 졸업

  1977   Georgetown 대학(법학)

o 경   력

  1969-   소위 임관

  1970-71   월남 근무

  1977-78   미 항소재판소 근무

  1978-83   NSC 근무

  1983-85   NSC 부보좌관

  1985-87   재무성 고문관

  1987-89   Sidney & Austin 법률회사

  1989-   국무부 정무차관

o 가족관계 : 부인 및 4자녀

0038

Solomon 國務部 東亞.太 次官補

ㅇ 姓　　名 :　Richard H. SOLOMON

ㅇ 生年月日 :　1937. 6. 13.

ㅇ 學　　歷 :

　1966　　　M.I.T. 博士學位 取得

ㅇ 經　　歷 :

　1966-71　　Michigan大 政治學 教授

　1971-76　　NSC 아시아 擔當 補佐官

　1972-74　　SAIS 客員敎授

　1976-86　　Rand 硏究所 硏究員, 國際安保政策 責任硏究員

　1986-88　　國務部 政策企劃室長

　1989-　　　國務部 東亞.太 次官補

ㅇ 訪韓記錄 :

　1988.7.　　슐츠 國務長官 訪韓時 隨行

　1989.12.　　몰타 美.蘇 頂上會談 結果 說明 目的

　1990.5.　　管轄 地域 國家 巡訪 目的

　1990.8.　　亞.太 閣僚會談(싱가폴) 및 美.蘇 外務長官 會談(이르쿠츠크)
　　　　　　　參席後

0039

Kelly 近東.南亞 次官補

o 성   명 : John H. KELLY

o 직   책 : 近東.南亞 次官補

o 생년월일 : 1939.7.20.

o 출 생 지 : Fond Du Lac, 위스컨신

o 학   력 :

1961   에모리 대학 졸업

o 경   력

1964   외교관 생활 시작

1965-67   터키 근무(부영사)

1969-71   태국 근무(영사)

1972-76   국무부, 국방부 근무

1976-80   파리주재 미대사관 근무

1980-81   국무부장관 비서실장

1982-83   선임 공보 부차관보

1983-85   수석 구주 부차관보

1986-88   레바논 주재 미대사

1989-   近東.南亞 次官補

0040

Rowen 국제안보 담당 차관보

o 성   명 : Henry S. ROWEN

o 직   책 : 국방부 국제안보 담당 차관보

o 생년월일 : 1925.10.11.

o 출 생 지 : Boston. Massachusetts

o 학   력 :

   1949   미 MIT 대 졸업

   1955   영 Oxford 대(철학 석사)

o 경   력 :

   1950-61   Rand Corp. 연구원

   1961-64   국방부 안보담당 부차관보

   1965-66   예산국 부국장

   1967-72   Rand Corp. 연구소장

   1972-81   Stanford 대 Hoover 연구소 교수

   1981-83   CIA 국가 정보회의(NIC) 의장

   1983-89   Stanford 대 Hoover 연구소 연구원

   89-현재   국방부 국제안보 담당 차관보

o 가족관계 : 부인 및 6자녀

0041

2. 걸프事態 關聯 支援 推進 現況

0042

걸프事態 關聯 支援 推進現況

1. 支援 計劃

가. 一次 支援計劃(90.9.24. 發表)

(單位 : 만불)

區　　分	現　金	物　資	EDCF	쌀	其　他	合　計
美　　　國	5,000				3,000 (輸 送)	8,000
周　邊　國		3,700	4,000			7,700
방글라데시				500		500
I　O　M	50					50
行　政　費	50					50
豫　備　費	200			500		700
91年度計劃					5,000	5,000
	5,300	3,700	4,000	1,000	8,000	22,000

나. 追加支援 計劃(91.1.30. 發表)

　　ㅇ 多國籍軍에 2億8千万弗 相當 支援

　　　- 1억7천만불 : 國防部 在庫 軍需物資 및 裝備提供

　　　- 1억1천만불 : 現金 및 輸送支援

　　ㅇ 追加支援은 多國籍軍 특히 美國支援이며 周邊國 經濟支援은 불포함

다. 我國의 總 支援規模는 5億弗임.

0043

2. 支援現況

가. 支援事業 執行狀況(91.3.5. 現在)

(單位 : 萬弗)

區 分	現 金 (執行)	輸 送 (執行)	物 資 (執行)	借 款 (執行)	合 計	進陟度(%)
美 國	5,000 (5,000)	5,500 (3,556)	-	-	10,500 (8,556)	81.5
周 邊 國	-	-	3,700 (900)	4,000 (0)	7,700 (900)	11.7
. 이집트	-	-	1,500 (0)	1,500 (0)	3,000 (0)	0
. 터 키	-	-	500 (500)	1,500 (0)	2,000 (500)	25
. 요르단	-	-	500 (200)	1,000 (0)	1,500 (200)	13.3
. 시리아	-	-	1,000 (0)	-	1,000 (0)	0
. 모로코	-	-	200 (200)	-	200 (200)	100
I O M	50 (50)				50 (50)	100
行 政 費	50 (40)	-	-	-	50 (40)	
豫 備 費 . ICRC, UNESCO	200 (6)	-	-	-	200 (6)	3
綜 合	5,300 (5,096)	3,000 (3,556)	3,700 (900)	4,000 (0)	18,500 (9,552)	51.6

※ 91년도 支援豫定分中 前線國家 支援 2,500萬弗 및 쌀 1,000萬弗등 3,500萬弗은
除外

- 단, 1차 支援時 91년도 支援 配定額中 2,500萬弗은 對美輸送 支援으로
  전환, 3.5. 現在 不執行

0044

나. 推進現況

(1) 美 國

　○ 現金 5,000만불 支援(90.12)

　○ 多國籍軍 輸送費, 91.3.5. 現在 3,556만불 支援(제1차 支援約束時
　　總 5,500만불 配定)

(2) 周 邊 國

　가) 이집트

　　○ 軍需 物資 (700만불)
　　　- 이집트측은 品目選定을 위한 4명의 군수전문가단 訪韓을 希望해
　　　　왔으므로 접수용의 表明했으나 常今 回信 없음.

　　○ 民需用 物資 (800만불)
　　　- 住民登錄 電算化 事業費로의 轉用이 擧論되었으나 이집트 政府內
　　　　協議 常今 進行中

　　○ EDCF 借款 (1,500만불)
　　　- 이집트는 EDCF 借款을 無償援助 資金으로 轉換要請한바 있으나
　　　　豫算 뒷받침없어 不可함을 通報 (91.2.9)

　나) 터 키

　　○ 民需用 物資 (500만불)
　　　- 터키측, 앰블런스.미니버스.트럭등 23개 品目 提示(90.12.18. 接受)
　　　- 500만불 상당의 對 터키 支援品目 確定, 現在 發送 進行中
　　　　(一部品目 旣到着, 91.1.22. 物品 發注 最終 契約)

0045

o EDCF 借款(1,500만불)

- 터키측, 아국산 上水道用 파이프(Ductile Pipe) 購入에 使用
  希望 (90.12.14)

- 國産 파이프 供給不足으로 다른 事業計劃書 提出토록 要請

다) 요르단

o 民需用 物資(500만불)

- 요르단측, 설탕, 미니버스, 各種 生必品等 總24個 品目 提示
  (90.12.24)

- 1차 支援品(설탕, 미니버스 200만불 相當)은 91.1.25. 物品
  發注 契約 締結, 發送中

- 其他品目은 요르단측에서 品目確定後 追後 發送豫定

o EDCF 借款(1,000만불)

- 廢水處理工場 事業計劃書 提示(90.12.11)

- 關係機關(財務部, 輸出入銀行) 檢討完了, 政府間 協定締結
  準備中

라) 시 리 아

o 民需用 物資(400만불) 및 軍需物資 (600만불)

- 90.11.2~11.5간 政府調査團 訪問, 對시리아 物資支援計劃 通報
  (1,000만불)

- 시리아 國防長官, 全額 미니버스로 支援希望 (90.11.21자 駐 레바논
  大使代理앞 書信)

- 我側, 外交經路(駐日大使館)을 통해 提議토록 要請했으나(90.11.24)
  尙今 回信 未接受

- 駐日 大使館에 시리아측 立場 打診토록 指示 (91.2.13)

0046

마) 모 로 코

　　o　軍需物資（200만불）

　　　- 希望品目　7개提示(방독면，침투보호의，텐트등)

　　　- 200만불　상당의　對　모로코　支援品目確定，發送　進行中(91.1.14.

　　　　物品　發注　契約　畢)

(3)　쌀　支援

　　o　방글라데시에　500만불，豫備費로　500만불　상당의　쌀支援이　豫定되었으나

　　　쌀　輸出節次上의　特殊性으로　現在　執行　不可狀態

　　　- 쌀　支援은　FAO 및　農産物　輸出國과　協議가　必要하나　美國側에서

　　　　難色을　表明　하였으므로　現實的으로　執行이　어려움

(4)　걸프事態　難民關聯　國際機構　支援現況(56만불)

　　가)　支援計劃上　50만불　配定(IOM 支援)

　　나)　執行現況

　　　　o　IOM(국제이민기구)　:　50만불

　　　　o　UNESCO　:　3만불（豫備費）

　　　　o　ICRC　:　3만불（豫備費）

(5)　調査團　派遣等　行政費　執行現況　:　약　30만불

0047

3. 걸프戰 終戰에 따른 中東地域 秩序 再編 構想

0048

걸프戰 終戰에 따른 中東地域 秩序再編 構想

1. 美側 構想

2. 카나다側 構想

3. 프랑스側 構想

4. 팔레스타인 問題 暫定解決 方案

5. 터어키의 戰後 걸프 地域 安保體制 構想

6. 걸프戰 平和的 解決 仲裁 動向

添 附 : 1. Baker 長官 美 上.下院 外交委 證言文 1部

2. Clark 外相 카나다 國際 問題 硏究所 招請 午餐 演說文

3. Kissinger Newsweek紙 寄稿文 寫本 1部.

0049

1. 美側 構想

 * 2.6, 2.7, Baker 國務長官, FY92 豫算提出 關聯 上.下院
   外交委에서 證言

 가. 戰後 處理問題 接近 基本姿勢

  ○ 向後 地上戰 開始時 많은 死傷者 발생등 제반 어려움과
    미래에 대한 불안감 增大로 인해 戰後 處理問題에 대한
    接近에 있어 愼重함(Sense of Modesty)의 필요성을 강조함.
    - 域內 國家의 主權尊重 및 平和定着 노력 필요

 나. 終戰後 當面 諸般 挑戰

  (걸프地域을 包含한 中東地域 全體의 安全保障 體制 樹立)

  ○ 安全保障 體制의 目的과 원칙
    - 侵略의 沮止
    - 領土의 不可侵性
    - 國家간 제분쟁의 평화적 해결

  ○ 域內 國家, 國際機構 및 國際社會의 役割
    - 上記 原則과 目標達成에는 域內 모든 國家들과 GCC
      等이 主導的 역할 수입 필요
      . 戰後 이라크, 이란등의 建設的 役割 기대
    - UN과 友邦國들은 强力한 支援 계속 제공필요

  ○ 美國은 트루만 行政府 以來 中東地域에 海軍力을 配置
    하고 사우디 等 域內 國家들과 兩者關係를 강화시켜
    왔으나 終戰後 美 地上軍을 계속 유지할 계획은 없음.

0050

o 終戰 直後의 過渡期的 狀況에 있어서의 平和維持軍 구성
  문제
  - UN 또는 GCC 旗幟아래 域內 國家 地上軍으로 編成된
    平和 維持軍을 일정기간 또는 반영구적으로 駐屯케하는
    方案과
  - 域外 友邦國들의 地上軍으로 구성된 平和維持軍 配置
    또는 決議案 또는 安全保障 確約等 政治的 보장 방안
    等을
    관련국들간 廣範圍한 協議를 통해 決定이 필요함.

(在來式 武器 및 大量 殺傷武器의 擴散 防止)

o 戰後 域內 國家들의 大量 殺傷武器 生産 및 保有能力을
  없애고 域內 國家間 武器 保有競爭 억제와 중동지역에
  일종의 信賴構築 措置의 적용 방안 검토가 要求됨.
  - 化學武器 協定 早期妥結 및 尖端技術 移轉 統制等

(經濟 復舊 및 再建 措置)

o 쿠웨이트 및 이라크 經濟復舊에 協力 支援
  - 經濟 再建後 域內 自由貿易 및 투자확대
  - 水資源 開發에도 力點

o 中東地域 銀行 設立을 통한 경제재건 및 開發 방안제시
  - 과거 경험상 地域銀行 設立 및 IBRD/IMF와의 協調
    關係 중요성 감안

0051

(이스라엘과 아랍國家 및 팔레스타인 民族間 和解)

o 相互間 尊重.忍耐 및 信賴를 基盤으로한 이스라엘과
  아랍국간 對話進展은 中東地域 全般의 平和定着 과정의
  필수적 부분임.
  - 이스라엘과 팔레스타인 民族間 和解를 위한 兩側의
    具體的 行動, 동 과정에 있어서의 아랍 國家들의 역할,
    域內 軍備統制 推進의 영향, 最適 外交的 手段 講究
    等이 검토 대상

(美國의 對中東 原油 依存度 減縮)

o 美國의 對中東 原油 依存度 減縮을 위한 綜合對策 施行이
  요구됨.
  - 에너지의 節約, 效率性 增大 방안, 원유 비축분 증대,
    代替燃料 사용 증대등의 綜合 시행

0052

2. 카나다측 構想

    * 2.8. 멀루니 首相은 오타와 Confederation Club 招請 演説에서
      闡明

      - Clark 外務長官, 퀘벅시 소재 카나다 國際問題 研究所 招請
        演説時 同一 內容 發表

  가. 걸프전 終戰 관련 4대 基本原則

      o 이라크군의 쿠웨이트로 부터의 完全 撤收 目標는 妥協의
        여지가 없음.

      o 걸프 地域의 諸般 問題 解決 방안은 관련국 및 國民들의
        支持를 받는 것이어야 함.

      o UN을 中心으로 한 諸般問題 解決이 바람직함.

      o 中東地域 安保體制는 政治, 經濟, 軍事 및 人道的 問題等
        관련 問題를 包括的으로 다루어야 함.

  나. 終戰 直後 推進 課題

      (人道的 援助 提供)

      o 國際 難民 고등판무관실(UNHCR), UNDRO, 國際 赤十字社
        等과의 협조를 통한 民間人 戰爭 被害者들에 대한 인도적
        援助 提供 노력 전개 필요

(平和 維持軍 構成)

o UN 旗幟下에 域內國家 地上軍들로 구성된 平和維持軍에
　 의한 쿠웨이트 國境線 安全保障 활동 적극 지원
　 - 域外 國家들의 參加도 考慮

(環境 汚染 除去 努力)

o 이라크의 걸프만에의 原油 放流로 인한 海洋汚染 被害
　 縮小를 위한 國際的 노력 지원
　 - 專門家 팀等 現地派遣

다. 中.長期的 中東地域 安保體制 樹立

(地域 安保 體制 樹立)

o 地域 安保 體制는 UN과 聯合軍 파견국들간의 國際的 協約
　 等에 의한 國際的 保障이 필요함.
　 - 걸프 地域에의 항구적 外國軍 駐屯은 불요

o 유럽에서의 CSCE 成功 經驗을 참고로 한 中東地域 전역을
　 대상으로 한 '地中海에서의 安保協力 會議'(Conference on
　 Security and Cooperation in the Mediterranean) 構想
　 檢討 提議

o 國境 保障, 國家間 紛爭의 平和的 解決, 會員國間 信賴
　 構築 方案 確立等이 同 安保 體制의 主要 任務가 될 것임.

o 域內 國家들간 진정한 대화를 기초로한 域內 安保 問題에
　 대한 巨視的 接近은 中東地域內 民主主義的 경향 확대에
　 기여할 것임.

0054

(이스라엘-아랍 民族間 對立 解消)

o 包括的이고 항구적인 이스라엘-아랍 民族間 대립 해소
　없이는 地域 安保 體制의 성공이 미지수임.
　　- UN 安保理 決意 242호 및 338호를 기초로 한 交涉 解決
　　　方案이 바람직
　　- 同 問題 討議를 위한 國際會議 開催 歡迎

(域內 國家間 經濟的 不均衡 解消)

o 中東 地域內 모든 국가들의 균형적인 經濟 發展을 위해
　2차 대전후 마샬플랜과 유사한 域內 經協機構 設立 推進을
　積極 支援함.
　　- UN과 連繫된 地域 經濟協力機構 創設

라. 戰爭手段 및 大量 殺傷武器 除去에 관한 頂上會談 開催 提議

o 이라크를 포함한 中東地域 國家들에 武器를 販賣한 서방
　先進國들의 무모했던 과거 形態의 變更이 절실히 요구됨.

o 中東地域 平和案에는 大量 殺傷武器의 전파와 재래식 병기의
　備蓄을 엄격히 제한하는 裝置 마련이 포함되어야 함.
　　- 同件 관련 多者間 協議는 이미 開始

o 카나다는 同 頂上會談의 積極的 推進을 위해, Clark 外相이
　來週 런던 開催 英聯邦 外相會議 參席은 물론, 10여일간
　관계국을 巡訪, 同件 協議 豫定임.

0055

3. 프랑스側 構想

＊ 미테랑 大統領, 2.7. T.V. 會見時 立場 表明

(基本 立場)

o 쿠웨이트 駐屯 이라크군 逐出을 통한 쿠웨이트 主權回復 이라는
  UN 決議案의 名分을 尊重 參戰한 바, 同 目標가 達成되면 戰後
  處理를 위해 地域 安保機構 設立, 쿠웨이트, 이라크 經濟再建
  및 이스라엘-아랍 國家間 和解 모색을 위한 국제회의 개최가
  必要함.

(國際會議를 통한 協議 議題)

o 紛爭 再發 防止를 위한 國際的 保障 問題
  - 現 國境線 尊重 및 地域 均衡 回復

o 固有 中東 問題
  - 팔레스타인-이스라엘 問題 및 레바논 問題 等

o 戰爭 被害 復舊 事業을 위한 지역 은행 또는 開發基金 參席문제
  - 石油로 인한 富의 均衡 분배 문제
  - 現 國際武器 販賣 方式에 대한 制度改善 및 통제 문제

0056

4. 팔레스타인 問題 暫定解決 方案

* Henry Kissinger 前 美 國務長官의 91.1.28.자 Newsweek지
   기고문

가. 基本 認識

   o 現 段階에서 팔레스타인 문제의 완전한 解決은 現實的으로
      不可能함.
      - 당사자간의 懸隔한 立場差異로 반목과 불화만 增幅

   o 美國의 仲裁와 걸프戰 終戰 以後 影響力이 증대될 온건
      아랍국의 役割을 활용함.

   o 終戰後 수개월내 해결 노력 개시 필요
      - 너무 시간을 끌면 사담후세인 류의 過激 勢力 影響力
         回復 危險

나. 具體的 內容

   o 유엔 事務總長의 후견하에 美, 이스라엘 및 걸프 戰時
      美國과 공동 보조를 취한 아랍국(온건 아랍국)간의 會議
      召集

   o 온건 아랍국은 일정期間(例 ; 5-10년간) 아랍측에 返還될
      領土의 受託者(trustee)役割 擔當

   o 온건 아랍국은 유엔 監視下에 同 地域의 非武裝化 實施
      - 이스라엘, 同 檢證 過程 參與

0057

o 이스라엘은 Gaza 全域과 West Bank中 人口 密集地域을 아랍
  側에 返還
  - West Bank 中 이스라엘 安保에 直決되는 地域만 繼續
    維持

o 이스라엘이 返還한 領土를 다스릴 政府 構成 問題는 合意에
  의해 決定 단, 暫定 期間中에는 完全 獨立國家 수립은 보류
  - 受託國들은 PLO側이 받아들일 수 있는 人士를 包含,
    政府 構成 豫想

0058

5. 터어키의 戰後 걸프 地域 安保體制 構想

   가. 戰後 걸프 地域 安保體制

      (終戰後 이란, 사우디 勢力增大)

      o 이라크는 敗戰에 따른 體制崩壞 내지는 군사력 약화로 地域
        安保體制에 큰 影響力을 미치지 못할 것이므로 短期的으로는
        이란, 사우디 兩國의 勢力 均衡으로 地域安保體制가 構築
        될 것으로 보임.
        - 軍事力이 우세한 이란의 勢力이 크게 浮上 豫想

      (이라크 領土保存 및 이라크의 이란 牽制勢力으로서의 價値)

      o 이란, 시리아, 터키의 理解關係 상충으로 인하여 戰後
        이라크 領土分割내지는 이라크 北部에 Kurd 獨立國 또는
        自治區 創設 가능성은 많지 않으며, 이라크의 領土는 종전
        대로 보존될 것으로 보임.

      o 戰後 勢力 膨脹이 예상되는 이란을 견제하기 위해서는
        아랍국인 이라크의 領土保存 및 일정 수준의 軍事力 보유가
        필요할 것이며, 이점에서 아랍 諸國과 美國의 理解가 일치
        될 수 있을 것임.

      o 戰後 이라크의 軍事力은 오직 防衛力만 보유하고 인접국에
        위협을 주는 攻擊力은 가지 못하도록 하는 國際的인 制限
        措置가 취해질 가능성이 많음.

0059

(集團安保體制 胎動 可能性)

o 戰後 쿠웨이트, 이라크 國境에는 多國的軍을 대신해서
   아랍 연맹 또는 유엔에서 平和維持軍을 派遣할 가능성이
   있음.

o 長期的으로 이라크 및 이란의 勢力을 牽制하기 위하여
   美國을 背後 勢力으로 하고 사우디, 쿠웨이트등 GCC 國家와
   이집트등을 잇는 安保體制가 집단적으로 또는 개별적으로
   이루어질 가능성이 있음.

o 이 경우 아랍 地域의 特性에 비추어 볼때, 集團安保機構의
   創設보다는 오히려 다수의 양자 安保條約締結 형태를
   취하면서 集團安保의 효과를 거양토록 하는 방안이 採擇될
   가능성이 높음.

(長期的 安保體制)

o 장기적으로 볼때, 戰後 걸프 地域은 이라크의 領土가 보존
   되고 또한 그 勢力이 弱化된 상태에서 Status quo ante로
   돌아갈 것으로 豫想되며, 이란, 이라크, 사우디, 시리아
   等이 Main Actor로 勢力均衡을 이루면서 地域安保體制가
   維持되어 나갈 것으로 보임.

나. 터키의 意圖 및 役割

(터키의 安保維持)

o 터키는 東南部 地域安保에 威脅을 줄 수 있는 隣接國
   (시리아, 이라크, 이란)의 軍事强國化를 불원하고 있으
   므로 이라크의 敗戰, Saddam 政權崩壞를 內心 歡迎할 것임.

0060

o 연이나, 이라크의 분할 또는 極度의 勢力弱化는 이란 및
  시리아 牽制勢力의 사실상의 消滅을 의미하므로, 터키로서는
  이를 받아들이기가 어려울 것임.

o 다만, 可能性은 稀薄하나 시리아 및 이란이 이라크 敗戰後
  힘의 공백상태(power vacuum)을 이용, 領土擴張等 勢力
  擴大 기도시 터키는 이에 介入하게될 것이며, 武力行事도
  불사할 것임.

(걸프戰을 利用한 實利追求)

o 터키는 걸프 地域 3개국과 接境하고 있는 지리적 위치를
  십분활용, NATO 會員國으로서의 戰略的 중요성을 美國等
  西方 陣營에 認識시키고, 美國, 西歐諸國等과의 關係
  긴밀화 도모 및 軍事經濟 援助獲得으로 政治軍事 强大國
  化를 기도할 것임.

(地域安保 體制에서의 터키의 役割)

o 터키는 걸프 地域이 터키의 安保 및 經濟的 利益에 직결
  되는 地域이므로, 戰後 處理에 참여, 對아랍권 立地强化를
  기도할 것으로 보이며, 걸프 地域에 인접한 親西方 軍事
  强國으로서 터키는 地域安保體制 再編 過程에서 큰 역할을
  擔當코져 努力할 것으로 보임.

o 연이나, 터키의 過去 아랍 支配歷史, 터키가 비아랍국인
  점, 이에따른 體制의 相異 및 理解關係 상충등으로 인하여
  터키의 役割이 아랍측의 우려내지 반발을 야기시킬 가능성이
  있음. 걸프戰 開戰後 터키의 미국에 대한 Incirlik 空軍
  基地 使用許可가 다수의 아랍 諸國의 반발을 야기한 것이
  하나의 사례임.

0061

6. 걸프戰 平和的 解決 仲裁 動向

　가.　蘇聯 特使 이라크 訪問 結果

　　o 이라크 訪問中인 '프리마코프' 蘇聯特使, 후세인 大統領을
　　　面談하고 메시지 傳達

　　o 사담 후세인 大統領의 反應
　　　- 이라크는 事態의 平和的, 政治的 解決策 摸索을 위해
　　　　蘇聯을 비롯한 其他 國家의 平和案에 協力할 용의가 있음.
　　　- 그러나 多國的軍 爆擊이 우선 中止되어야 하며 이라크는
　　　　어떠한 犧牲이 따르더라도 侵略에 對抗할 것임.

　　o 美國의 反應
　　　- 事態 解決은 이라크가 쿠웨이트 撤收 문제에 대해 어떤
　　　　立場을 취하는가에 달려 있으며, 걸프戰과 팔레스타인
　　　　問題를 連繫시키려는 동일한 戰略의 反復으로 평가

　　o 유엔 事務總長
　　　- 이라크의 平和的 解決 움직임 歡迎하나, 쿠웨이트로부터
　　　　完全 撤收가 前提條件이 되어야 할 것임.

　　o 한편, 蘇聯도 提案의 내용에 대해, 유엔 決議와 相反되는
　　　內容을 包含하고 있지 않으며, 이라크의 쿠웨이트로 부터
　　　撤收가 前提 條件임을 명백히 밝힘.

　나.　非同盟 15개국 外相會議

　　* 2.11. 高位實務者 會談, 2.12. 閣僚會議, 베오그라드

0062

(론카르 유고 外相 基調演說 要旨)

o 現 걸프戰 解決을 위한 4段階 解決 方案 提示
  - 1段階 : 이라크의 쿠웨이트 撤軍 및 適法政府 回復
  - 2段階 : 交戰 當事者間의 敵對行爲 中止
  - 3段階 : 事態의 平和的, 政治的 解決
  - 4段階 : 中東地域 全體 問題, 특히 팔레스타인 問題
          解決을 위한 平和 節次 開始

o 事態의 더이상 惡化 防止를 위해 이라크측이 UN 安保理
  決意 660호의 이행을 촉구함.
  - 이라크의 쿠웨이트로 부터의 先撤軍 原則 强調
  - 이라크측이 要求한 팔레스타인 問題 解決을 위한 國際
    會議 開催 方案도 包含

o 印度 및 이란측 제시 4段階 解決 原則
  - 1段階 : 이라크의 撤軍 約束 公表
  - 2段階 : 敵對 行爲 中止
  - 3段階 : UN 監視下의 兩側 撤軍 實施
  - 4段階 : 中東問題 解決을 위한 地域會議 開催

o 上記 유고측과 이란, 인도측 解決原則과의 調整을 통한
  統一된 方案 導出에 失敗하고 聯合國 및 유엔 安保理에
  2개의 平和使節團을 각각 파견키로 決定하고 會議를 종료함.

添 附 : 1. Baker 長官 美 上.下院 外交委 證言文 1部
       2. Clark 外相 카나다 國際 問題 研究所 招請 午餐 演說文
       3. Kissinger Newsweek紙 寄稿文 寫本 1部.   끝.

0063

SECRETARY'S FEBRUARY 6 TESTIMONY ON THE GULF

THE FOLLOWING IS AN ORAL MESSAGE FROM THE SECRETARY TO
THE FOREIGN MINISTER, ALONG WITH THE GULF PORTION OF THE
SECRETARY'S TESTIMONY BEFORE THE HOUSE FOREIGN AFFAIRS
COMMITTEE.

BEGIN TEXT OF ORAL MESSAGE:

-- I WANT TO SHARE WITH YOU THE TEXT OF A STATEMENT I MADE IN
TESTIMONY BEFORE CONGRESS. IN THE STATEMENT, I EMPHASIZED
SEVERAL POINTS:

-- FIRST, OUR COMMITMENT TO FULL IMPLEMENTATION OF THE UNSC
RESOLUTIONS RELATED TO IRAQ'S AGGRESSION AGAINST KUWAIT REMAINS
UNSHAKEABLE. THE INTERNATIONAL COALITION CONTINUES TO HOLD
STEADILY AND RESOLUTELY TO THIS COURSE.

-- SECOND, THE COALITION IS SHARING RESPONSIBILITY FOR THE
ECONOMIC BURDENS OF THE CONFLICT.

-- THIRD, THE COALITION'S MILITARY EFFORT TO REVERSE
IRAQ'S AGGRESSION FULLY REFLECTS OUR POLITICAL PURPOSES. WE
HAVE NO QUARREL WITH THE PEOPLE OF IRAQ. OUR GOAL IS THE
LIBERATION OF KUWAIT, NOT THE DESTRUCTION OF IRAQ OR CHANGES IN
ITS BORDERS.

-- AND FOURTH, WE MUST ALL PUT JUST AS MUCH EFFORT AND
IMAGINATION INTO SECURING THE PEACE AS WE HAVE PUT INTO WINNING
THE WAR.

-- ON THE LAST POINT, I SOUGHT IN MY STATEMENT SIMPLY TO
HIGHLIGHT A NUMBER OF THE CHALLENGES THAT WE WILL ALL HAVE TO
ADDRESS ONCE IRAQ IS EVICTED FROM KUWAIT. WHAT I OUTLINED WAS
NOT A BLUEPRINT FOR POSTWAR ACTION, BUT THE HIGHLIGHTS OF AN
AGENDA THAT WILL REQUIRE VERY CAREFUL CONSULTATION AND
COORDINATION AMONG US.

-- WE ARE WORKING TO DEVELOP OUR OWN THINKING, ALTHOUGH MUCH
OBVIOUSLY DEPENDS ON THE ACTUAL SHAPE OF THE OUTCOME OF THE
CRISIS. I LOOK FORWARD TO STAYING IN TOUCH WITH YOU ON THESE
IMPORTANT QUESTIONS IN THE WEEKS AND MONTHS AHEAD.

-- IN THE MEANTIME, OUR FIRST PRIORITY REMAINS REVERSAL OF
IRAQ'S AGGRESSION AND COMPLETE IMPLEMENTATION OF THE UNSC
RESOLUTIONS. WITH CONTINUED SOLIDARITY WITHIN THE
INTERNATIONAL COALITION, THERE CAN BE NO DOUBT ABOUT THE
OUTCOME. END TEXT OF ORAL MESSAGE.

BEGIN TEXT OF GULF PORTION OF SECRETARY'S ORAL TESTIMONY:

MR. CHAIRMAN,

IT IS A PRIVILEGE TO APPEAR BEFORE THIS COMMITTEE TO TESTIFY ON
BEHALF OF OUR FOREIGN AFFAIRS FUNDING PROPOSAL FOR FY 1992.
WITH YOUR PERMISSION, I WOULD HAVE MY DETAILED WRITTEN

0064

STATEMENT ENTERED INTO THE RECORD. THIS YEAR, EVEN MORE SO
THAN MOST YEARS, THE FUNDS REQUESTED SHOULD BE SEEN AS AN
INVESTMENT IN A BETTER FUTURE -- A WORLD OF SECURE NATIONS,
FREE PEOPLES, AND PEACEFUL CHANGE.

I REALIZE THAT AS ARMIES FIGHT IN THE PERSIAN GULF SUCH A WORLD
SEEMS FAR DISTANT. YET I BELIEVE THAT IT IS VITALLY IMPORTANT
TO SEE THE CHALLENGES WE FACE ALSO AS OPPORTUNITIES TO BUILD A
MORE SECURE AND JUST WORLD ORDER. AND SO, TODAY I WOULD LIKE
TO MAKE A FEW COMMENTS CONCERNING OUR IDEAS ABOUT POST-CRISIS
CHALLENGES AND ARRANGEMENTS.

THE GULF WAR

THE INTERNATIONAL COALITION HAS BEEN WAGING WAR AGAINST IRAQ
FOR THREE WEEKS NOW WITH VERY CLEAR OBJECTIVES: TO EXPEL IRAQ
FROM KUWAIT; TO RESTORE THE LEGITIMATE GOVERNMENT OF KUWAIT;
AND TO ENSURE THE STABILITY AND SECURITY OF THIS CRITICAL
REGION. I WANT TO MAKE SEVERAL OBSERVATIONS ABOUT THE COURSE
OF THE CONFLICT SO FAR.

FIRST, THE INTERNATIONAL COALITION HAS HELD STEADILY TO ITS
PURPOSE AND ITS COURSE. AN OUTSTANDING ACHIEVEMENT OF THE
CURRENT CRISIS HAS BEEN THE ABILITY OF THE UNITED NATIONS TO
ACT AS ITS FOUNDERS INTENDED. BEFORE JANUARY 15, A DOZEN
SECURITY COUNCIL RESOLUTIONS GUIDED THE UNITED STATES AND OTHER
NATIONS AS TOGETHER WE WAGED A CONCERTED DIPLOMATIC, POLITICAL,
AND ECONOMIC STRUGGLE AGAINST IRAQI AGGRESSION. WE DID SO
BECAUSE WE ALL SHARE A CONVICTION THAT THIS BRUTAL AND
DANGEROUS DICTATOR MUST BE STOPPED AND STOPPED NOW. SINCE
JANUARY 16, IN ACTIONS AUTHORIZED BY SECURITY COUNCIL
RESOLUTION 678, WE HAVE BEEN ABLE TO WAGE WAR BECAUSE WE ARE
EQUALLY CONVINCED THAT ALL PEACEFUL OPPORTUNITIES TO END
SADDAM'S AGGRESSION HAD BEEN EXPLORED AND EXHAUSTED.

LET ME GIVE YOU SOME IDEA OF THOSE EXHAUSTIVE EFFORTS, BOTH BY
THE UNITED STATES AND OTHER NATIONS. IN THE 166 DAYS BETWEEN
THE INVASION OF KUWAIT ON AUGUST 2, 1990 AND THE EXPIRATION OF
THE UN DEADLINE FOR IRAQI WITHDRAWAL ON JANUARY 15, 1991, I
PERSONALLY HELD OVER 200 MEETINGS WITH FOREIGN DIGNITARIES,
CONDUCTED 10 DIPLOMATIC MISSIONS, AND TRAVELLED OVER 100,000
MILES. FOR OVER SIX AND ONE HALF HOURS, I MET WITH THE IRAQI
FOREIGN MINISTER -- SIX AND ONE-HALF HOURS IN WHICH THE IRAQI
LEADERSHIP REJECTED THE VERY CONCEPT OF WITHDRAWAL FROM KUWAIT,
EVEN THE MENTION OF WITHDRAWAL. AS YOU KNOW MANY OTHERS ALSO
TRIED -- THE ARAB LEAGUE, THE EUROPEAN COMMUNITY, THE UN
SECRETARY GENERAL, KINGS, PRESIDENTS, AND PRIME MINISTERS.
NONE SUCCEEDED BECAUSE SADDAM HUSSEIN REJECTED EACH AND EVERY
ONE.

SECOND, THE COALITION IS SHARING RESPONSIBILITY FOR THE
ECONOMIC BURDENS OF CONFLICT. SUPPORT FOR U.S. MILITARY
OUTLAYS COVERS BOTH 1990 COMMITMENTS FOR DESERT SHIELD AND 1991
COMMITMENTS FOR THE PERIOD OF JANUARY THROUGH MARCH FOR DESERT
SHIELD/STORM. IN ADDITION, FUNDS HAVE ALSO BEEN FORTHCOMING TO
OFFSET THE ECONOMIC COSTS CONFRONTING THE FRONT LINE STATES IN

0065

THE REGION.

TO DATE, WE HAVE PLEDGES OF OVER $50 BILLION TO SUPPORT OUR
MILITARY EFFORTS AND OVER $14 BILLION TO ASSIST THE FRONT LINE
STATES AND OTHERS WITH THEIR ECONOMIC NEEDS.

THIRD, OUR UNFOLDING MILITARY STRATEGY FULLY REFLECTS OUR
POLITICAL PURPOSES. THIS IS THE PLACE TO RESTATE, AS THE
PRESIDENT HAS DONE SO OFTEN, THAT WE HAVE NO QUARREL WITH THE
IRAQI PEOPLE. OUR GOAL IS THE LIBERATION OF KUWAIT, NOT THE
DESTRUCTION OF IRAQ OR CHANGES IN ITS BORDERS.

A THOROUGHLY PROFESSIONAL AND EFFECTIVE MILITARY CAMPAIGN IS
UNDERWAY. OUR YOUNG MEN AND WOMEN AND THE FORCES OF OUR
COALITION PARTNERS ARE WRITING NEW ANNALS OF BRAVERY AND
SKILL. BUT THE TASK IS FORMIDABLE, AND NO ONE SHOULD
UNDERESTIMATE SADDAM'S MILITARY CAPABILITIES. IRAQ IS NOT A
THIRD RATE MILITARY POWER. BILLIONS HAVE BEEN DIVERTED FROM
PEACEFUL USES TO GIVE THIS SMALL COUNTRY THE FOURTH LARGEST
ARMY IN THE WORLD. IRAQ HAS MORE MAIN BATTLE TANKS THAN THE
UNITED KINGDOM AND FRANCE COMBINED. IT HAS MORE COMBAT
AIRCRAFT THAN EITHER GERMANY, FRANCE, OR THE UNITED KINGDOM.
EJECTING IRAQ FROM KUWAIT WILL NOT BE EASY, BUT, AS THE
PRESIDENT SAID, "SO THAT PEACE CAN PREVAIL, WE WILL PREVAIL."

WE ARE ALSO TRYING OUR BEST TO WAGE A JUST WAR IN A JUST WAY.
OUR TARGETS ARE MILITARY, AND WE ARE DOING ALL WE CAN TO
MINIMIZE CIVILIAN CASUALTIES AND AVOID DAMAGE TO RELIGIOUS AND
CULTURAL SITES. AND AS GENERAL SCHWARZKOPF HAS POINTED OUT,
THE COALITION FORCES ARE EVEN PUTTING THEMSELVES IN DANGER TO
MINIMIZE THE RISK TO INNOCENT LIVES.

IN SHOCKING CONTRAST, SADDAM HUSSEIN'S CONDUCT OF THE WAR HAS
BEEN NOT UNLIKE HIS CONDUCT BEFORE THE WAR: A RELENTLESS
ASSAULT ON THE VALUES OF CIVILIZATION. HE HAS LAUNCHED
MISSILES AGAINST ISRAELI CITIES AND SAUDI CITIES, MISSILES
AIMED NOT AT TARGETS OF MILITARY VALUE BUT FULLY INTENDED TO
MASSACRE CIVILIANS. HE HAS ABUSED AND PARADED PRISONERS OF WAR
AND HE SAYS HE IS USING THEM AS "HUMAN SHIELDS" -- ACTIONS
TOTALLY IN VIOLATION OF THE GENEVA CONVENTION. AND HE HAS EVEN
ATTACKED NATURE ITSELF, ATTEMPTING TO POISON THE WATERS OF THE
PERSIAN GULF WITH THE PETROLEUM THAT IS THE PATRIMONY OF THE
REGION'S ECONOMIC FUTURE.

WE HAVE HEARD, AND WE TAKE AT FACE VALUE, SADDAM'S THREATS TO
USE CHEMICAL AND BIOLOGICAL WEAPONS. WE HAVE WARNED HIM -- AND
HE WOULD BE WELL ADVISED TO HEED OUR WARNING -- THAT WE WILL
NOT TOLERATE THE USE OF SUCH WEAPONS. ANY USE OF CHEMICAL OR
BIOLOGICAL WEAPONS WILL HAVE THE MOST SEVERE CONSEQUENCES, AND
WE WILL CONTINUE TO INSIST THAT IRAQ FULFILL ITS OBLIGATIONS
UNDER THE GENEVA CONVENTION WITH RESPECT TO COALITION POW'S.

I THINK THAT OUR CONDUCT OF THE WAR IS IN ITSELF A GREAT
STRENGTH, THE STRENGTH THAT COMES FROM DOING THE RIGHT THING IN
THE RIGHT WAY. AND SADDAM'S CONTINUING BRUTALITY REDOUBLES OUR
RESOLVE AND THE ENTIRE COALITION'S CONVICTION ABOUT THE

0066

RIGHTNESS OF OUR COURSE. ENDING SADDAM'S AGGRESSION WILL ALSO
BE A BLOW TO STATE-SPONSORED TERRORISM.

THIS IS ALSO THE PLACE TO NOTE OUR DEEP APPRECIATION AND GREAT
ADMIRATION FOR THE EXTRAORDINARY RESTRAINT OF THE GOVERNMENT OF
ISRAEL. ISRAELI CITIES HAVE BEEN ATTACKED BY SADDAM HUSSEIN
BECAUSE PART OF HIS STRATEGY HAS BEEN TO CONSOLIDATE HIS
AGGRESSION BY TURNING THE GULF CRISIS INTO AN ARAB-ISRAELI
CONFLICT. DESPITE ITS CLEAR RIGHT TO RESPOND, THE ISRAELI
GOVERNMENT HAS ACTED WITH RESTRAINT AND RESPONSIBILITY. THE
UNITED STATES HAS BEEN AND WILL CONTINUE TO BE IN CLOSE CONTACT
AT THE HIGHEST LEVELS WITH ISRAEL. WE HAVE OFFERED AND ISRAEL
HAS ACCEPTED BATTERIES OF PATRIOT MISSILES -- SOME WITH
AMERICAN CREWS -- TO DEFEND AGAINST SCUD ATTACKS. WE CONTINUE
TO DEVOTE SPECIAL MILITARY EFFORTS TO DESTROYING THE SCUDS AND
THEIR LAUNCHERS.

EVERYONE SHOULD KNOW: WHEN WE SPEAK ABOUT OUR UNSHAKEABLE
COMMITMENT TO ISRAELI SECURITY, WE MEAN IT.

THE FOURTH OBSERVATION I WOULD MAKE IS THIS: THE GREAT
INTERNATIONAL COALITION THAT IS NOW WINNING THE WAR MUST ALSO
BE STRONG ENOUGH TO SECURE THE PEACE. WINSTON CHURCHILL ONCE
OBSERVED THAT "WE SHALL SEE HOW ABSOLUTE IS THE NEED OF A BROAD
PATH OF INTERNATIONAL ACTION PURSUED BY MANY STATES IN COMMON
ACROSS THE YEARS, IRRESPECTIVE OF THE EBB AND FLOW OF NATIONAL
POLITICS." IF WE ARE GOING TO REDEEM THE SACRIFICES NOW BEING
MADE BY THE BRAVE MEN AND WOMEN WHO DEFEND OUR FREEDOM WITH
THEIR LIVES, THEN WE MUST FASHION A PEACE WORTHY OF THEIR
STRUGGLE. AND THAT CAN BE DONE IF WE CAN HOLD TOGETHER IN
PEACE THE COALITION TEMPERED BY WAR.

I BELIEVE THAT WHEN CONGRESS VOTED THE PRESIDENT AUTHORITY TO
USE FORCE IN SUPPORT OF THE UNITED NATIONS RESOLUTIONS, IT
VOTED ALSO FOR PEACE -- A PEACE THAT MIGHT PREVENT SUCH WARS IN
THE FUTURE. I BELIEVE THAT THE AMERICAN PEOPLE SUPPORT OUR
ROLE IN THE COALITION NOT ONLY TO DEFEAT AN AGGRESSOR BUT TO
SECURE A MEASURE OF JUSTICE AND SECURITY FOR THE FUTURE.

POST-WAR CHALLENGES

MR. CHAIRMAN, WE AND EVERY NATION INVOLVED IN THIS CONFLICT ARE
THINKING ABOUT THE POST-WAR SITUATION AND PLANNING FOR THE
FUTURE. IT WOULD BE IRRESPONSIBLE NOT TO DO SO. AT THE SAME
TIME, IT WOULD BE BOTH PREMATURE AND UNWISE FOR US TO LAY OUT A
DETAILED BLUEPRINT FOR THE POSTWAR GULF OR, FOR THAT MATTER,
THE REGION AS A WHOLE.

THE WAR ITSELF AND THE WAY IT ENDS WILL GREATLY INFLUENCE BOTH
THE SECURITY OF THE GULF AND THE REST OF THE AREA. THE DEEPEST
PASSIONS HAVE BEEN STIRRED. THE MILITARY ACTIONS NOW UNDERWAY
NECESSARILY INVOLVE MANY CASUALTIES, GREAT HARDSHIPS, AND
GROWING FEARS FOR THE FUTURE. TOUGH TIMES LIE AHEAD.

WE SHOULD THEREFORE APPROACH THE POSTWAR PROBLEMS WITH A DUE
SENSE OF MODESTY. RESPECT FOR THE SOVEREIGNTY OF THE PEOPLES

0067

OF THE GULF AND MIDDLE EAST MUST BE UPPERMOST. IN ANY EVENT,
MODERN HISTORY HAS SHOWN THAT NO SINGLE NATION CAN LONG IMPOSE
ITS WILL OR REMAKE THE MIDDLE EAST IN ITS OWN IMAGE. AFTER
ALL, THAT IS PARTLY WHY WE ARE FIGHTING SADDAM HUSSEIN.

YET AMONG ALL THE DIFFICULTIES WE FACE, ONE FACT STANDS OUT:
THE PEOPLES OF THE GULF AND INDEED THE ENTIRE MIDDLE EAST
DESPERATELY NEED PEACE. I TRULY BELIEVE THAT THERE MUST BE A
WAY, WORKING IN CONSULTATION WITH ALL OF THE AFFECTED NATIONS,
TO SET A COURSE THAT BRINGS GREATER SECURITY FOR ALL AND
ENDURING PEACE. WE SHOULD THEREFORE MAKE EVERY EFFORT NOT JUST
TO HEAL THE PERSIAN GULF AFTER THIS WAR BUT ALSO TO TRY TO HEAL
THE REST OF THE REGION WHICH NEEDS IT SO BADLY.

SO I WOULD LIKE TO DISCUSS SEVERAL CHALLENGES THAT I BELIEVE WE
MUST ADDRESS IN THE POST WAR PERIOD.

ONE CHALLENGE WILL BE GREATER SECURITY FOR THE PERSIAN GULF.
AFTER TWO WARS IN TEN YEARS, THIS VITAL REGION NEEDS NEW AND
DIFFERENT SECURITY ARRANGEMENTS. IN OUR VIEW, THERE ARE THREE
BASIC ISSUES TO BE RESOLVED: THE PURPOSES OR PRINCIPLES OF THE
SECURITY ARRANGEMENTS; THE ROLE OF THE LOCAL STATES, REGIONAL
ORGANIZATIONS, AND THE INTERNATIONAL COMMUNITY; AND IN THE
AFTERMATH OF THE WAR, THE MILITARY REQUIREMENTS UNTIL LOCAL
STABILITY IS ACHIEVED, AND THEREAFTER.

I THINK WE WOULD FIND ALREADY A WIDE MEASURE OF AGREEMENT ON
THE PRINCIPLES. THEY WOULD INCLUDE:

O   DETERRENCE OF AGGRESSION FROM ANY QUARTER.

O   TERRITORIAL INTEGRITY. THERE MUST BE RESPECT FOR EXISTING
SOVEREIGNTY OF ALL STATES AND FOR THE INVIOLABILITY OF BORDERS.

O   PEACEFUL RESOLUTION OF DISPUTES. BORDER PROBLEMS AND OTHER
DISPUTES THAT HAVE LONG HISTORIES -- AND THERE ARE MANY BEYOND
THE IRAQ-KUWAIT EXAMPLE -- SHOULD BE RESOLVED BY PEACEFUL
MEANS, AS PRESCRIBED BY THE U.N. CHARTER.

THESE PRINCIPLES MUST BE PUT INTO ACTION FIRST AND FOREMOST BY
THE LOCAL STATES SO THAT CONFLICTS CAN BE PREVENTED AND
AGGRESSION DETERRED. WE WOULD EXPECT THE STATES OF THE GULF
AND REGIONAL ORGANIZATIONS SUCH AS THE GULF COOPERATION COUNCIL
TO TAKE THE LEAD IN BUILDING A REINFORCING NETWORK OF NEW AND
STRENGTHENED SECURITY TIES. NO REGIONAL STATE SHOULD BE
EXCLUDED FROM THESE ARRANGEMENTS. POST-WAR IRAQ COULD HAVE AN
IMPORTANT CONTRIBUTION TO PLAY. AND SO COULD IRAN AS A MAJOR
POWER IN THE GULF.

THERE IS A ROLE, TOO, FOR OUTSIDE NATIONS AND THE INTERNATIONAL
COMMUNITY, INCLUDING THE UNITED NATIONS, TO ENCOURAGE SUCH
ARRANGEMENTS AND TO STAND BEHIND THEM.

AS FOR THE UNITED STATES, WE HAVE DEPLOYED SMALL NAVAL FORCES
IN THE PERSIAN GULF EVER SINCE THE TRUMAN ADMINISTRATION IN
1949. WE HAD AND CONTINUE TO HAVE VERY STRONG BILATERAL TIES

0068

WITH SAUDI ARABIA AND OTHER LOCAL STATES. AND THROUGH THE
YEARS, WE HAVE CONDUCTED JOINT EXERCISES WITH AND PROVIDED
MILITARY EQUIPMENT FOR OUR FRIENDS IN THE REGION. THE
PRESIDENT HAS SAID THAT WE HAVE NO INTENTION OF MAINTAINING A
PERMANENT GROUND PRESENCE ON THE ARABIAN PENINSULA ONCE IRAQ IS
EJECTED FROM KUWAIT AND THE THREAT RECEDES.

BEFORE SECURITY IS ASSURED, HOWEVER, IMPORTANT QUESTIONS MUST
BE ANSWERED. WE WILL BE GOING THROUGH AN IMPORTANT
TRANSITIONAL PHASE IN THE IMMEDIATE AFTERMATH OF THE WAR AS WE
TRY TO ESTABLISH STABILITY. LET ME LIST JUST A FEW OF THE
QUESTIONS THAT NEED TO BE ANSWERED.

O SHOULD THERE BE A PERMANENT, LOCALLY STATIONED GROUND FORCE
MADE UP OF LOCAL TROOPS UNDER U.N. AUSPICES OR UNDER REGIONAL
AUSPICES, SUCH AS THE GCC?

O HOW CAN THE INTERNATIONAL COMMUNITY REINFORCE DETERRENCE IN
THE GULF, WHETHER BY CONTRIBUTING FORCES OR THROUGH OTHER
POLITICAL ARRANGEMENTS, SUCH AS RESOLUTIONS OR SECURITY
COMMITMENTS?

NO ONE HAS THE ANSWERS YET TO THESE AND OTHER QUESTIONS. SOME
MAY NEVER BE ANSWERED. BUT HOWEVER WE EVENTUALLY PROCEED, WE
WILL CONDUCT EXTENSIVE CONSULTATIONS AMONG ALL OF THE CONCERNED
PARTIES TO SUCH ARRANGEMENTS.

2 A SECOND CHALLENGE WILL SURELY BE REGIONAL ARMS PROLIFERATION
AND CONTROL. THIS INCLUDES BOTH CONVENTIONAL WEAPONS AND
WEAPONS OF MASS DESTRUCTION. THE TERRIBLE FACT IS THAT EVEN
THE CONVENTIONAL ARSENALS OF SEVERAL MIDDLE EASTERN STATES
DWARF THOSE OF MOST EUROPEAN POWERS. FIVE MIDDLE EASTERN
COUNTRIES HAVE MORE MAIN BATTLE TANKS THAN THE UNITED KINGDOM
OR FRANCE. THE TIME HAS COME TO TRY TO CHANGE THE DESTRUCTIVE
PATTERN OF MILITARY COMPETITION AND PROLIFERATION IN THIS
REGION AND TO REDUCE ARMS FLOWS INTO AN AREA THAT IS ALREADY
OVERMILITARIZED. THAT SUGGESTS THAT WE AND OTHERS INSIDE AND
OUTSIDE THE REGION MUST CONSULT ON HOW BEST TO ADDRESS SEVERAL
DIMENSIONS OF THE PROBLEM:

O HOW CAN WE COOPERATE TO CONSTRAIN IRAQ'S POST-WAR ABILITY TO
RETAIN OR REBUILD ITS WEAPONS OF MASS DESTRUCTION AND MOST
DESTABILIZING CONVENTIONAL WEAPONS?

O HOW CAN WE WORK WITH OTHERS TO ENCOURAGE STEPS TOWARD
BROADER REGIONAL RESTRAINT IN THE ACQUISITION AND USE OF BOTH
CONVENTIONAL ARMAMENTS AND WEAPONS OF MASS DESTRUCTION? WHAT
ROLE MIGHT THE KINDS OF CONFIDENCE BUILDING MEASURES THAT HAVE
LESSENED CONFLICT IN EUROPE PLAY IN THE GULF AND THE MIDDLE
EAST?

O FINALLY, WHAT GLOBAL ACTIONS WOULD REINFORCE STEPS TOWARD
ARMS CONTROL IN THE GULF AND MIDDLE EAST? THESE COULD INCLUDE
RAPID COMPLETION OF PENDING INTERNATIONAL AGREEMENTS LIKE THE
CHEMICAL WEAPONS CONVENTION, AS WELL AS MUCH TIGHTER SUPPLY
RESTRAINTS ON THE FLOW OF WEAPONS AND DUAL-USE TECHNOLOGY INTO

0063

THE REGION. AND WHAT IMPLICATIONS DOES THAT HAVE FOR ARMS
TRANSFER AND SALES POLICIES?

3 A THIRD CHALLENGE WILL BE ECONOMIC RECONSTRUCTION AND
RECOVERY. AN ECONOMIC CATASTROPHE HAS BEFALLEN THE GULF AND
THE NATIONS TRADING WITH IT. KUWAIT HAS BEEN LOOTED AND
WRECKED. HUNDREDS OF THOUSANDS OF WORKERS HAVE LOST JOBS AND
FLED. TRADE FLOWS AND MARKETS HAVE BEEN DISRUPTED.

I AM CONFIDENT THAT THE PEOPLE OF KUWAIT WILL REBUILD THEIR
COUNTRY. AS WE HAVE WORKED WITH THE KUWAITIS IN THEIR MOMENT
OF TRIAL, SO WE SHALL LOOK FORWARD TO COOPERATING WITH THEM IN
THEIR HOUR OF RECOVERY.

AND NO ONE SHOULD FORGET THAT FOR THE SECOND TIME IN A DECADE,
THE PEOPLE OF IRAQ WILL BE RECOVERING FROM A DISASTROUS
CONFLICT. THE TIME OF RECONSTRUCTION AND RECOVERY SHOULD NOT
BE THE OCCASION FOR VENGEFUL ACTIONS AGAINST A NATION FORCED TO
WAR BY A DICTATOR'S AMBITION. THE SECURE AND PROSPEROUS FUTURE
EVERYONE HOPES TO SEE IN THE GULF MUST INCLUDE IRAQ.

OF NECESSITY, MOST OF THE RESOURCES FOR RECONSTRUCTION WILL BE
DRAWN FROM THE GULF. YET, SHOULD WE NOT BE THINKING ALSO OF
MORE THAN RECONSTRUCTION? IT MIGHT BE POSSIBLE FOR A COALITION
OF COUNTRIES USING BOTH LOCAL AND EXTERNAL RESOURCES TO
TRANSFORM THE OUTLOOK FOR THE REGION -- IN EXPANDING FREE TRADE
AND INVESTMENT IN ASSISTING DEVELOPMENT, AND IN PROMOTING
GROWTH-ORIENTED ECONOMIC POLICIES WHICH HAVE TAKEN ROOT ACROSS
THE GLOBE.

ANY ECONOMIC EFFORT MUST HAVE A SPECIAL PLACE FOR WATER
DEVELOPMENT. WELL OVER HALF THE PEOPLE LIVING IN THE MIDDLE
EAST DRAW WATER FROM RIVERS THAT CROSS INTERNATIONAL BOUNDARIES
OR DEPEND ON DESALINATION PLANTS. WE HAVE ALL BEEN INCENSED BY
SADDAM HUSSEIN'S DELIBERATE POISONING OF THE GULF WATERS, WHICH
COULD AFFECT A LARGE PORTION OF SAUDI ARABIA'S DESALINIZED
DRINKING WATER.

FINALLY, WE WILL WANT TO CONSULT WITH GOVERNMENTS BOTH FROM THE
MIDDLE EAST AND FROM OTHER REGIONS ABOUT SPECIFIC ARRANGEMENTS
THAT MIGHT BEST SERVE THE PURPOSES OF REGION-WIDE ECONOMIC
COOPERATION. SUCH COOPERATION WOULD SURELY BE HELPFUL IN
REINFORCING OUR OVERALL OBJECTIVE: REDUCING ONE BY ONE THE
SOURCES OF CONFLICT AND REMOVING ONE BY ONE THE BARRIERS TO
SECURITY AND PROSPERITY THROUGHOUT THE AREA.

4. A FOURTH CHALLENGE IS TO RESUME THE SEARCH FOR A JUST PEACE AND
REAL RECONCILIATION FOR ISRAEL, THE ARAB STATES, AND THE
PALESTINIANS. BY RECONCILIATION, I MEAN NOT SIMPLY PEACE AS
THE ABSENCE OF WAR, BUT A PEACE BASED ON ENDURING RESPECT,
TOLERANCE, AND MUTUAL TRUST. AS YOU KNOW, I PERSONALLY HAD
DEVOTED CONSIDERABLE EFFORT BEFORE THE WAR TO FACILITATING A
DIALOGUE BETWEEN ISRAEL AND THE PALESTINIANS -- AN ESSENTIAL
PART OF AN OVERALL PEACE PROCESS. LET'S NOT FOOL OURSELVES.
THE COURSE OF THIS CRISIS HAS STIRRED EMOTIONS AMONG ISRAELIS
AND PALESTINIANS THAT WILL NOT YIELD EASILY TO CONCILIATION.

0070

YET IN THE AFTERMATH OF THIS WAR, AS IN EARLIER WARS, THERE MAY
BE OPPORTUNITIES FOR PEACE -- IF THE PARTIES ARE WILLING. AND
IF THEY REALLY ARE WILLING, WE ARE COMMITTED TO WORKING CLOSELY
WITH THEM TO FASHION A MORE EFFECTIVE PEACE PROCESS.

THE ISSUES TO BE ADDRESSED ARE OF COURSE FAMILIAR AND MORE
CHALLENGING THAN EVER.

O HOW DO YOU GO ABOUT RECONCILING ISRAELIS AND PALESTINIANS?
WHAT CONCRETE ACTIONS CAN BE TAKEN BY EACH SIDE?

O WHAT WILL BE THE ROLE OF THE ARAB STATES IN FACILITATING
THIS PROCESS AND THEIR OWN NEGOTIATIONS FOR PEACE WITH ISRAEL?

O HOW WILL REGIONAL ARMS CONTROL ARRANGEMENTS AFFECT THIS
PROCESS?

O WHAT IS THE BEST DIPLOMATIC VEHICLE FOR GETTING THE PROCESS
UNDERWAY?

AGAIN, WE WILL BE CONSULTING AND WORKING VERY CLOSELY WITH OUR
FRIENDS AND ALL PARTIES WHO HAVE A CONSTRUCTIVE ROLE TO PLAY IN
SETTLING THIS CONFLICT.

5 A FIFTH AND FINAL CHALLENGE CONCERNS THE UNITED STATES: WE
SIMPLY MUST DO MORE TO REDUCE OUR ENERGY DEPENDENCE. AS THE
PRESIDENT HAS STRESSED, ONLY A COMPREHENSIVE STRATEGY CAN
ACHIEVE OUR GOALS. THAT STRATEGY SHOULD INVOLVE ENERGY
CONSERVATION AND EFFICIENCY, INCREASED DEVELOPMENT,
STRENGTHENED STOCKPILES AND RESERVES, AND GREATER USE OF
ALTERNATIVE FUELS. WE MUST BRING TO THIS TASK THE SAME
DETERMINATION WE ARE NOW BRINGING TO THE WAR ITSELF.

AS YOU CAN SEE, MR. CHAIRMAN, SOME OF THESE ELEMENTS ARE
POLITICAL, SOME ARE ECONOMIC, AND SOME OF NECESSITY ARE RELATED
TO SECURITY. THAT SUGGESTS THAT WE SHOULD VIEW SECURITY NOT
JUST IN MILITARY TERMS BUT AS PART AND PARCEL OF THE BROADER
OUTLOOK FOR THE REGION. WE'RE NOT GOING TO HAVE LASTING PEACE
AND WELL-BEING WITHOUT SOUND ECONOMIC GROWTH. WE'RE NOT GOING
TO HAVE SOUND ECONOMIC GROWTH IF NATIONS ARE THREATENED OR
INVADED -- OR IF THEY ARE SQUANDERING PRECIOUS RESOURCES ON
MORE AND MORE ARMS. AND SURELY FINDING A WAY FOR THE PEOPLES
OF THE MIDDLE EAST TO WORK WITH EACH OTHER WILL BE CRUCIAL IF
WE ARE TO LIFT OUR EYES TO A BETTER FUTURE.

0071

CNW(F)—0016   910209 16∞
(15부재)

(CNW-0186 의 첨부물)

THE RIGHT HONOURABLE JOE CLARK,

AT A LUNCHEON HOSTED BY

THE CANADIAN INSTITUTE OF INTERNATIONAL AFFAIRS

AT THE AUBERGE DES GOUVERNEURS

QUEBEC CITY, Quebec
February 8, 1991

0072

I am very pleased to be with you here today under the auspices of the Canadian Institute of International Affairs. The Institute has earned the reputation over the years of being a leading forum for the discussion of the world's great questions and the issues that they confront our country with.

Nothing could be more normal under the circumstances than to pursue with you the indispensable dialogue which the government wishes to sustain with Canadians at a time when our country is passing through a crucial period in the history of international relations over the past 40 years.

It was with full consideration for the significance of its action that the government made the weighty decision to involve our forces in the fight. One must have the courage of one's convictions. When the international community unanimously calls for the defence of peace, and when the basic principles underlying the international order are involved, Canada, including Quebec, must respond. As an architect of the UN system, we must fulfil our international responsibilities to the letter and must do our part to apply the principles upheld by the UN.

The forceful occupation of the territory of a United Nations member is unacceptable and violates the basic principles of the international order. Faced with the invasion of Kuwait, the international community had a certain options, one of which was inaction and passivity. This would have been an unpardonable abdication, recognition of the secular power of the strong over the weak. An immediate, unilateral counter-strike by a limited number of countries would have amounted to a small group of countries appropriating the role of world policeman. These options were both unacceptable and would both have had disastrous consequences for the future of world relations.

With wisdom but not without some reticence, the community of states resolved to resort wholly to the United Nations to face this threat to its collective security. This was a great victory for the UN system and for countries like Canada, which have based their diplomacy on the construction of a credible, effective multilateral system.

Rarely have such unanimity and such determination been shown within the Security Council, and with the support of the vast majority of UN members. Let us not forget that countries as disparate as Pakistan and Argentina, Senegal and Bulgaria, Australia and Spain have played an active part in the 29-country coalition established to apply the sanctions.

0073

The specific problems that arise will largely depend on the situation as it stands once the war is over. It is already clear that certain problems will be unavoidable.

1) A GLOBAL APPROACH TO SECURITY

First, let us consider security. While a peacekeeping force is a factor in maintaining equilibrium, it cannot in and of itself claim to fully guarantee the security of the Gulf states. Regional arrangements must thus be complemented by international guarantees which could take the form of international accords committing some of the countries in the coalition under the authority of the United Nations. Such multilateral arrangements would no doubt be more acceptable to the people of the region. In the same spirit, Canada feels that it would be preferable for these guarantees not to include the permanent deployment of foreign forces in the Gulf.

On a longer-range basis, however, these countries must work to establish mechanisms and structures that will enable them to resolve their disputes peacefully and contribute to greater trust among them. While the experience of the Conference on Security and Co-operation in Europe (CSCE) cannot be transferred to this region as is, some of its lessons may offer promising avenues.

Several European countries are engaged in actively exploring this concept. After the war ends, they may propose the creation of a CSCM, a Conference on Security and Co-operation in the Mediterranean, which would also include the Persian Gulf region for this purpose. This is an ambitious project, and Canada is carefully monitoring its development.

In the same spirit, when visited recently by my colleague, Dr. Meguid, the Egyptian Minister of Foreign Affairs, we agreed on the importance of beginning immediately a study of post-war security structures. This would include a consideration of possible mechanisms to incorporate into a regional security structure. Border guarantees, a peaceful mechanism for the resolution of disputes, and the establishment of confidence-building measures would form the bases for this structure. Such a mechanism would also allow the discussion of non-military matters, as in the case of the CSCE's second and third baskets.

Such a global approach to security matters, based on the establishment of genuine dialogue among the various regional partners, would serve to raise such issues as the development of democratic institutions in the region. But if they are to have any chance at all of succeeding, efforts to achieve greater regional security and stability must courageously address the very roots of the problems that exist in the Middle East. These root causes are well known.

2) THE ISRAELI-ARAB CONFLICT

The thorniest issue involves relations between Israel and the Arab countries. After decades of conflict, the build-up of hatred and misunderstanding has been enormous.

No regional security plan can expect to succeed unless it is firmly determined to make progress toward a comprehensive, lasting, negotiated settlement of the Israeli-Arab conflict, including the Palestinian question. Such a negotiated settlement must be founded on Resolutions 242 and 338 of the Security Council. In this regard, even before the Gulf war, Canada let it be known that it favoured holding an international conference. While we should not exclude other options, a well-organized conference with reasonable chances of success could indeed be useful and contribute to the peace process.

3) ECONOMIC DISPARITIES

When faced with numerous conflicts, especially those involving less developed countries, Canada has always emphasized social and economic imperatives. This need is even more urgent in the Middle East. Reconstruction is doomed to fail if it ignores social and human dimensions and does not address economic disparities.

The region requires a new framework, which must be defined by the nationals and the states that make up the region and the people who live in them. There can be no peace without prosperity, and no stability without justice either within states or between states. Democracy also promotes justice, prosperity and peace. Long-term security cannot be built solely on military structures and political agreements. Long-term security, in the Middle East as elsewhere, can rest only on genuine co operation between states, a guarantee of dialogue and confidence. It is in this context that I developed the concept of co-operative security before the most recent General Assembly of the United Nations.

Our role is to encourage the countries of this region to strive toward such an objective. For instance, after the hostilities have ceased, the Gulf states and indeed the entire Middle East might consider creating an organization for the purpose of economic cooperation. Such an organization, which might be affiliated with the United Nations and maintain contact with the

0075

major international economic and financial institutions, would
help to ensure greater economic stability in the region.

LESSONS OF THE CRISIS

Finally, we must begin now to learn the important lessons of
this conflict. We bear a considerable burden of responsibility.
Over the years, to varying degrees, we have all helped to create
a military apparatus in this region, especially in Iraq, that
is beyond human comprehension. Military assistance in the
region has exceeded economic assistance. This must stop. The
governments most concerned are already making a commitment in
this regard.

To be credible, any peace plan must include strict measures
to check the proliferation of weapons of mass destruction and the
stockpiling of conventional weapons in the region. Multilateral
negotiations have already begun regarding these crucial issues,
such as the proliferation of nuclear, chemical and biological
weapons and missile launching techniques. So far, however, their
success has been limited owing to the lack of political will or
the conflicting interests of the various parties involved. It is
urgent that we make further efforts to display a strong political
will.

In this belief, Canada plans to promote a world summit on
disarmament of war and weapons of mass destruction in the coming
months. This summit would become a showcase for a new political
consultation. It would aim to develop a strict plan or action
that would result in the adoption by 1995 of an integrating
framework for systems ensuring the non-proliferation and control
of weapons, including conventional weapons.

I have broadly outlined the views and initiatives that the
Prime Minister and I will seek to promote in the coming months.

Canada and the world community must invest as much energy--
and even more--in winning the postwar as we are in winning the
war.

If this war is to have any meaning, it must serve to build
peace. It is on our ability to build this peace that we will
be judged. We are aware of this, and Canada does not intend
to spare any effort to meet this extraordinary challenge.

Office of the
Prime Minister

Cabinet du
Premier ministre

CANADA

NOTES FOR AN ADDRESS

BY PRIME MINISTER BRIAN MULRONEY

ON THE SITUATION IN THE PERSIAN GULF

OTTAWA

FEBRUARY 8, 1991

CHECK AGAINST DELIVERY

Ottawa Canada K1A 0A2

9/15

0077

1

The diplomatic community has never, in the modern era, seen such a feverish and intense period as that between last August and mid-January. Every possible effort was made to avoid war. Every available means was sought to obtain the withdrawal of Iraq from Kuwait. The disappointing and painful recourse to force is the result of our having reached the limits of diplomacy -- not the absence of efforts to apply it. The blame for this failure can be placed squarely on the shoulders of the Iraqi President.

Why, you might ask, were the sanctions not prolonged? The answer is simple: we tried, but we had to face facts -- sanctions could not succeed where diplomacy had failed. For the entire period during which they were in force, he was also pillaging Kuwait, building up huge reserves for his forces and compelling the Kuwaiti population to take flight. Within a short time, the coalition would have liberated nothing but a desert and a few inhabitants in total subjection to Saddam HUSSEIN.

No, the United Nations had no choice, under the Charter, but to use force in the interest of justice and thus begin an operation to restore peace and international security.

The Canadian forces are an integral part of this operation. I take this opportunity to pay tribute to the men and women, Quebeckers among them, who are doing their duty with such a noble attitude over there. I know they will count on your confidence and your encouragement. Their commitment will be a source of pride and inspiration for generations to come.

The soldiers who are courageously discharging their mission are entitled to expect the politicians to do everything possible to prevent us from finding ourselves in such straits in the future. They are perfectly justified in this.

THE BUILDING OF PEACE

Paradoxical as it may seem, this war expresses the firm desire of the international community to build a better world founded on justice and the peaceful resolution of conflicts. This determination must go far beyond the restoration of Kuwaiti sovereignty. We have waited too long for this kind of attitude, this demonstration of responsibility on the part of the United Nations not to feel collegially committed to ensuring that this new spirit also manifests itself in the search for long-term solutions to the inextricable problems of the Middle East.

Canada is playing an active part in this undertaking. I would like to share with you today my thoughts on the matter,

0078

3

along with certain initiatives that the Prime Minister and I might promote in the coming months.

To begin with, we must, above all, be realistic. For Canada at this stage to claim to have the answers to the problems of the Middle East would be presumptuous. Why? Simply because it is first and foremost the business of the countries in the region to together find solutions to the current situation. No lasting solution can be imposed from without. A commitment on the part of the countries immediately involved is essential to stability and security in this region.

This having been said, the task is a considerable one and will also require the co-operation of the countries beyond the Middle East. In fact, many of the causes of instability in this region, such as the central problem of the proliferation of arms, call for solutions that would involve the whole international community. We will also have to count on the mobilization of international resources, notably those of the United Nations, to respond to the humanitarian and security problems that have been aggravated by Saddam Hussein's adventurism.

Let us now look at what the post-war issues will be, and what kind of contribution a country like ours can make.

IMMEDIATE POST-WAR ISSUES

To begin with, three pressing questions will arise once the objectives of the Security Council resolutions have been achieved and the ceasefire has been established:

- humanitarian assistance will have to be provided to the civilian populations and to displaced persons;

- a peacekeeping force will have to be established;

- the damage caused to the environment by the huge oil slicks in the Gulf will have to be repaired

1) HUMANITARIAN ASSISTANCE

In terms of humanitarian assistance, we must continue the magnificent co-ordination and co-operation effort that the various international organizations have begun. These organizations (the High Commissioner for Refugees, the International Committee of the Red Cross, UNDRO [the United Nations Disaster Relief Organization] and so on) have already done a tremendous job and continue to provide effective assistance. Canada has made a substantial contribution to these

人道

0079

efforts, supplying about $75 million. We intend to continue our
commitment. To meet the needs of countries such as Turkey,
Jordan and Egypt, however, we will have to mobilize the resources
of the entire international community, especially countries that
have shown considerable surplus oil revenues and those whose
military commitment within the coalition has been limited.

2)A PEACEKEEPING FORCE

Moreover, the borders of Kuwait must initially be guaranteed
by a peace-keeping force, ideally under the authority of the
United Nations. Canada feels that this force must consist mainly
of troops from the countries of the region. Their expertise,
however, is limited. That is why Canada, which has a well
established reputation in this field, has offered its services to
the Secretary-General of the United Nations and to the countries
of the region. We are prepared to assist both in setting up such
a peace-keeping force and in the planning operations that its
deployment requires. We are also prepared to co-operate with the
United Nations in calling a meeting of experts in Canada with the
responsibility of analyzing needs and identifying the various
alternatives that are worth exploring.

It is of great importance to Canada that the United
Nations, with their renewed credibility, play a central role in
implementing postwar arrangements. Their commitment guarantees
the new international order that we seek to consolidate.

3)RESTORATION OF THE ENVIRONMENT

On the environmental front, we must collectively tackle
the clean-up of the damage caused by the insane dumping of
unprecedented quantities of crude oil into the Gulf. A team of
Canadian specialists is already on site and is busy planning this
operation together with colleagues from many countries. But we
must also look further ahead and examine how to strengthen
present conventions on the use of the environment for military
purposes. We have already taken the initiative of contacting
certain countries to pursue this project further. At the same
time, we will examine the possibility of reinforcing the
international mechanisms currently provided to respond to such
emergencies.

MEDIUM-RANGE CHALLENGES: SECURITY IN THE GULF AND THE MIDDLE EAST

But these immediate post-war problems seem almost laughable
compared to the challenges of establishing lasting peace and
security in this region of the world.

0080

Since August 2, when he invaded Kuwait, Saddam Hussein has ignored every effort of the international community to end his illegal occupation of that country. His intransigence presents the world community with two crucial challenges: first, to win the war and free Kuwait; and, second, to secure the peace, by reinforcing the principle of collective security enshrined in the United Nations Charter and by creating a system of order in the Middle East based on justice and equity. We must win the war and win the peace. While victory must come first, a just peace is of no less importance.

The action against Saddam Hussein is being carried out under the authority of the United Nations Charter. The express purpose of that Charter is to spare future generations from "the scourge of war". But the world has been powerless to deter or stop aggression while the Security Council was deadlocked in ideological competition. That deadlock has been broken and the dreams of the visionaries who created the United Nations can now be realized. But old ways die hard.

No one has thrown down a more hostile or brazen challenge to the values enshrined in the U.N. Charter than Saddam Hussein. Never has the need been more urgent for the world community to respond effectively. The U.N. must succeed in this direct challenge to its authority. Failure would mean that the United Nations would be ignored in the future by major powers and potential aggressors alike. Failure would once again condemn the U.N. to impotence, and make it incapable of protecting any country's security, including Canada's. A discredited U.N. would make the world an even more dangerous and unpredictable place than it is already, as nations around the world, left to their own devices to ensure their security, armed themselves against potentially hostile neighbours.

The stakes in the war in the Gulf go well beyond the Middle East. The case for U.N. action against Saddam Hussein could not be stronger. He has turned his country into a police state, launched an eight year long war with Iran, which cost more than a million casualties, and used poison gas against Iranian troops in contravention of the Geneva conventions, and then turned that gas on his own people. His forces have perpetrated terrible atrocities against the people of Kuwait, as documented by Amnesty International.

We have all witnessed the indiscriminate missile attacks against the civilian populations of Saudi Arabia and Israel, the latter a non-combatant country. We have all been angered by the pictures we have seen of the prisoners of war he has abused. We have all been disgusted by his deliberate and senseless destruction of marine life of the Persian Gulf. We have all been chilled by his threats, repeated most recently last week, to use chemical and biological weapons against the men and women of the coalition forces and against the people of Israel. And, in the backs of our minds, we are all alarmed by his nuclear ambition.

The International community has a moral obligation to step in and put an end to Saddam Hussein's brutality against Kuwait. Canada shares in that obligation and will fulfil its responsibilities. There are times, regrettably, when we have to fight for peace and this is one of those times. Super-powers, major powers, middle powers and

10/15

mini-powers from around the world -- sustained by the moral authority of the United Nations and the most basic principles of international law -- have joined in the fight against Saddam Hussein. It is a war that must end in victory by the forces of international law and the standard-bearers of human decency. And it will end in victory.

In the past few weeks, coalition aircraft have reduced or destroyed Iraq's nuclear, chemical and biological weapons production capabilities. As well, they have substantially reduced Saddam Hussein's ability to threaten population centres in Israel and Saudi Arabia with SCUD missiles. The effectiveness of Iraq's navy has been curtailed and coalition forces currently have air supremacy over the skies of Iraq and occupied Kuwait. Surprises are still possible, however, and vigilance continues to be necessary. Saddam Hussein's enormous, heavily equipped army -- perhaps the fifth largest force in the world -- remains dug in deep in Kuwait and along the Iraq-Kuwait border.

The next few weeks will likely be the decisive phase of the war. Canada will do its full share to achieve victory in the Gulf. Because victory in the Gulf is victory in the cause of international law and order. Victory will send powerful new messages around the world.

To other potential aggressors who might hope that aggression still pays, the message will be clear: times have changed. To military powers, who feel they need not rely on the U.N., the message will be persuasive: there is no force more compelling than global consensus and unity. And to all countries, large and small, victory will send a third message: the United Nations works, as its architects intended, and we can all count on the U.N. to help us meet the challenges of the next century.

To meet those challenges, the world must learn the larger lessons of this war. This war cannot be allowed simply to set the stage for the next war as so often has been the case in the Middle East. Durable peace in this unfortunate region requires more than dealing with Saddam Hussein. Peace requires a broader focus and a longer time-frame. The war is far from over, and the post-war picture far from clear. We must be very cautious in any assessments we make at this stage. But, despite the uncertainties, it is not too early, especially for a region as complex and volatile as the Middle East, to begin planning for the post-war peace.

I want to outline, today, Canada's perspective on some of the issues that must be addressed if the war is to end successfully and produce a durable peace. Canada's approach is based on four principles. First, there can be no compromise when it comes to Saddam Hussein's complete withdrawal from Kuwait. That is a precondition to peace. Second, solutions to the problems of the region must have the support of the governments and of the people concerned. Third, the United Nations must be an integral part of the solution to these problems, because it is under its auspices that the new international order must be built, if it is to endure. And fourth, regional security for the region must cover the whole range of inter-related issues -- political, economic, military and humanitarian -- that have plagued this region and fuelled this conflict.

11/15

- 3 -

We must address three main issues: the short-term needs for humanitarian aid and peacekeeping, the longer-term security requirements and, finally, the larger issues that go beyond the region. In the short-term, three immediate needs can be anticipated: assistance for people affected and displaced by the war, coordinated through international agencies; a peacekeeping force, under U.N. auspices; and a cooperative effort to clean up the environmental damage done by the war, especially to the Persian Gulf itself. Canada has committed $77.5 million in economic and humanitarian assistance to countries most affected by the war -- primarily Jordan, Egypt and Turkey.

When the fighting stops, we will provide humanitarian assistance to the direct victims of the war. We would welcome, as well, a broad-based effort under the auspices of the U.N. Disaster Relief Organization and the High Commission for Refugees for people harmed by the war -- migrant workers, Kuwaitis and Iraqis. The coalition is at war with Saddam Hussein -- not with the people of Iraq. The people of Iraq must be eligible for short-term assistance, as needed, when the fighting stops.

Over the longer term, Iraq's oil revenues, freed from the burden of wasteful arms purchases and the costs of war with its neighbours, should be able to finance its own reconstruction effort. The relief and reconstruction of Kuwait will require expertise, skills and material; Canada is willing to participate. We assume that this effort can be financed largely by the Government of Kuwait and the other Arab governments of the Gulf. Once the fighting stops, observers must be available to oversee the disengagement of soldiers and the repatriation of prisoners of war. Peacekeeping will also be needed while longer-term security arrangements are designed and put in place. Peacekeeping forces should be drawn primarily from Arab states, from Moslem non-Arab states, and possibly from the Nordics and others with peacekeeping experience.

We have told Secretary General Perez de Cuellar that Canada is willing to participate in the design and training of that force and to contribute to it ourselves, if necessary and appropriate. And we have offered to host a small gathering of specialists, under U.N. auspices, to review requirements and suggest ideas. I will discuss these issues with Mr. Perez de Cuellar when he visits Ottawa next week.

We will, also, contact the countries of the region and other potential participants in the coming days. Canada will contribute expertise and equipment to Bahrain and Qatar to help clean up the environmental damage caused by the vandalism done by Saddam Hussein to the Persian Gulf. We will provide personnel and equipment to help map the oil slick and coordinate the effort to deal with it. We will also provide equipment and expertise to help save affected wild-life. I will, also, discuss with the U.N. Secretary-General whether a conference of legal experts should be convened to explore ways of strengthening international law to prevent the environment from being used as a weapon of war or an instrument of extortion. Canada would be willing to host such a meeting.

12/15

0083

- 4 -

Over the longer-term, the security of all of the countries in the region will depend on solutions to the interlinked problems -- political, economic and military -- that have made it so unstable for so long. Military security arrangements must be based on the principle of collective security, as provided for in the U.N. Charter. These arrangements must go beyond the simple containment of Iraq to include a system of regional security based on guaranteed borders and collective defence. All of the countries of the region must have the opportunity to participate fully in the design and implementation of any security regime. Respect for the sovereignty of these countries is of fundamental importance.

International guarantees, preferably under the aegis of the U.N. Security Council would be advisable. Developing a regional security system for countries as divided as those in the Middle East will be an enormous challenge to diplomatic creativity and perseverance. But there is no viable alternative. And there is a recent precedent. It has been done, in equally difficult circumstances, in Europe. Slowly and steadily, over two decades, the Conference on Security and Cooperation in Europe laid the basis for the thaw in East-West relations and for the cooperation which has followed. The CSCE model cannot simply be transferred to the Middle East. But we have learned some lessons in the CSCE process that are relevant: for example, procedures for the peaceful settlement of disputes and for the advance notification of military manoeuvres, to name only two of many.

Canada played an active role in development of the CSCE, especially in its human rights work, and we are prepared to contribute expertise on this and other elements of a regional security system for the Middle East. No plan for regional security can hope to succeed in the absence of progress on the Arab-Israeli dispute, the most worrisome fault line in the Middle East. Saddam Hussein has tried cynically to exploit this conflict to attract support from the Arab world and to sow dissension among coalition members. We believe that U.N. resolutions 242 and 338 continue to form the appropriate basis for a solution of this issue.

One lesson that is clear from this crisis is that in an era of increasingly sophisticated high technology weapons everyone is vulnerable, the possession of territory in the cauldron of the Middle East does not alone guarantee security. Canada continues to support the convening, at an appropriate time once hostilities are over, of a properly structured conference to facilitate efforts to achieve a settlement between the parties directly concerned.

The Middle East is a region of vast riches and disparate poverty. This disparity contributes to social instability and feeds the politics of extremism. A more equitable distribution of the benefits of wealth and the burdens of growth in the area would contribute to the security of all states, as long as resources were used for development and not for more weapons. At the end of World War II, the Marshall Plan built the foundations of security and stability in Europe. A similar approach, perhaps based in existing regional institutions and financed in substantial measure from regional resources, would contribute to economic development and ultimately to peace in the region.

13/15

- 5 -

One of the main lessons to be learned from this war is the danger to us all of the proliferation of both conventional and non-conventional weapons and of missiles and other high technology delivery systems. Iraq has more combat aircraft than Germany, France or the United Kingdom. And it has more than twice as many main battle tanks as the United Kingdom and France, combined. And Iraq is far from being the only country in the region that is very heavily armed.

Iraq also has weapons of mass destruction. These weapons of mass destruction have not been used but the threat to use them against civilians and combatants alike has been made repeatedly. These threats raise the risk of a very dangerous escalation at a time of great tension and animosity. When the war is over, the world community must cooperate to prevent the proliferation of these weapons and to roll back that proliferation which has already occurred. Controlling the most dangerous, non-conventional weapons -- chemical, biological and nuclear and the means to deliver them -- is already the subject of negotiations. But success to date has been spotty because political will has been lacking.

The world is being given a very expensive and very persuasive lesson on how dangerous these weapons are. Left to proliferate, they seriously threaten the peace around the world. The major arms-exporting firms and nations have contributed to the current crisis. The great majority of weapons in Iraq's arsenal come from suppliers in the countries of the five permanent members of the Security Council. This problem must be brought under control and the time to act is now.

Next week, I will propose to the U.N. Secretary General, Mr. Perez de Cuellar, that the United Nations convene a Global Summit on the Instruments of War and Weapons of Mass Destruction. The objective is to convene world leaders in order to mobilize political will and to re-energize international efforts that are underway to produce results urgently. A high level follow up meeting, or a series of such meetings, could be scheduled to ensure results.

We must act wisely so that this war leads to peace and not to another conflict. We have been to the brink of the precipice and we have seen the chaos that lies below. The world cannot simply return to business as usual, because business as usual in that region usually means war. And we cannot risk another war vastly more dangerous and destructive than this one.

Wars begin in the minds of man and women. Peace begins there, too. We must persuade people that true security comes from cooperation and common purpose, not bullets and ballistic missiles. We must change attitudes and create political will for peace.

- 6 -

Canada will work with diligence and determination to make the best use of the best hope there is for peace -- the United Nations and its capacity for collective security. An effective United Nations would make the entire world population the victors in this war. With the cooperation of all states, the objectives in creating the United Nations in 1945 can yet be realized. Future generations can be spared "the scourge of war". But this war -- a just war -- must first be won. Because in the crucible of that victory will be forged the bonds of peace.

Canadians can be counted on to do their part in winning the war. And, once the war is won, we will play our part in winning a durable and just peace.

- 30 -

15/15

.0086

A Postwar Agenda

A new balance of power could create prospects for progress in the Arab-Israeli conflict

BY HENRY A. KISSINGER

When I first heard that the war had begun, I thought of President Bush. In a movie, people run around during a crisis, picking up telephones and yelling instructions. In a real crisis, the top people are very much alone. Many officials head for the foxholes, occasionally throwing out memoranda designed to absolve them of responsibility for their actions. Usually there are only two or three people willing to make tough decisions. President Bush has earned the nation's gratitude for his fortitude in holding the coalition together during the months of buildup, gaining Congressional backing and steering the country to the point where allied and domestic support coincided. But even in the best-planned operation, there are hours in which a leader in his position must wonder why he ever expended so much time and effort trying to get elected.

I also thought of the challenges the President will have to face once the war is over. After all, the purpose of victory is to ensure a lasting peace. To that end, the United States should move to implement a number of measures in the immediate aftermath of the war:

■ An arms-control policy for the gulf to prevent a recurrence of the weapons race that contributed to this conflict.

■ Some kind of agreement on economic and social development under the auspices of the Gulf Cooperation Council, which embraces the nations of the gulf. Other Arab allies of the U.S. could join this effort, which would be designed to defuse the argument that this is a conflict of rich against poor.

■ A process to address the original Iraqi-Kuwaiti dispute. Direct negotiations between the two countries would be inherently unbalanced, because of the disparity in their size, which has only been compounded by Iraq's invasion and pillaging of its neighbor. But some issues are susceptible to legal determination, such as drilling rights or the location of the boundaries. These could be put to the International Court of Justice, while remaining issues are handled within the framework of the Gulf Cooperation Council.

■ An international program for imposing tough sanctions against terrorism. The world must not again stand impotently transfixed by thousands of hostages. Countries harboring terrorist groups must be confronted with severe reprisals, including military measures if other pressures fail.

THE WAR LOOKING AHEAD

Over the long run, our biggest challenge will be to preserve the new balance of power that will emerge from this conflict. And that will not prove easy, given conventional American thinking about foreign policy. Today, it translates into the notion of "a new world order," which would emerge from a set of legal arrangements and be safeguarded by collective security. The problem with such an approach is that it assumes that every nation perceives every challenge to the international order in the same way, and is prepared to run the same risks to preserve it. In fact, the new international order will see many centers of power, both within regions and between them. These power centers reflect different histories and perceptions. In such a world, peace can be maintained in only one of two ways: by domination or by equilibrium. The United States neither wants to dominate, nor is it any longer able to do so. Therefore, we need to rely on a balance of power, globally as well as regionally. We must prevent situations where the radical countries are tempted by some vacuum every few years, forcing us to replay the same crises over and over again, albeit with different actors.

This is why, in the final analysis, all of

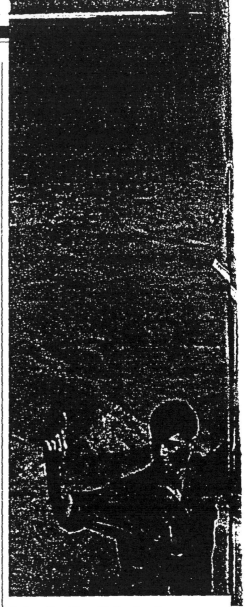

An Israeli soldier with Hawk anti-aircraft missiles near the Jordan Valley

the so-called diplomatic options would have made matters worse. Each would have left Iraq in a militarily dominant position. None addressed the root problem of the gulf's lack of security, which drew 415,000 Americans into the region in the first place—a deployment that certified the gap in military capability between Iraq and the moderate Arab countries. Any diplomatic solution that did not produce a dramatic reduction of Iraq's military power would have been a victory for Saddam Hussein. From then on, he would not have needed to engage in actual physical aggression. He could have let Iraq's demonstrated superiority speak for itself, progressively undermining the governments that supported the United States. He would have

0087

been able to exploit his position within OPEC to achieve an increase in oil prices, as well as a greater share of production. These two steps would have given Iraq vast additional resources to increase its already huge military buildup, including nuclear and missile programs. The United States would have been left with the choice of keeping major ground forces in the gulf, or of destabilizing the region by withdrawal. The practical result of the military operations now in motion will be to bring into balance the military capability of Iraq against its neighbors in the gulf.

Yet ironically, maintaining equilibrium in the region requires us to navigate between a solution that leaves Iraq too strong and an outcome that would leave Iraq too weak. After all, one of the causes of the present crisis is the one-sided way the Western nations rushed to the

A revived peace process should begin by redefining the objectives

defense of Iraq in its war against Iran, forgetting that if Iran was excessively weakened Iraq might become the next aggressor. It would be ironic if another bout of tunnel vision produced an Iraq so weak that its neighbors, especially Iran, seek to refill the vacuum.

Ideally, one military goal should be to pull the teeth of Iraq's offensive capability

without destroying its capacity to resist invasion from covetous neighbors. We should take care that Scud missiles are not reintroduced. We should prevent Iraq from importing high-technology equipment, including high-performance aircraft with long ranges, and from reacquiring the means to manufacture biological and nuclear weapons. However, Iraq's capacity to defend itself with conventional weapons against ground attack from its neighbors would in the long run not be a threat to stability but a contribution to it.

The new balance of power in the region cannot be based on the permanent presence of American ground forces. This was the weakness of diplomatic solutions that would have kept Iraq's military preponderance intact. A major Western ground force in the area would inevitably become the target of radical and nationalist agitation. The cultural gap between even the best-behaved American troops and the local population is unbridgeable. After a brief period, American ground forces would be considered foreign intruders. There would be a repetition of our experiences in Lebanon, including terrorism and sabotage. American ground forces in the area should be withdrawn after victory; residual forces should be stationed beyond the horizon—at sea or perhaps at a few remote air bases. Any monitoring of Iraqi withdrawal from Kuwait should be done by Arab members of the coalition.

The difficulty of stationing Western ground forces in the area for an extended period was one reason why sanctions almost surely could not have achieved our objective. It would have been impossible to keep over 400,000 troops in the area for the 12 to 18 months that even optimists thought were needed for sanctions to succeed. But if we started to withdraw any American forces during that time—or to rotate them, as the term of art had it—it would have set off a panic among our Arab allies.

Military equilibrium, however, cannot be the sole aim of American policy in the gulf. It is essential that America learn to become less dependent on oil and generate a viable energy program. We cannot suffer through an energy crisis every decade. We should stress conservation and develop alternative sources of energy, avoiding the self-indulgent attitudes of the 1980s, when plentiful oil caused the search for alternative energy sources to be largely abandoned.

We must also remember the possibility of renewed Soviet designs on the region. For the time being, domestic problems keep the Soviets from running any significant foreign risks. But 200 years of Russian expansionism toward the gulf indicate a certain proclivity. And this drive may be compounded as Moscow's preoccupation with its more than 50 million Muslim citizens grows. After some domestic equilibrium is restored, the Kremlin may become more active in the Middle East—especially in Iran, Iraq, Pakistan and Turkey, which border the Soviet Union. The intensity of that thrust will depend on internal developments within the Soviet Union. If the Muslim republics remain Soviet, Moscow will be wary of Muslim radicalism lest it inflame its own Muslim population. But if the Muslim republics break off and become independent, Moscow may seek favor in the breakaway states by embracing Islamic radicalism—especially if the Muslim world turns more extremist.

Finally, and perhaps most importantly, a new balance of power will revive prospects for progress on the Arab-Israeli conflict. A peace process dominated by Saddam Hussein, or heavily influenced by him, would have been a debacle. For it would have taught the lesson that radicalism, terrorism and force are the road to diplomatic progress in the Middle East. This is why President Bush was right in resisting the linkage of the Kuwait and Palestinian problems.

But with Saddam defeated, moderate Arab leaders will gain in stature, America's credibility will be enhanced and Israel will have a breathing space. This new equation should be translated into a major diplomatic effort within a few months of victory. Far from amounting to linkage and a submission to blackmail, such a move, after Saddam has been defeated, should be viewed as an opportunity resulting from the success of the moderate forces.

Progress will depend on a proper perception of the issues involved. The Arab-Israeli problem is usually stated as a negotiating issue: how to convene an international conference that returns Israel to the 1967 frontiers, defines a new status for Jerusalem, induces the Arabs to "accept" Israel and provides international guarantees for the resulting arrangements. I have

grave doubts about every one of these propositions.

First, I am very skeptical about an international conference. For the United States would be totally isolated at such a forum. The behavior of France just prior to the gulf war is a small foretaste of what would happen. Instead of being a mediator, America would be maneuvered into the role of Israel's lawyer, while Israel would regard any independent position we took as a betrayal of its interests. No sensible nation would voluntarily throw itself into such a maelstrom. Since everything depends on our influence with Israel anyway, I would much prefer a diplomatic process in which the United States, the moderate Arab countries and Israel are the principal participants.

Second, for Israel a return to pre-1967 borders and the creation of a Palestinian state are not negotiating issues but matters of life and death. The distance from the Jordan River to the sea is less than 50 miles; the corridor between Tel Aviv and Haifa in terms of the 1967 frontiers is about 10 miles wide. It would be difficult to squeeze two states into such a limited area in the best of circumstances. But the PLO has been in mortal conflict with Israel during the entire existence of both groups. How can such an arrangement possibly be compatible with security?

Moreover, a return to pre-1967 borders would still leave almost as many Arabs under Israeli control as live on the West Bank minus Gaza. How is one going to justify that one group of Arabs must live under Israeli rule while other Arabs are entitled to self-determination? Thus a restoration of pre-1967 borders, coupled with the formation of a Palestinian state, could easily turn into the first step to the further reduction of Israel, if not its ultimate destruction.

Third, acceptance of Israel is not only a legal but above all a psychological challenge. And I find it hard to believe that any legal formula can by itself provide for Israeli security. After all, Kuwait lived in a state of legal peace with Iraq without being able to prevent Iraqi aggression. And Saddam attacked Israel in a war from which Israel had kept totally aloof because it calculated that many Arabs would support Iraq against Israeli retaliation, no matter how justified. American leaders understandably felt this danger real enough to advise against retaliation. But when reaction to an unprovoked attack becomes an international issue, Israel is still certified

ERIC BOUVET—ODYSSEY-MATRIX
Iranians parading in Teheran before Friday prayers

If Iraq is left too weak, Iran may seek to fill the vacuum

as a pariah and is held hostage for the actions of others.

Fourth, how does one define "credible guarantees"? After all, even in the case of Kuwait, where there was unanimous international support for the victim (something that would be inconceivable with Israel), it took six months to organize resistance while the country was looted and pillaged and the population expelled.

For all these reasons, the peace process as currently conceived is likely to lead to a dead end. It forces each side to accept something they find unbearably difficult: for the Israelis, it is a Palestinian state; and for the Arabs, it is the Israeli state. I know of no conflict between Arab nations—let alone between the Arabs and Israel—that has ever been resolved by the method suggested for the Palestinian issue: namely, with one conclusive negotiation resulting in a legal document intended to last for all time.

A revived peace process should begin by redefining the objectives. A final settlement at this moment seems a legalistic mirage. On the other hand, the status quo will sooner or later sound the death knell for moderates on all sides. As it is, too many Israelis consider the peace process a one-sided means to gain acceptance without sacrifice. They are unwilling to give up any occupied territory, or will do so only if de facto Israeli control is maintained. Too many Arabs, especially in the PLO, see in the Middle East a replay of Vietnam, where peace talks were used to soften up the opponent for escalating pressures leading to his ultimate collapse.

An interim solution might seek to introduce the moderate Arab governments, fresh from the victory over Iraq, as a buffer between Israel and the PLO. It might reduce the amount of territory Israel is asked to give up in return for something less than formal peace. A possible approach, mediated by the United States, might unfold like this:

■ A conference would be assembled, under the aegis of the U.N. secretary-general, composed of the United States, Israel and the Arab states allied with America in the gulf crisis.

■ The moderate Arab countries would agree to act as trustees for territories that are returned to Arab control for a specified amount of time, say five to 10 years.

■ The moderate Arab states would also commit themselves to demilitarizing these areas under U.N. supervision.

■ Israel would give up all of Gaza and the most heavily populated areas of the West Bank, retaining only territories essential to its security. It would be allowed to participate in verifying the demilitarization of any territory it evacuates.

■ Precise government arrangements would be established by agreement, but would not for the interim period lead to a separate state. As a practical matter, the trustee powers would undoubtedly establish an administration containing individuals acceptable to the PLO.

If this particular scenario turned out to be impractical, some other interim approach must be sought to break the deadlock. The aftermath of an allied victory over Iraq will

AL JAWAD—SIPA
Syrian troops driving a tank from Damascus to Lebanon

Even Assad, hardly a moderate, might go along with an interim approach

offer a perhaps never-to-recur opportunity. Moderate Arab states are disillusioned with the PLO, which in effect has backed Iraq. They are also dismayed by the fact that the PLO has never unambiguously dissociated itself even from terrorism aimed at the moderate Arabs. As a result, these governments may no longer be prepared to give the PLO a veto over their actions.

As for Israel, it must avoid two possible nightmares. If it insists on holding onto every square inch of occupied territory, it could suffer the fate of South Africa and find itself ostracized, and even ultimately under U.N. sanctions. On the other hand, if it follows the maxims of conventional wisdom and gives up all the occupied territories, it runs the risk of winding up like Lebanon,

gradually squeezed to the point of obliteration. For its own sake, Israel must find a middle way. And there is no better moment to do that than when its most dangerous enemy has been defeated.

I do not envy the American negotiator assigned the task of distilling an interim settlement from the confusing passions of the Middle East. Still, with Iraq's military capacity reduced, the moderate Arab leaders, as well as Israel, should be able to turn to the peace process with authority and confidence. President Mubarak of Egypt, King Fahd of Saudi Arabia—and even King Hussein of Jordan, whatever the maneuvers imposed by his vulnerability— are unusually intelligent and prudent. Even President Assad of Syria, by no means a moderate, signed an interim agreement with respect to the Golan Heights which has been in force for 17 years and has been meticulously observed. All these leaders might in the end go along with an intermediate approach as the only way to break an even more dangerous deadlock. And there are surely Israeli leaders who recognize that a gradual approach will provide their best prospect for a satisfactory outcome—especially when the moderate Arabs are triumphant and radical Arabs are in retreat.

America should act as a mediator in this effort, having earned the trust of both sides. Our initial challenge may well be philosophical. The best way to produce a successful negotiation is to advance a new concept, to convince both sides that the proposed new course serves their common interest. If that demonstration cannot be made, no negotiating gimmick can serve as a substitute.

In several thousand years of recorded history, the Middle East has produced more conflicts than any other region. As the source of three great religions, it has always inspired great passions. It is therefore unlikely that any one negotiation can bring permanent tranquility to this turbulent area. An Arab-Israeli negotiation will not end all the turmoil, because many Middle East problems are quite independent of that conflict. Fundamentalism in Iran has next to nothing to do with the Palestinian issue, though Teheran has exploited it. And Saddam Hussein would have tried to dominate his neighbors even if the Palestinian problem did not exist. But what the Arab-Israeli conflict has done is to make it difficult for the voices of moderation in the Arab world to cooperate with their supporters in the West. Victory in the gulf will create a historic opportunity to alter that particular equation—and it should be seized. ■

0090

0091

第 1 次官補 訪美時
重點 協議 事項

1991. 3

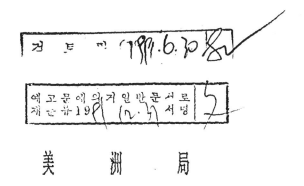

美 洲 局

目次

0092

5. 韓國軍 醫療 支援團 및 輸送團 追加 活動 問題

    가. 醫療支援團 쿠웨이트 移動 問題

    나. 空軍輸送團 活動 繼續 問題

6. 걸프事態 關聯 追加 支援 問題 (美側 擧論時 對應)

7. 外務長官 訪美問題

8. 我國의 유엔加入 問題

添附 : 1. 걸프事態 關聯 支援 推進 現況

      2. 걸프戰 終戰에 따른 中東地域 秩序 再編 構想

0093

1. 人事 말씀

○ 美軍을 비롯한 聯合軍이 걸프戰에서 가히 奇蹟이라 할 만한 최소한의
人命 被害를 내면서 迅速한 勝利를 거둠으로써 그간 世界 平和와 安定을
威脅하던 걸프事態가 終結되게 된 것을 祝賀함.

○ 今番 걸프事態는 지난 40여년간 東.西間 冷戰이 崩壊되고 새로운 國際
秩序가 形成되는 過程에서 發生하여 全 世界에 衝撃을 던져 주었음.

○ 그러나 부쉬 大統領의 迅速하고 決然한 指導力을 바탕으로 한 美國의
主導下에 國際社會가 유엔 決議에 따라 一致 團結하여 地域 覇權을
追求하는 이라크의 侵略을 撃退하고 걸프地域에서 平和와 安定이 回復
하므로써 앞으로의 世界에 있어 集團 安全保障 措置를 통해 地域紛爭을
解決하는 좋은 先例를 確立하였다고 봄.

○ 한편, 우리로서는 아직도 武力赤化統一 路線을 固守하고 있는 北韓이
걸프戰爭에서 敎訓을 얻어 非現實的인 政策을 하루속히 버리고 和解와
協力의 길로 나와 韓半島에서 冷戰의 殘滓를 말끔히 씻어낼 수 있는
契機가 마련되기를 期待함.

- 1 -

0094

2. 中東秩序 再編 方案 및 我國의 參與

가. 美國의 中東秩序 改編 構想

○ 베이커 國務長官은 지난 2.6. 및 2.7. 上.下院 外交委에서 戰後 걸프地域에 대한 美國의 構想을 發表한 것으로 알고 있음.

당시 베이커 國務長官은 걸프地域의 安全保障 裝置는 걸프協力 會議 (GCC) 等과 같이 域內 國家 全體의 參與를 基盤으로 해야 하며, 戰後 걸프協力 會議나 UN 傘下의 地上軍 維持 可能性을 밝히고, 國境 保障을 위해서 美國이 걸프地域에 海.空軍力을 駐屯시킬 수 있음을 暗示한 것으로 알고 있는바, 이에 관한 美國의 보다 具體的인 構想은 ?

* 베이커 國務長官이 밝힌 戰後 걸프 構想
  - 걸프地域 勢力均衡과 相互 侵略 防止를 위한 安全保障 裝置 마련
  - 化生放 武器의 供給 遮斷을 包含한 軍縮 協商
  - 域內國間의 貧富格差 解消를 위한 經濟 再建 計劃
  - 팔레스타인 問題 및 아랍-이스라엘 紛爭 解決 努力
  - 美國의 中東石油 依存度를 낮추는 政策 追求

○ 또한 유럽에서의 NATO 와 같은 安保機構 創設 論議에 대한 評價는 ?

* 同 構想에 대한 批判者들은 NATO 와 같은 機構 創設을 위해서는 美國과 유럽 諸國間에 民主主義, 自由라는 共同의 價値와 蘇聯 이라는 共同의 적의 存在가 必要하다고 主張

- 2 -

0095

o 또한 최근 言論報道에 의하면 Robert Gates NSC 安保 副補佐官을
中心으로 戰後 中東秩序 改編에 관한 構想이 거의 完成되었다는 바,
美國이 構想하고 있는 中東地域 集團 安全保障 體制와 유엔 平和
維持軍 設置 計劃等에 관해 說明을 듣고자 함.

o 금번에 이라크가 敗退하므로써 過去 急進的 아랍 民族主義가 衰退하고
걸프地域에서는 사우디를 中心으로 弱化된 勢力均衡(a healthy
balance of weakness)이 形成될 것이라는 展望도 있는데 이에 대한
美側의 評價는 ?

나. 中東地域 軍縮 推進 方向)

o 금번 걸프事態의 經驗을 통하여 核 및 化學武器 等 大量 殺傷 武器와
미사일 減縮, 그리고 미사일 運搬 體系에 관한 技術移轉 制限等의
必要性을 더욱 切實해졌는바, 向後 中東地域에서의 非在來式 武器
減縮은 어떻게 推進할 것인지 ?(특히, 이스라엘의 軍備나 核武器
保有와 關聯 美側의 構想)

- 3 -

0096

다. 팔레스타인 問題等 아랍-이스라엘間 和解 問題

　o 今番 걸프戰으로 아랍-이스라엘 問題, 특히 팔레스타인 問題는
　　이 地域의 安定을 위해서는 반드시 解決되어야 한다는 點이 크게
　　浮刻되었음.

　o 그러나, 걸프戰을 契機로 팔레스타인 특히 PLO가 이라크 支持로
　　立地가 弱化된 반면, 이스라엘은 美國과의 關係 緊密化 等 外交的으로
　　立志가 强化되므로써 解決이 더욱 어려워질 可能性도 대두되고 있는
　　바, 이 問題에 대한 美側의 解決 方案은 ?

라. 中東秩序 再編 過程에의 我國 參與問題

　o 우리 政府는 걸프事態 發生以來 5億弗의 財政支援과 醫療團 및
　　輸送團을 派遣하는 等 同 地域에서의 平和와 安定回復을 위한 國際的
　　努力에 積極 參與하여 왔음.

　o 우리는 앞으로 걸프地域에서 戰爭이 終結됨에 따라 이 地域의 安定을
　　하루속히 回復하기 위하여 우리의 能力 範圍內에서 할 수 있는 일이
　　무엇인가를 積極 檢討하고 있음. 이와관련 美側의 좋은 意見이
　　있으면 알려주기 바람.

- 4 -

0097

3. 戰後 中東建設 計劃 및 我國의 參與 問題

　가. 美國의 中東地域 經濟 復興計劃

　　　ο 世界經濟에 있어 막대한 重要性을 갖고 있는 中東地域에서 恒久的인
　　　　平和와 安定 維持를 위해서는 이 地域의 國家間 貧富의 差를 解消하고
　　　　經濟復興을 이룩하여야 한다는 主張이 강한바, 이를 위하여 美國이
　　　　2次大戰後 유럽에 대해 實施했던 Marshall Plan 과 같은 構想을 갖고
　　　　있는지 ?

　　　ο 이와관련 現在 美國은 戰後 中東地域 經濟 復興計劃을 뒷받침하기
　　　　위해 가칭 中東經濟開發 復興銀行 設立을 推進한다는 說이 있는데
　　　　이에 대한 美側의 說明을 要請함. 또한 이에 대한 우리의 役割 및
　　　　參與 方案에 관한 美側의 意見은 ?

　　　ο 또한 中東地域 經濟 復舊에 대한 IMF 나 IBRD 등 旣存의 機構의
　　　　役割과 關聯 美國의 構想은 ?

　나. 戰後 復舊事業 參與 問題

　　　ο 쿠웨이트 再建은 政治, 經濟, 社會等 廣範한 領域에 걸쳐 이루어질
　　　　것으로 展望되며, 向後 5年間 500-5,000億弗의 復舊費가 所要될 것으로
　　　　推定된다함.

- 5 -

0098

ㅇ 美國 企業들은 지금까지 締結된 약 200건의 復舊事業 契約中 약 70%를
獨占한 것으로 報道되고 있음. 이와 關聯한 建設 輸出等 多樣한 經驗을
가진 우리 企業들도 쿠웨이트 緊急 復舊事業에 積極的으로 參與하기를
원하고 있는바, 美側의 支援이 있기를 期待함.

ㅇ 이라크의 復舊問題에 대해서도 美側의 構想이 있으면 알려주기 바람.

다. 걸프事態 財政支援 供與國 調整委員會(GCFCG) 의 向後 運營 및 活動 計劃

ㅇ GCFCG 는 걸프事態로 被害를 입고 있는 戰線國家에 대한 經濟支援을
效果的으로 執行하는 동시에 이를 加速化시키는데 크게 寄與해 온
것으로 評價함.

ㅇ 美側은 걸프戰이 終結됨에 따라 GCFCG 의 役割 및 活動을 再調整할
計劃이 있는지 ?   앞으로 同 機構가 中東 經濟復舊를 위한 機構로
institutionalize 될 가능성은 ?

4. 新世界 秩序 宣言을 위한 頂上會談 開催 問題

ㅇ 最近 言論 報道에 의하면 美國은 多國籍軍 派遣國과 其他 支援 供與國
首腦들이 參與하는 頂上會談을 開催할 計劃이라는 바, 이의 事實 與否는 ?
또한, 同 報道內容이 事實일 경우 開催時期, 參與國家 등 計劃은 ?

- 6 -

0099

o 한편, 베이커 長官은 걸二地域이 平和構造 樹立等 協議를 위하여 3.6-16 間 中東地域을 巡訪하고 있는 것으로 알고 있는바, 이에 관한 자세한 說明을 구함.

o 고르바쵸프 大統領은 얼마전 美.蘇 關係가 아직도 깨어지기 쉬운(fragile) 關係라는 發言을 했는바, 걸프事態 이후 美.蘇 關係에 대한 美側의 立場 및 對蘇政策을 알려주기 바람.

5. 韓國軍의 醫療支援團 및 軍輸送團 追加 活動問題

가. 醫療支援團 쿠웨이트 移動 問題

o 現在 사우디 알 누아이리아에서 活動中인 我國軍 醫療支援團은 任務 開始後 걸프戰이 終了될때까지 784名(사우디軍 524名, 이라크軍 47名, 其他 多國籍軍 213名)을 治療하였음.

o 同 醫療團은 戰爭이 終結되었음에도 人道的 見地에서 診療 活動을 繼續하고 있으며, 앞으로도 당분간 活動 豫定인바, 이와 關聯 美側의 特別한 意見이 있는지 ?

o 한편, 우리 政府는 쿠웨이트內 緊急 醫療 需要에 副應키 위해 同 醫療團을 쿠웨이트로 移動시키는 方案도 考慮하고 있는바, 이에대한 美側의 立場은 ?

- 7 -

0100

나. 空軍輸送團 活動 繼續 問題

  ○ 우리 政府는 지난 2.21. UAE 알 바인 基地에 派遣되어 지금까지
    多國籍軍에 대한 後方輸送 支援 業務를 擔當하고 있는 我國의 軍
    輸送團을 걸프 配置 美軍에 대한 輸送支援 業務를 繼續하기 위해
    당분간 Al Ain 에 繼續 配置할 생각인바, 輸送支援 活動 繼續 必要性에
    대한 美側의 立場은 ?

6. 걸프事態 關聯 我國의 支援

가. 第1次 支援 執行 現況

  ○ 90年度 對美 支援分으로 策定된 現金 5千萬弗과 輸送支援 3千萬弗은
    全額 執行이 되었으며, 91년도 多國籍軍에 대한 支援으로 配定되었던
    2,500萬弗도 1.23. Baker 長官의 要請에 따라 現在 美國에 대한 輸送
    支援으로 配定, 現在 약 500萬弗을 執行하였으며, 輸送 支援等 現在도
    繼續하고 있음.

- 8 -

0101

º 기타 多國籍軍에 대한 支援 및 戰線國家에 대한 支援은 早期 執行을
위해 關聯國과 協議를 繼續하고 있음.

＊ 90.10.27 - 11.8 간 정부 조사단 1차 파견
91. 2.24 - 3.9 간 정부 조사단 2차 파견(UAE, 이집트, 사우디,
요르단)

＊ 戰線國家 執行上 問題點

- 걸프事態 被害國에 대한 支援事業 協議次 我國은 政府調査團을
  90.10.27-11.8 및 91.2.24-3.9 간 派遣, 支援計劃을 協議
  하였으며, 駐在公館을 통해 早期支援을 希望하는 立場을 전하고
  早速한 支援事業 및 品目 選定을 督促해온 결과 터키, 요르단,
  모로쿠에 대한 支援은 比較的 순조로이 執行되고 있음.

- 그러나 이집트의 경우, 3차에 걸쳐 品目選定 및 借款利用計劃書
  提出을 督促하였으나 이집트 政府內 部處間 協議 지체로 인해
  상금 進陟이 없음.

- 未修交國인 시리아의 경우 國防長官으로 부터 支援希望品目
  提示가 있었으나 外交채널을 통한 시리아 政府의 公式立場
  表明은 없음.

  · 我國은 駐日, 요르단 및 이란 公館을 통해 시리아 政府와
    協議 推進中

- 9 -

0102

○ 한편 우리 政府는 91년도에 支援하기로 한 5千萬弗中 2,500萬弗은
   對美 輸送支援으로 配定하였으며, 나머지 2,500萬弗은 戰線國家에
   대한 執行計劃을 蒐集中에 있음.

나. 我國의 2次 支援 執行 方案 (美側 擧論時 對應)

○ 우리 政府는 지난 2.20. 對美 追加支援 280百万弗中 現金 및 輸送
   支援 110百万弗을 現金 60百万弗, 輸送支援 50百万弗로 支援할 것을
   提示하였는 바, 이에 대한 美側의 立場은 ?

○ 또한 170百万弗의 軍需物資 支援의 執行方案에 대한 美側의 立場은 ?

○ 한편, 英國은 지난 2.13. John Weston 外務部 政務擔當 副次官을
   我國에 派遣, 32百萬 내지 40百万弗의 戰費支援을 要請해 왔음.
   우리 政府로서는 걸프戰에서의 英國의 寄與度等을 감안 英國에 대한
   戰費 支援을 積極 檢討하고 있으나, 우리의 經濟與件上 旣約束한
   500百万弗 以外의 追加 支援은 現實的으로 不可能한 實情임.

○ 우리는 美國이 이러한 우리의 立場을 充分히 理解하여 美國에 대한
   軍需物資 支援 約束인 170百万弗에서 一部를 英國에 대한 戰費
   支援으로 轉用하는 我側 提議를 受諾할 것을 要望함.

- 10 -

0103

다. 美側의 追加支援 要請에 대한 우리 立場 (美側 擧論時 對應)

o 막대한 戰爭 所要 經費에 비추어 볼때, 韓國이 支援金이 相對的으로
   크다도 볼 수는 없으나, 아래와 같이 韓國이 처한 事情下에서는
   最大限의 金額이며, 이 規模를 上廻하는 어떤 金額도 韓國內에서 매우
   深刻한 政治的, 財政的 問題를 야기하지 않고는 推進될 수 없으므로
   美國이 韓國의 支援金 增額을 무리하게 시도하지 않는 것이 切實히
   要望됨.

   1) 日本과의 단순 GNP 對備만으로 韓國의 支援 能力을 計算하는 것은
      現實的이지 못하며, 貿易收支, 對外資産, 政府 財政 狀態等을
      考慮해야 함. (89년 基準 貿易黑字 日本/韓國 = 641億弗/46億弗,
      對外純資産 日本/韓國 = 2,930億弗/-31億弗等)

   2) 韓國은 美國의 同盟國中 가장 높은 GNP 對備 防衛費 負擔을 안고
      있을뿐 아니라, 韓.美 兩者間 安保協力을 위한 防衛費 分擔이 매년
      急增하고 있음.

   3) 작년말 豫算 編成 당시 政治, 社會的으로 극히 重要한 秋穀 收買價도
      약 3億弗 정도의 豫算 사정으로 農民의 期待에 副應치 못함으로써
      人口의 15%에 해당되는 農村 人口로부터 심각한 反撥을 야기시켰으며,
      國會에서 野黨으로부터 殺人的 農政이라는 非難을 받고, 國會가
      停會되는 事態까지 發生했음.

   4) 우리나라는 今年들어 1月달에 17億 8千 4百萬 $의 赤字에 이어
      2月에도 16.1億弗의 赤字를 記錄, 總 33億 8千 5百萬 $의 赤字를
      記錄하는 等 매우 어려운 狀況임.

- 11 -

0104

o 한편, 我國의 최근 對蘇 經協은 原則的으로 商業 베이스에서 이루어진
  것이며, 政府 財政 支出이 아닌바, 消費財 輸出用 戰隊借款 15億弗,
  資本財 輸出用 年拂輸出 5億弗, Libo 金利에 따른 銀行間 借款 10億弗로
  構成되어 있음.

o 이러한 經濟協力은 韓國뿐만 아니라, 各國이 商業的 次元에서 施行하는
  協力 形態이며, 蘇聯 極東 地域의 原木, 天然가스, 석탄 등 韓國으로
  搬入 可能한 資源을 考慮하면, 借款 償還에 있어 큰 어려움이 없을
  것으로 볼 뿐만 아니라, 韓.蘇間 協力은 蘇聯의 對北韓 軍事 援助
  抑制, 北韓의 核安全 協定 締結 誘導等 政治的으로 肯定的인 影響도
  期待됨.

o 韓國의 걸프事態 解決 支援 努力은 단순히 石油 供給의 安定이라는
  經濟的 次元을 넘어 中東事態의 安定이 가져오는 國際 政治的 効果,
  韓.美 同盟關係等을 考慮한 措置이며, 可能한 最大限의 支援을 한다는
  點에 대하여 與野를 막론하고 異意가 없음을 다시한번 强調코자 함.

- 12 -

0105

7. 外務長官 訪美 問題

　ㅇ 新任 李相玉 外務長官이 조기에 美國을 訪問 韓.美 外務長官 會談을 조속
　　開催하여 戰後 中東秩序 再編 및 復舊計劃, 韓.美 頂上會談 問題, 韓半島
　　問題, 通商問題 및 亞.太 問題에 대해 率直한 意見을 交換하고 韓.美
　　兩國關係 强化 方案에 관해서도 協議를 할 必要가 있음.

　ㅇ 韓.美 外務長官 會談 開催에 편리한 時期를 協議하기를 원하며, 李相玉
　　長官 訪美時 부쉬 大統領, 퀘일 副統領, 체니 國防長官, Scowcroft 白堊館
　　安保補佐官 等 行政府 高位人士 및 議會 指導者들의 面談이 可能하도록
　　美側의 積極的인 協調가 있기를 期待함.

8. 我國의 유엔加入 問題

添附 : 1. 걸프事態 關聯 支援 推進 現況

　　　 2. 걸프戰 終戰에 따른 中東地域 秩序 再編 構想

　　　　　　　　　　　　　　　　　　　　- 끝 -

- 13 -

0106

걸프 事態 關聯 支援 推進現況

1. 支援 計劃

가. 一次 支援計劃(90.9.24. 發表)

(單位 : 만불)

區 分	現 金	物 資	EDCF	쌀	其 他	合 計
美 國	5,000				3,000 (輸 送)	8,000
周 邊 國		3,700	4,000			7,700
방글라데시				500		500
I O M	50					50
行 政 費	50					50
豫 備 費	200			500		700
91年度計劃					5,000	5,000
	5,300	3,700	4,000	1,000	8,000	22,000

나. 追加支援 計劃(91.1.30. 發表)

ㅇ 多國籍軍에 2億8千万弗 상당 支援

- 1억7천만불 : 國防部 在庫 軍需物資 및 裝備提供
- 1억1천만불 : 現金 및 輸送支援

ㅇ 追加支援은 多國籍軍 특히 美國支援이며 周邊國 經濟支援은 불포함

다. 我國의 總 支援規模는 5億弗임.

0107

2. 支援現況

가. 支援事業 執行狀況(91.1.30. 現在)

(單位 : 만불)

區 分	現 金 (執行)	輸 送 (執行)	物 資 (執行)	借 款 (執行)	合 計	進涉度(%)
美 國	5,000 (5,000)	3,000 (2,585)	-	-	8,000 (7,585)	94.8
周 邊 國	-	-	3,700 (900)	4,000 (0)	7,700 (900)	11.7
. 이집트	-	-	1,500 (0)	1,500 (0)	3,000 (0)	0
. 터 키	-	-	500 (500)	1,500 (0)	2,000 (500)	25
. 요르단	-	-	500 (200)	1,000 (0)	1,500 (200)	13.3
. 시리아	-	-	1,000 (0)	-	1,000 (0)	0
. 모로코	-	-	200 (200)	-	200 (200)	100
I O M	50 (50)				50 (50)	100
行 政 費	50 (30)	-	-	-	50 (30)	60
豫 備 費 . ICRC, UNESCO	200 (6)	-	-	-	200 (6)	3
綜 合	5,300 (5,086)	3,000 (2,585)	3,700 (900)	4,000 (0)	16,000 (8,571)	53.6

※ 91년도 支援豫定分 5,000만불, 쌀 1,000만불등 6,000만불은 除外

나. 推進現況

(1) 美 國

　○ 現金 5,000만불 支援(90.12)

　○ 多國籍軍 輸送費, 91.1.31. 現在 2,585만불 支援(3,000만불 配定)

0108

(2) 周邊國

　가) 이집트

　　ㅇ 軍需 物資 (700만불)

　　　- 이집트측은 品目選定을 위한 4명의 군수전문가단 訪韓을 希望해
　　　　왔으므로 접수용의 表明했으나 常今 回信 없음. (90.12.12. 督促)

　　ㅇ 民需用 物資 (800만불)

　　　- 住民登錄 電算化 事業費로의 轉用이 擧論되었으나 이집트 政府內
　　　　協議 常今 進行中

　　ㅇ EDCF 借款 (1,500만불)

　　　- 이집트는 EDCF 借款을 無償援助 資金으로 轉換要請한바 있으나
　　　　豫算 뒷받침없어 不可함을 通報 (91.2.9)

　나) 터 키

　　ㅇ 民需用 物資 (500만불)

　　　- 터키측, 앰블런스.미니버스.트럭등 23개 品目 提示 (90.12.18. 接受)
　　　- 500만불 상당의 對 터키 支援品目 確定, 現在 發送 進行中
　　　　(一部品目 旣到着, 91.1.22. 物品 發注 最終 契約)

　　ㅇ EDCF 借款 (1,500만불)

　　　- 터키측, 아국산 上水道用 파이프 (Ductile Pipe) 購入에 使用
　　　　希望 (90.12.14)
　　　- 國産 파이프 供給不足으로 다른 事業計劃書 提出토록 要請

　다) 요르단

　　ㅇ 民需用 物資 (500만불)

　　　- 요르단측, 설탕, 미니버스, 各種 生必品等 總24個 品目 提示
　　　　(90.12.24)

0109

- 1차 支援品(설탕, 미니버스 200만불 상당)은 91.1.25. 物品
  發注 契約 締結, 發送中
- 其他品目은 요르단側에서 品目確定後 追後 發送豫定

○ EDCF 借款(1,000만불)
- 廢水處理工場 事業計劃書 提示(90.12.11)
- 關係機關(財務部, 輸出入銀行) 檢討完了, 政府間 協定締結
  準備中

라) 시 리 아

○ 民需用 物資(400만불) 및 軍需物資 (600만불)
- 90.11.2-11.5간 政府調査團 訪問, 對시리아 物資支援計劃 通報
  (1,000만불)
- 시리아 國防長官, 全額 미니버스로 支援希望 (90.11.21자 駐 레바논
  大使代理앞 書信)
- 我側, 外交經路(駐日大使館)을 통해 提議토록 要請했으나(90.11.24)
  尙今 回信 未接受
- 駐日 大使館에 시리아측 立場 打診토록 指示 (91.2.13)

마) 모 로 코

○ 軍需物資 (200만불)
- 希望品目 7개提示(방독면, 침투보호의, 텐트등)
- 200만불 상당의 對 모로코 支援品目確定, 發送 進行中(91.1.14.
  物品 發注 契約 畢)

(3) 쌀 支援

○ 방글라데시에 500만불, 豫備費로 500만불 상당의 쌀支援이 豫定되었으나
  쌀 輸出節次上의 特殊性으로 現在 執行 不可狀態
- 쌀 支援은 FAO 및 農産物 輸出國과 協議가 必要하나 美國側에서
  難色을 表明 하였으므로 現實的으로 執行이 어려움

0110

(4) 걸프事態 難民關聯 國際機構 支援現況(56만불)

　가) 支援計劃上 50만불 配定(IOM 支援)

　나) 執行現況

　　o　IOM(국제이민기구) : 50만불

　　o　UNESCO : 3만불 (豫備費)

　　o　ICRC : 3만불 (豫備費)

(5) 調査團 派遣等 行政費 執行現況 : 약 30만불

0111

걸프戰 終戰에 따른 中東地域 秩序再編 構想

1. 美側 構想

2. 카나다側 構想

3. 프랑스側 構想

4. 팔레스타인 問題 暫定解決 方案

5. 터어키의 戰後 걸프 地域 安保體制 構想

6. 걸프戰 平和的 解決 仲裁 動向

添 附 : 1. Baker 長官 美 上.下院 外交委 證言文 1部

        2. Clark 外相 카나다 國際 問題 研究所 招請 午餐 演說文

        3. Kissinger Newsweek紙 寄稿文 寫本 1部.

0112

1. 美側 構想

   * 2.6, 2.7, Baker 國務長官, FY92 豫算提出 關聯 上.下院
     外交委에서 證言

   가. 戰後 處理問題 接近 基本姿勢

      o 向後 地上戰 開始時 많은 死傷者 발생등 제반 어려움과
        미래에 대한 불안감 增大로 인해 戰後 處理問題에 대한
        接近에 있어 愼重함(Sense of Modesty)의 필요성을 강조함.
        - 域內 國家의 主權尊重 및 平和定着 노력 필요

   나. 終戰後 當面 諸般 挑戰

      (걸프地域을 包含한 中東地域 全體의 安全保障 體制 樹立)

      o 安全保障 體制의 目的과 원칙
        - 侵略의 沮止
        - 領土의 不可侵性
        - 國家간 제분쟁의 평화적 해결

      o 域內 國家, 國際機構 및 國際社會의 役割
        - 上記 原則과 目標達成에는 域內 모든 國家들과 GCC
          等이 主導的 역할 수임 필요
        . 戰後 이라크, 이란등의 建設的 役割 기대
        - UN과 友邦國들은 强力한 支援 계속 제공필요

      o 美國은 트루만 行政府 以來 中東地域에 海軍力을 配置
        하고 사우디 等 域內 國家들과 兩者關係를 강화시켜
        왔으나 終戰後 美 地上軍을 계속 유지할 계획은 없음.

0113

o 終戰 直後의 過渡期的 狀況에 있어서의 平和維持軍 구성
  문제
  - UN 또는 GCC 旗幟아래 域內 國家 地上軍으로 編成된
    平和 維持軍을 일정기간 또는 반영구적으로 駐屯케하는
    方案과
  - 域外 友邦國들의 地上軍으로 구성된 平和維持軍 配置
    또는 決議案 또는 安全保障 確約等 政治的 보장 방안
    等을
    관련국들간 廣範圍한 協議를 통해 決定이 필요함.

(在來式 武器 및 大量 殺傷武器의 擴散 防止)

o 戰後 域內 國家들의 大量 殺傷武器 生産 및 保有能力을
  없애고 域內 國家間 武器 保有競爭 억제와 중동지역에
  일종의 信賴構築 措置의 적용 방안 검토가 要求됨.
  - 化學武器 協定 早期妥結 및 尖端技術 移轉 統制等

(經濟 復舊 및 再建 措置)

o 쿠웨이트 및 이라크 經濟復舊에 協力 支援
  - 經濟 再建後 域內 自由貿易 및 투자확대
  - 水資源 開發에도 力點

o 中東地域 銀行 設立을 통한 경제재건 및 開發 방안제시
  - 과거 경험상 地域銀行 設立 및 IBRD/IMF와의 協調
    關係 중요성 감안

0114

(이스라엘과 아랍國家 및 팔레스타인 民族間 和解)

o 相互間 尊重, 忍耐 및 信賴를 基盤으로한 이스라엘과
  아랍국간 對話進展은 中東地域 全般의 平和定着 과정의
  필수적 부분임.
  - 이스라엘과 팔레스타인 民族間 和解를 위한 兩側의
    具體的 行動, 동 과정에 있어서의 아랍 國家들의 역할,
    域內 軍備統制 推進의 영향, 最適 外交的 手段 講究
    等이 검토 대상

(美國의 對中東 原油 依存度 減縮)

o 美國의 對中東 原油 依存度 減縮을 위한 綜合對策 施行이
  요구됨.
  - 에너지의 節約, 效率性 增大 방안, 원유 비축분 증대,
    代替燃料 사용 증대등의 綜合 시행

0115

2. 카나다측 構想

* 2.8. 멀루니 首相은 오타와 Confederation Club 招請 演說에서 闡明

 - Clark 外務長官, 퀘벡시 소재 카나다 國際問題 研究所 招請 演說時 同一 內容 發表

가. 걸프전 終戰 관련 4대 基本原則

　　o 이라크군의 쿠웨이트로 부터의 完全 撤收 目標는 妥協의 여지가 없음.

　　o 걸프 地域의 諸般 問題 解決 방안은 관련국 및 國民들의 支持를 받는 것이어야 함.

　　o UN을 中心으로 한 諸般問題 解決이 바람직함.

　　o 中東地域 安保體制는 政治, 經濟, 軍事 및 人道的 問題等 관련 問題를 包括的으로 다루어야 함.

나. 終戰 直後 推進 課題

(人道的 援助 提供)

　　o 國際 難民 고등판무관실(UNHCR), UNDRO, 國際 赤十字社 等과의 협조를 통한 民間人 戰爭 被害者들에 대한 인도적 援助 提供 노력 전개 필요

0116

(平和 維持軍 構成)

o UN 旗幟下에 域內國家 地上軍들로 구성된 平和維持軍에
   의한 쿠웨이트 國境線 安全保障 활동 적극 지원
   - 域外 國家들의 參加도 考慮

(環境 汚染 除去 努力)

o 이라크의 걸프만에의 原油 放流로 인한 海洋汚染 被害
   縮小를 위한 國際的 노력 지원
   - 專門家 팀等 現地派遣

다. 中.長期的 中東地域 安保體制 樹立

(地域 安保 體制 樹立)

o 地域 安保 體制는 UN과 聯合軍 파견국들간의 國際的 協約
   等에 의한 國際的 保障이 필요함.
   - 걸프 地域에의 항구적 外國軍 駐屯은 불요

o 유럽에서의 CSCE 成功 經驗을 참고로 한 中東地域 전역을
   대상으로 한 '地中海에서의 安保協力 會議' (Conference on
   Security and Cooperation in the Mediterranean) 構想
   檢討 提議

o 國境 保障, 國家間 紛爭의 平和的 解決, 會員國間 信賴
   構築 方案 確立等이 同 安保 體制의 主要 任務가 될 것임.

o 域內 國家들간 진정한 대화를 기초로한 域內 安保 問題에
   대한 巨視的 接近은 中東地域內 民主主義的 경향 확대에
   기여할 것임.

0117

(이스라엘-아랍 民族間 對立 解消)

o 包括的이고 항구적인 이스라엘-아랍 民族間 대립 해소
  없이는 地域 安保 體制의 성공이 미지수임.
  - UN 安保理 決意 242호 및 338호를 기초로 한 交涉 解決
    方案이 바람직
  - 同 問題 討議를 위한 國際會議 開催 歡迎

(域內 國家間 經濟的 不均衡 解消)

o 中東 地域內 모든 국가들의 균형적인 經濟 發展을 위해
  2차 대전후 마샬플랜과 유사한 域內 經協機構 設立 推進을
  積極 支援함.
  - UN과 連繫된 地域 經濟協力機構 創設

라. 戰爭手段 및 大量 殺傷武器 除去에 관한 頂上會談 開催 提議

o 이라크를 포함한 中東地域 國家들에 武器를 販賣한 서방
  先進國들의 무모했던 과거 形態의 變更이 절실히 요구됨.

o 中東地域 平和案에는 大量 殺傷武器의 전파와 재래식 병기의
  備蓄을 엄격히 제한하는 裝置 마련이 포함되어야 함.
  - 同件 관련 多者間 協議는 이미 開始

o 카나다는 同 頂上會談의 積極的 推進을 위해, Clark 外相이
  來週 런던 開催 英聯邦 外相會議 參席은 물론, 10여일간
  관계국을 巡訪, 同件 協議 豫定임.

0118

3. 프랑스側 構想

* 미테랑 大統領, 2.7. T.V. 會見時 立場 表明

(基本 立場)

o 쿠웨이트 駐屯 이라크군 逐出을 통한 쿠웨이트 主權回復 이라는
  UN 決議案의 名分을 尊重 參戰한 바, 同 目標가 達成되면 戰後
  處理를 위해 地域 安保機構 設立, 쿠웨이트, 이라크 經濟再建
  및 이스라엘-아랍 國家間 和解 모색을 위한 국제회의 개최가
  必要함.

(國際會議를 통한 協議 議題)

o 紛爭 再發 防止를 위한 國際的 保障 問題
  - 現 國境線 尊重 및 地域 均衡 回復

o 固有 中東 問題
  - 팔레스타인-이스라엘 問題 및 레바논 問題 等

o 戰爭 被害 復舊 事業을 위한 지역 은행 또는 開發基金 參席문제
  - 石油로 인한 富의 均衡 분배 문제
  - 現 國際武器 販賣 方式에 대한 制度改善 및 통제 문제

0119

4. 팔레스타인 問題 暫定解決 方案

＊ Henry Kissinger 前 美 國務長官의 91.1.28.자 Newsweek지
기고문

가. 基本 認識

  ㅇ 現 段階에서 팔레스타인 문제의 완전한 解決은 現實的으로
    不可能함.
    - 당사자간의 懸隔한 立場差異로 반목과 불화만 增幅

  ㅇ 美國의 仲裁와 걸프戰 終戰 以後 影響力이 증대될 온건
    아랍국의 役割을 활용함.

  ㅇ 終戰後 수개월내 해결 노력 개시 필요
    - 너무 시간을 끌면 사담후세인 류의 過激 勢力 影響力
      回復 危險

나. 具體的 內容

  ㅇ 유엔 事務總長의 후견하에 美, 이스라엘 및 걸프 戰時
    美國과 공동 보조를 취한 아랍국(온건 아랍국)간의 會議
    召集

  ㅇ 온건 아랍국은 일정期間(例 ; 5-10년간) 아랍측에 返還될
    領土의 受託者(trustee)役割 擔當

  ㅇ 온건 아랍국은 유엔 監視下에 同 地域의 非武裝化 實施
    - 이스라엘, 同 檢證 過程 參與

0120

ㅇ 이스라엘은 Gaza 全域과 West Bank中 人口 密集地域을 아랍
側에 返還
- West Bank 中 이스라엘 安保에 直決되는 地域만 繼續
維持

ㅇ 이스라엘이 返還한 領土를 다스릴 政府 構成 問題는 合意에
의해 決定 단, 暫定 期間中에는 完全 獨立國家 수립은 보류
- 受託國들은 PLO側이 받아들일 수 있는 人士를 包含,
政府 構成 豫想

0121

5. 터어키의 戰後 걸프 地域 安保體制 構想

가. 戰後 걸프 地域 安保體制

(終戰後 이란, 사우디 勢力增大)

o 이라크는 敗戰에 따른 體制崩壞 내지는 군사력 약화로 地域
  安保體制에 큰 影響力을 미치지 못할 것이므로 短期的으로는
  이란, 사우디 兩國의 勢力 均衡으로 地域安保體制가 構築
  될 것으로 보임.
  - 軍事力이 우세한 이란의 勢力이 크게 浮上 豫想

(이라크 領土保存 및 이라크의 이란 牽制勢力으로서의 價値)

o 이란, 시리아, 터키의 理解關係 상충으로 인하여 戰後
  이라크 領土分割내지는 이라크 北部에 Kurd 獨立國 또는
  自治區 創設 가능성은 많지 않으며, 이라크의 領土는 종전
  대로 보존될 것으로 보임.

o 戰後 勢力 膨脹이 예상되는 이란을 견제하기 위해서는
  아랍국인 이라크의 領土保存 및 일정 수준의 軍事力 보유가
  필요할 것이며, 이점에서 아랍 諸國과 美國의 理解가 일치
  될 수 있을 것임.

o 戰後 이라크의 軍事力은 오직 防衛力만 보유하고 인접국에
  위협을 주는 攻擊力은 가지 못하도록 하는 國際的인 制限
  措置가 취해질 가능성이 많음.

0122

(集團安保體制 胎動 可能性)

　○ 戰後 쿠웨이트, 이라크 國境에는 多國的軍을 대신해서
　　아랍 연맹 또는 유엔에서 平和維持軍을 派遣할 가능성이
　　있음.

　○ 長期的으로 이라크 및 이란의 勢力을 牽制하기 위하여
　　美國을 背後 勢力으로 하고 사우디, 쿠웨이트등 GCC 國家와
　　이집트등을 잇는 安保體制가 집단적으로 또는 개별적으로
　　이루어질 가능성이 있음.

　○ 이 경우 아랍 地域의 特性에 비추어 볼때, 集團安保機構의
　　創設보다는 오히려 다수의 양자 安保條約締結 형태를
　　취하면서 集團安保의 효과를 거양토록 하는 방안이 採擇될
　　가능성이 높음.

(長期的 安保體制)

　○ 장기적으로 볼때, 戰後 걸프 地域은 이라크의 領土가 보존
　　되고 또한 그 勢力이 弱化된 상태에서 Status quo ante로
　　돌아갈 것으로 豫想되며, 이란, 이라크, 사우디, 시리아
　　等이 Main Actor로 勢力均衡을 이루면서 地域安保體制가
　　維持되어 나갈 것으로 보임.

나. 터키의 意圖 및 役割

(터키의 安保維持)

　○ 터키는 東南部 地域安保에 威脅을 줄 수 있는 隣接國
　　(시리아, 이라크, 이란)의 軍事強國化를 불원하고 있으
　　므로 이라크의 敗戰, Saddam 政權崩壞를 內心 歡迎할 것임.

0123

o 연이나, 이라크의 분할 또는 極度의 勢力弱化는 이란 및
   시리아 牽制勢力의 사실상의 消滅을 의미하므로, 터키로서는
   이를 받아들이기가 어려울 것임.

o 다만, 可能性은 稀薄하나 시리아 및 이란이 이라크 敗戰後
   힘의 공백상태(power vacuum)을 이용, 領土擴張等 勢力
   擴大 기도시 터키는 이에 介入하게될 것이며, 武力行事도
   불사할 것임.

(걸프戰을 利用한 實利追求)

o 터키는 걸프 地域 3개국과 接境하고 있는 지리적 위치를
   십분활용, NATO 會員國으로서의 戰略的 중요성을 美國等
   西方 陣營에 認識시키고, 美國, 西歐諸國等과의 關係
   긴밀화 도모 및 軍事經濟 援助獲得으로 政治軍事 强大國
   化를 기도할 것임.

(地域安保 體制에서의 터키의 役割)

o 터키는 걸프 地域이 터키의 安保 및 經濟的 利益에 직결
   되는 地域이므로, 戰後 處理에 참여, 對아랍권 立地强化를
   기도할 것으로 보이며, 걸프 地域에 인접한 親西方 軍事
   强國으로서 터키는 地域安保體制 再編 過程에서 큰 역할을
   擔當코져 努力할 것으로 보임.

o 연이나, 터키의 過去 아랍 支配歷史, 터키가 비아랍국인
   점, 이에따른 體制의 相異 및 理解關係 상충등으로 인하여
   터키의 役割이 아랍측의 우려내지 반발을 야기시킬 가능성이
   있음. 걸프戰 開戰後 터키의 미국에 대한 Incirlik 空軍
   基地 使用許可가 다수의 아랍 諸國의 반발을 야기한 것이
   하나의 사례임.

0124

6. 걸프戰 平和的 解決 仲裁 動向

가. 蘇聯 特使 이라크 訪問 結果

○ 이라크 訪問中인 '프리마코프' 蘇聯特使, 후세인 大統領을
  面談하고 메시지 傳達

○ 사담 후세인 大統領의 反應
  - 이라크는 事態의 平和的, 政治的 解決策 摸索을 위해
    蘇聯을 비롯한 其他 國家의 平和案에 協力할 용의가 있음.
  - 그러나 多國的軍 爆擊이 우선 中止되어야 하며 이라크는
    어떠한 犧牲이 따르더라도 侵略에 對抗할 것임.

○ 美國의 反應
  - 事態 解決은 이라크가 쿠웨이트 撤收 문제에 대해 어떤
    立場을 취하는가에 달려 있으며, 걸프戰과 팔레스타인
    問題를 連繫시키려는 동일한 戰略의 反復으로 평가

○ 유엔 事務總長
  - 이라크의 平和的 解決 움직임 歡迎하나, 쿠웨이트로부터
    完全 撤收가 前提條件이 되어야 할 것임.

○ 한편, 蘇聯도 提案의 내용에 대해, 유엔 決議와 相反되는
  內容을 包含하고 있지 않으며, 이라크의 쿠웨이트로 부터
  撤收가 前提 條件임을 명백히 밝힘.

나. 非同盟 15개국 外相會議

  ＊ 2.11. 高位實務者 會談, 2.12. 閣僚會議, 베오그라드

0125

(론카르 유고 外相 基調演説 要旨)

o 現 걸프戰 解決을 위한 4段階 解決 方案 提示
  - 1段階 : 이라크의 쿠웨이트 撤軍 및 適法政府 回復
  - 2段階 : 交戰 當事者間의 敵對行爲 中止
  - 3段階 : 事態의 平和的, 政治的 解決
  - 4段階 : 中東地域 全體 問題, 특히 팔레스타인 問題
        解決을 위한 平和 節次 開始

o 事態의 더이상 惡化 防止를 위해 이라크측이 UN 安保理
  決意 660호의 이행을 촉구함.
  - 이라크의 쿠웨이트로 부터의 先撤軍 原則 强調
  - 이라크측이 要求한 팔레스타인 問題 解決을 위한 國際
    會議 開催 方案도 包含

o 印度 및 이란측 제시 4段階 解決 原則
  - 1段階 : 이라크의 撤軍 約束 公表
  - 2段階 : 敵對 行爲 中止
  - 3段階 : UN 監視下의 兩側 撤軍 實施
  - 4段階 : 中東問題 解決을 위한 地域會議 開催

o 上記 유고측과 이란, 인도측 解決原則과의 調整을 통한
  統一된 方案 導出에 失敗하고 聯合國 및 유엔 安保理에
  2개의 平和使節團을 각각 파견키로 決定하고 會議를 종료함.

添 附 : 1. Baker 長官 美 上.下院 外交委 證言文 1部
       2. Clark 外相 카나다 國際 問題 研究所 招請 午餐 演説文
       3. Kissinger Newsweek紙 寄稿文 寫本 1部.   끝.

       예고 : 91. 12. 31 일반

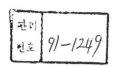
第5次 걸프事態 財政支援 供與國 調整委 會議

代表參考資料

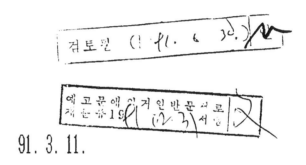

검토필 (1 91. 6 30.)

예고문에 의거 일반문서로
재분류 199

91. 3. 11.

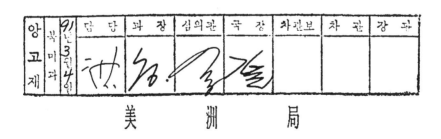

앙고제	91년 3월 4일 북미과	담 당	과 장	심의관	국 장	차관보	차 관	장 관
		洪						

美 洲 局

- 目 次 -

0128

Ⅰ. 議　題

1. Welcoming remarks by hosts

2. Introduction by chair

3. Political overview

4. Presentation by IMF and World Bank

5. Commitments and disbursements

    가. Report of working committee on commitments and disbursements

    나. Additional commitments for 1991

    다. Tour de table on commitments, disbursements, and terms and
        conditions

6. Other business and concluding remarks by chair

7. Closing remarks by hosts

0130

Ⅱ. 基調 發言

1. 國 文

發言權을 주신 議長께 感謝드립니다.

우선 아름다운 룩셈부르크시에서 금번 第5次 調整委 會議를 主催한 룩셈부르크 政府의 勞苦에 치하의 말씀을 드립니다.

大韓民國 政府와 國民은, 걸프戰이 多國籍軍의 最終 勝利와 유엔 安保理의 平和 決議案 採擇으로 걸프地域에 平和定着 過程이 開始된 것을 매우 多幸스럽게 생각하며 이를 忠心으로 歡迎하는 바입니다.

本人은 國際正義와 UN 決議의 履行을 위해 온갖 努力과 犧牲을 아끼지 않은 聯合國 여러나라 國民들과 특히 聯合國 將兵들의 勞苦에 대한 大韓民國 政府의 깊은 感謝의 뜻을 다시한번 傳하고자 합니다.

먼저 걸프事態로 인한 周邊 被害國들에 대한 韓國의 支援 執行狀況을 報告드리겠습니다.

大韓民國 政府는 前線國家들에 支援키로한 約束 金額의 執行 加速化를 위해 지난 2月24日부터 3月9日까지 韓國 政府의 高位實務 代表團이 이집트, 요르단등 前線國을 巡訪하였습니다. 同 代表團은 이들 國家들과 90年度分 殘餘 執行額의 效果的이고 迅速한 支援方法에 대해 진지한 討議를 가졌으며, 이러한 協議結果를

0132

토대로 對外協力基金(EDCF) 4,000万弗 支援과 生必品 等 物資支援을 위한 3,900万弗의 早期 執行을 위한 구체적 節次를 加速化 해 나갈수 있을 것으로 展望됩니다. 이러한 方法에는 職業訓鍊所 設立, 醫療 機資材 供給, EDCF 資金의 條件 緩和등도 包含되어 있읍니다. 또한 91年度 周邊國 經濟 支援額 으로 約束한 2,500万弗의 早期 執行計劃도 동시에 協議中입니다.

멀포드 議長, 키미트 議長, 그리고 友邦國 代表 여러분 !

本人은 이러한 韓國 政府의 支援이 이들 國家의 經濟的 被害를 克服하는 데 다소 도움이 되기를 希望하면서 걸프戰 終戰에 따라 周邊 被害國에 대한 보다 효과적인 支援과 장기적으로 中東地域 全體의 經濟復興과 均衡있는 經濟發展을 위해 지난 5次에 걸친 調整委會議를 보다 發展的인 裝置로 轉換하는 方案을 檢討할 시점이 도래했음을 指摘코자 합니다.

이 會議가 단순한 情報 交換과 討論場으로서의 性格에서 한걸음 더 나아가 여러 關聯國들의 主導에 따라 實効的인 財政支援 裝置로 發展될 경우 韓國 政府도 이에 적극 參與할 예정입니다.

아울러 쿠웨이트 解放직후 쿠웨이트 國民들을 위해 韓國 政府가 취한 몇가지 조치를 말씀드리고자 합니다.

0133

韓國 政府는 사우디와 美國 政府와 協議하여 쿠웨이트 奪還직후 쿠웨이트내 緊急 醫療需要를 감안, 현재 사우디에서 活動中인 韓國軍 醫療支援團을 쿠웨이트로 移動시켜 쿠웨이트 住民들에 대한 醫療支援 活動을 개시키로 하였습니다.

또한 이라크측의 쿠웨이트 原油 放流로 인한 걸프地域 海上 汚染防止를 지원키 위해 사우디, 바레인, 카타르등에 필요한 物資를 支援키로 하였으며, 쿠웨이트에 대해 의류등 緊急 物資를 支援키로 決定하였습니다.

이 기회를 빌어 本人은 걸프戰이 終了함에 따라 걸프地域에 하루속히 戰爭의 상처가 치유되고 平和와 安定이 回復되기를 바라며, 특히 불의의 侵略을 받아 한때 나라를 잃고 온갖 고초를 겪어온 쿠웨이트 國民들이 조속히 나라를 再建하여 安定된 生活을 되찾게 되기를 祈願합니다.

또한 大韓民國 政府는 終戰後 걸프地域의 平和와 秩序維持 및 經濟再建을 위해 가능한 支援을 아끼지 않을 것임을 다짐하는 바입니다.

感謝합니다. 議長

0134

2. 英 文

Thank you, Mr. Chairman, for giving me the floor.

I would like to express my appreciation to the Government of Luxemburg for hosting the Fifth Meeting of the Gulf Crisis Financial Coordinating Group in this beautiful city of Luxemburg.

It is with great sense of relief that the Government and people of the Republic of Korea welcome the victory of the coalition forces in the Gulf War and the onset of a peace process through adoption of the peace resolution by the U.N. Security Council. I wish to extend once again our deep appreciation to the peoples and the valiant soldiers of the coalition countries for their devoted efforts for international justice and the implementation of the U.N. Security Council resolutions.

Let me first brief you on the disbursement status of Korea's financial support to the front-line states.

0135

To expedite the disbursement of the financial support Korea has promised to render to the front-line states, a high-level Government delegation visited Egypt and Jordan from Feb. 24 to March 9. The delegation had earnest consultations with those governments on the ways to make effective and speedy disbursement of Korea's outstanding pledge for the year 1990, which is 40 million U.S. dollars in EDCF(Economic Development Cooperation Fund) and 39 million dollars in kind. Among the ways discussed were establishment of vocational training centers, supply of medical equipments, and easing the terms and conditions of EDCF loan. Also being discussed are ways to expedite the disbursement of 25 million U.S. dollars pledged as financial support to the front-line states for 1991. A government delegation of Egypt is also going to visit soon my country to finalize the process of our economic aid to Egypt.

Chairman Mulford, Chairman Kimmitt, Distinguished Delegates,

I sincerely hope that our contribution to the front-line states will be helpful to their efforts to recover from the economic losses. Now that the War is over, it is my view that the time has come for us to examine the possibility of modifying the Meetings of this Coordinating Group so that they could meet the task of making effective support to the front-line

0136

states and of mapping out a balanced long-term plan to assist the economic rehabilitation of the Middle East region. When this Coordinating Group Meeting, which has provided a good forum of consultation and exchange of information, develops into a more efficient and suitable apparatus with active participation of Member Countries of the Group, Korea will be more than willing to join in their efforts.

Now let me mention some measures the Korean Government has taken for the Kuwaiti people after their liberation.

Considering the urgent need of medical service in Kuwait, we have decided in principle, after consultation with the Governments concerned, to relocate the Korean Military Medical Support Group, now in service in Saudi Arabia, to Kuwait to provide medical support there.

To help clear away the massive discharge of Kuwaiti crude oil by Iraq and prevent further contamination of the Gulf, we have decided to provide Saudi Arabia, Bahrain and Qatar with equipments and materials to fight maritime contamination. We also decided to provide emergency supplies of clothing and the like to Kuwait.

0137

Taking this opportunity, I wish to reiterate our earnest wish that scars of the War will be healed and peace and order restored in the Gulf region in the earliest possible future. Our special concern and heartfelt consolation is extended to the people of Kuwait and other countries in the region, who underwent all kinds of sufferings before and during the War. We sincerely hope that they will soon be able to rehabilitate their war-torn economy and lead secure and prosperous life as before.

Korea will not spare any effort within its capacity to help the maintenance of peace and order and the post-war economic reconstruction of the Gulf region.

Thank you.

0138

Ⅲ. 各 議題別 政府立場

1. 90년도 이집트, 터키, 요르단別 配定 問題

(Allocations to Egypt, Turkey and Jordan in 1990)

가. 我國 政府 立場

○ 各國別 支援額 詳細

- 이집트 : 總 3,000万弗   (EDCF 1,500万弗, 生必品等 物資

1,500万弗)

- 터 키 : 總 2,000万弗   (EDCF 1,500万弗, 生必品 500万弗)

- 요르단 : 總 1,500万弗   (EDCF 1,000万弗, 生必品 500万弗)

- 시리아 : 總 1,000万弗   (生必品等 物資 1,000万弗)

* 軍需物資 支援은 政府 調査團 巡訪後 生必品 支援과 統合 支援
키로 決定

나. 美側 立場

○ 이집트, 터어키, 요르단의 支援額 對比 被害額('90)은 아래와 같음.

(單位 : 100万弗)

受援國 區 分	이 집 트	터 어 키	요 르 단
支 援 額	3,199	872	246
被 害 額	1,125	1,675	1,365
差 額	2,074	- 803	-1,119

0140

ㅇ 對이집트 支援 편중으로 터어키, 요르단에 대한 配定 增額을 希望

- 1,2차 調整會議時까지 요르단의 經濟 制裁 措置에 대한 微溫的
  態度 指摘 結果

다. 美側 資料

各國別 對 前線國家 支援 發表額 對比 總 所要額

（單位 : 100万弗）

年度	前線國家	計	이집트	터어키	요르단	其 他
'90	支援發表額	7,228	3,169	852	231	2,976
	所要額	4,165	1,125	1,675	1,365	-
	差 額	3,063	2,044	- 823	-1,134	-2,976
'91	支援發表額	3,083	617	100	163	2,203
	所要額	9,415	2,250	4,235	2,930	-
	差 額	-6,332	-1,633	-4,135	-2,767	2,203
'90	支援發表額	10,311	3,786	952	394	5,179
-'91	所要額	13,580	3,375	5,910	4,295	-
	差 額	-3,269	411	-4,958	-3,901	5,179

13

0141

'90年度 各國別 對 前線國家 支援額 및 執行 豫算額

(單位 : 100만불)

	前線國家 / 國家	計	이집트	터어키	요르단	其 他 (人道的支援 包含)
GCC 國家	小 計	6,000	2,680	550	0	2,770
	사우디	2,500	1,675	oil	0	825
	쿠웨이트	2,500	555	300	0	1,645
	U A E	1,000	450	250	0	300
EC	小 計	564	189	102	131	142
	EC 豫算	78	0	0	0	78
	各國小計	486	189	102	131	64
	프랑스	100	50	30	0	20
	獨 逸	335	131	72	131	0
	이태리	24	0	0	0	24
	和 蘭	22	7	0	0	15
	英 國	5	0	0	0	5

14

0142

國家	前線國家	計	이집트	터어키	요르단	其他(人道的支援包含)
其他유럽	스웨덴	21	0	0	0	21
	스위스	9	0	0	0	9
日本		600	300	200	100	0
카나다		34	0	0	0	34
韓國		90	30	20	15	25
總支援額		7,228	3,199	872	246	2,926
總所要額		4,165	1,125	1,675	1,365	-
差額		3,063	2,074	- 803	-1,119	-2,926

15

0143

2. 90年度 支援額 執行 加速化 問題

(Acceleration of Disbursements in 1990)

가. 我國 政府 立場
○ 2次에 걸친 政府 調査團의 受援國 巡訪을 통한 受援國과의 協議를 통해 90年度 支援額 執行 繼續中임을 發表 ○ EDCF 借款은 受援國 希望 Project의 妥當性 檢討等에 多少 時日 所要 - 物資 支援 執行時期는 受援國 希望品目 確認直後 執行 加速化 豫定 ○ EDCF 借款 部分을 제외한 나머지 支援 發表 部分의 90.3限 執行 可能性 强調

나. 美側 立場

○ 各國別 支援 發表額과 실제 執行額間 差異를 줄이기 위해 '90년도 支援額의 91.2.5.한 執行을, 91年度 支援額은 90.3월 말까지 執行 希望

○ 周邊國 經濟支援 問題는 對이라크 經濟 制裁 措置에 따른 被害 보전 이므로 이미 被害는 發生했으며 同 被害는 時間의 經過에 따라 누증 되고 있다는 判斷을 前提

16

o 걸프戰 勃發로 인한 被害加重을 감안 早速한 對前線國家 被害 보전

重要性 強調 및 追加 支援 勸誘

다. 美側 資料

'90年度 各國別 對 前線國家 支援 旣執行額 및 所要額 現況

(單位 : 100万弗)

國家	前線國家	計	이집트	터어키	요르단	其他(人道的支援包含)
GCC國家	小計	2,640	2,165	475	0	0
	사우디	1,175	1,175	0	0	0
	쿠웨이트	765	540	225	0	0
	U A E	700	450	250	0	0
EC	小計	94	0	0	7	87
	EC 次元	78	0	0	0	78
	各國 小計	16	0	0	7	9
	獨逸	7	0	0	7	0
	이태리	4	0	0	0	4
	英國	5	0	0	0	5

17

國家 \ 前線國家		計	이집트	터어키	요르단	其他 (人道的支援 包含)
其他 유럽	小 計	30	0	0	0	30
	스 웨 덴	21	0	0	0	21
	스 위 스	9	0	0	0	9
日 本		22	0	0	0	22
카 나 다		6	0	0	0	6
總 支援執行		3,493	2,615	725	7	146
支援所要規模		4,165	1,125	1,675	1,365	-
差 額		- 672	1,490	- 950	-1,358	146

※ 被害額 算定時 基準 油價 : $31/barrel

18

3. 91年度 支援 發表額 및 執行額

(Committments and Disbursements in 1991)

가. 我國 政府 立場

◦ 91년도 周邊國 經濟支援에 割當된 金額 2,500万弗의 早期 配分 및
執行 意圖 說明

◦ 支援國, 支援 品目 및 支援 方法 等은 아직 未定임도 添言

나. 美側 立場

◦ 91年度 支援 發表額에 대한 91.3月末 以前 執行을 促求중임.

◦ 걸프戰 勃發에 따라 友邦國의 追加 支援 誘導에 積極 努力할 것으로 豫想됨.

19

다. 美側 資料

'91年度 各國別 對 前線國家 支援額

(單位 : 100万弗)

前線國家 國 家		計	이집트	터어키	요르단	其 他 (人道的支援 包含)
GCC 國家	小 計	0	0	0	0	0
	사우디	0	0	0	0	0
	쿠웨이트	0	0	0	0	0
	U A E	0	0	0	0	0
EC	小 計	1,549	520	0	13	1,016
	EC 次元	678	0	0	0	678
	各國小計	871	520	0	13	338
	프랑스	0	0	0	0	0
	獨 逸	522	509	0	13	4

20

0148

	前線國家 國家	計	이집트	터어키	요르단	其他 (人道的支援 包含)
其他 유럽	이태리	126	0	0	0	126
	네덜란드	33	11	0	0	22
	未 定	190	0	0	0	190
	小 計	0	0	0	0	0
	스웨덴	0	0	0	0	0
	스위스	0	0	0	0	0
日 本		1,400	97	100	150	1,053
카 나 다		34	0	0	0	34
韓 國		25	0	0	0	25
總 支援額		3,083	617	100	163	2,203
總 所要額		9,415	2,250	4,235	2,930	-
差 額		-6,332	-1,633	-4,135	-2,767	2,203

21

0149

4. 支援 方法 詳細

(Terms and Conditions of Assistance)

```
┌─────────────── 가. 我國 政府 立場 ───────────────┐
```

ㅇ EDCF 借款 供與 條件 說明

그룹 分類	分　　類	支援條件	
		金利	償還期間(据置)
Ⅰ	UN 分類 最貧國	2.5%	25年 (7年)
Ⅱ	'87 1인당 GNP 940불 以下	3.5%	20年 (5年)
Ⅲ	'87 1인당 GNP 1,950불 以下	4.2%	20年 (5年)
Ⅳ	'87 1인당 GNP 1,941불 以上	5.0%	20年 (5年)

＊ 이집트는 그룹 Ⅱ, 터어키 및 요르단은 그룹Ⅲ에 속함.

ㅇ 生必品, 쌀등 現物 支援은 受援國 希望에 따른 無償 供與 性格의
  支援임을 强調

나. 美側 立場

ㅇ 前線國家의 現 被害 狀況을 考慮, 外債 蕩減, 現物 無償 供與 等을 勸誘

ㅇ 借款 提供時 特殊 考慮를 適用, 可能한 最低 金利 및 長期 償還 條件
  으로 提供 希望

22

0150

다. 美側 資料

90/91年度 對 前線國家 支援 方法

(單位 : 100万弗)

	Balance of Payment			Project Financing	Co-Financing	Unspecified	TOTAL
	Grants	In Kind	Loans				
GCC STATES	1,075	1,420	100	1,050	0	2,703	6,348
Saudi Arabia	1,000	1,160		500		188	2,848
Kuwait	75	10	100	550		1,765	2,500
U A E		250				750	1,000
EC	662	6	111	0	7	1,397	2,183
EC Budget	78					682	760
Bilateral:	584	6	111	0	7	715	1,423
France						200	200
Germany	414		13			468	895
Italy	88		62				150
Luxembourg	4						4
Netherlands	56				7		63

23

0151

걸프사태 재정지원 공여국 조정위원회 회의, 1990-91. 전6권 (V.5 제5차. Luxemburg, 1991.3.11 : 자료) 271

	Balance of Payment			Project Financing	Co-Financing	Unspecified	TOTAL
	Grants	In Kind	Loans				
Ireland		6					6
U.K.						5	5
Belgium						33	33
Denmark	21					9	30
Portugal	1						1
Spain			36				36
OTHER EUROPE /Australia	45	1	0	0	0	179	225
Sweden	45						45
Switzerland						109	109
Australia		1				13	14
Austria						11	11
Finland						11	11
Iceland						3	3
Norway						32	32
JAPAN	90	1	648	194	157	13	2,116
CANADA	66						66
KOREA		75	40				115
TOTAL	1,938	1,488	882	1,244	164	5,305	11,021

2④   0152

272 걸프 사태 재정지원 공여국 조정위원회 회의 2

5. 追加 支援 努力에 대한 討議

(Discussion of Additional Assistance Efforts)

┌─────────────────────────┐
│ 가. 我國 政府 立場 │
└─────────────────────────┘

ㅇ 修交 基盤 造成을 위한 시리아에 대한 特別 考慮 方針 美側에 旣傳達

ㅇ 今番 我國의 支援은 우리 與件上 最大限의 支援이므로 現 時點에서
  受援國의 擴大는 考慮치 않고 있음.

나. 美側 立場

ㅇ 上記 資料와 같이 支援國의 兩者 關係를 考慮한 前線國家 以外 國家에
  대한 直接 支援도 勸誘

ㅇ 脫 冷戰 時代 조류에 따른 民主化 等 過渡期的 狀況을 겪고 있는
  東歐諸國의 被害 보전에 대한 關心 集中 必要性을 積極 強調
  - 1,2,3次 調整委 會議時 美側 同 必要性 數次 強調

25

0153

다. 美側 資料

前線國家 以外 國家에 대한 支援額

(單位 : 100万弗)

受 援 國	支 援 國	支援 發表額	執 行 額
시 리 아	사 우 디	1,050	550
	쿠 웨 이 트	500	250
	小　　計	1,550	800
모 로 코	쿠 웨 이 트	200	100
	프 랑 스	230	0
	小　　計	430	100
레 바 논	쿠 웨 이 트	33	0
計		2,013	900

26

0154

걸프事態 關聯 周邊國 經濟支援 現況

(91. 2. 5. 現在)

(單位 : 10億弗)

支援 供與國	約束 金額	이집트, 터키,요르단	未割當	其 他	執行額
걸프 沿岸國	9.3	6.1	0.2	3.0	5.4
EC 國家	2.3	2.0	0.2	0.1	0.68
日 本	2.1	2.0	0.1	0	0.4
其 他	0.4	0.2	0.2	0	0.1
計	14.1	10.3	0.7	3.1	6.6

※ 多國籍軍 活動支援, 兩者關係 關聯 支援, IMF/IBRD 基金 支援은 除外

27

0155

Ⅳ. 걸프事態 財政支援 供與國 調整委 會議

1. 槪 要

가. 槪 要

(目 的)

о 對이라크 經濟制裁 措置로 被害를 입고 있는 소위 戰線國家(Front Line States) 等 걸프事態 被害國家에 대한 財政支援과 對이라크 國際的 團結 誇示라는 두가지 目的을 總括 調整하기 위하여 "Gulf Crisis Financial Coordination Group" 創設

(構 成)

о 美, 韓, 日, 英, 獨, 佛, 카, 伊太利, EC, 사우디, 쿠웨이트, 카타르, UAE 및 GCC 등 14個國家 및 國際機構 參加

* 濠洲 1.24. 第6次 調整委 實務會議時부터 參加

о Mulford 美 財務次官과 Kimmitt 國務部 政務次官을 共同議長으로 關聯國.國際機構 參加

о IMF 및 IBRD 는 技術的 助言과 分析等 支援

29

(組織.運營機能)

ㅇ 運營委員會 : 參加國 財務部 및 外務部 代表로 構成

    - 受援國에 대한 援助支援 調整運營 (政治的 考慮 並行)

    - 財政支援 需要 增加의 分析.評價(財政需要는 一次的으로 美 政府에 의해 分析)

    - 受援國의 援助 使用 監督

ㅇ 事務局 : IMF 와 IBRD 를 事務局으로 活用

    - 技術的이고 分析的인 支援에 局限

나. 美側意圖 및 背景

ㅇ 肯定的으로 보아 戰線國 財政支援 問題를 效率的으로 調整 運營하려는 努力의 一環으로 評價

    - 유엔 制裁措置의 效率化를 위한 經濟的 解決方案 講究 努力

ㅇ 그러나 Gulf 事態關聯, 財政的 援助에 대한 美國의 主導的 役割 確保 意圖도 內在

    - 日本, 獨逸等의 IMF, IBRD 等 旣存機構를 통한 支援 選好 活動을 사전에 霧散시키려는 意圖

30

o 또한 걸프事態의 長期化에 對備, 美國 主導下의 多者間 協力體를 사전
  構築하려는 意圖도 있을 것으로 評價
  - 漸增하는 費用을 關聯國에 分擔시키고, 必要時 中東 安保體制
    構築을 위한 事前 布石으로 連結될 수 있는 裝置 마련

다. 그간의 我國 立場

o 原則的으로 我國의 政治.經濟的 能力 範圍內에서 受援國에 대한
  直接 支援規模와 방식을 취해나가는 것이 바람직하다는 原則 고수
  - 兩者關係와 多國籍 努力間의 均衡을 취할 必要

o 여사한 調整機構 創設이 걸프事態의 早期 解決에 도움이 된다면,
  동 Group 創設에 반대할 이유 없음.
  - 이 境遇에도 支援方法.內容에 있어서 援助 供與國의 立場에 대해
    融通性이 附與되는 協議會의 性格의 裝置가 適合

라. 措置事項

o 第2次 會議(10.12) 에서 아래와 같은 我國立場을 밝힘.
  - 걸프事態의 早期解決을 위해 도움이 되는 協議裝置 마련에
    기본적으로 同意
    (Korea basically agrees to the foundation of a consultative
    body for an early resolution of the Gulf crisis.)

31   0159

- 그러나 各國의 政治.經濟的 與件等 個別事情과 이 문제의 限時的 性格等을 감안하여, 拘束力있는 組織이 非常設 協議會議 形式으로 運營함이 바람직

  (However, considering the political and economical situation of individual countries and the fact that the current crisis is a temporary one, it would be desirable that the body be operated on an ad-hoc basis without binding force.)

- 이 協議會에서는 援助國間의 關聯 情勢 交換 및 援助計劃에 관해 論議토록 하고, 技術的 助言 및 分析은 IMF/IBRD 에 依存토록 함.

  (The consultative body shall serve as a forum for exchange of relative information among supporing countries and for discussion on support programs. The body shall ask IMF/IBRD for technical advice and analysis.)

- 걸프事態의 推移와 同 協議會議의 運營經過等을 綜合的으로 考慮 하여 向後 協議裝置의 發展을 檢討토록 함.

  (A review of the consultative body will be necessary in the future reflecting the development of the crisis and the performance of the body.)

ㅇ 上記 一般的인 立場 表明과 아울러, 日本, 獨逸等 主要 援助 供與國의 動向을 觀察하면서 我國의 立場을 具體化시켜 나감.

0160

32

2. 第1次 會議 開催 結果 (90.9.26. 워싱턴)

　ㅇ 美側, 걸프事態 解決위한 政治的, 軍事的 方案이외에 戰線國家에 대한

　　經濟的 支援을 통해 유엔 制裁措置를 보다 實効化할 수 있는 經濟的

　　解決 方案의 必要性 強調

　ㅇ 主要 協議.決定事項

　　- 具體的 方案 推進에 있어 融通性 附與 (公式的, 常設機構 性格 止揚)

　　- 戰線國家 範圍를 우선 이집트, 터키, 요르단 3국으로 局限

　　- 支援時期는 短期的으로 90년 말까지, 中期的으로 91년까지 區分

　　- 第2次 會議를 10.12(금) 워싱턴에서 開催키로 決定

　　　* 會議 參加國 代表들은 美國의 一方的인 會議召集 運營等 主導에

　　　　다소의 不滿을 표시하였으나, 支援對象 供與國 選定, 支援時期等

　　　　主要事案에 있어서는 美國의 提案에 일단 응하기로 함.

3. 第2次 會議 結果 (90.10.12. 워싱턴) 및 美側과의 主要 協議事項

　ㅇ 今番 我國支援 規模는 國內 經濟.安保 여건상 최대한의 支援임을 強調

　　- 美側, 我國의 支援決定에 謝意 表明

　　- 我側 支援 規模에 現在로는 滿足 表示 (Mulford 財務次官)

33

0161

ㅇ 支援 對象國 選定 및 支援額 決定時 我國의 裁量權 行使에 理解 表示
   - 修交 目的을 위한 對시리아 援助 方針 通報에 首肯
   - 援助 對象國에 세네갈 포함 勸誘

ㅇ 軍 醫療陣 派遣 關聯, 派遣, 駐屯 및 補給經費의 美側 또는 駐屯國 負擔 要請
   - 美側, 복잡하고 미묘한 問題이므로 深思熟考後 美側 立場 通報 豫定 言明

ㅇ 쌀 支援關聯, 美側은 農務部가 食糧 現物市場 攪亂을 理由로한 問題提起 可能性 憂慮 表示
   - 人道的 考慮에 의한 支援임을 強調하고 兩國間 緊密協議를 거쳐 措置 토록 合意

ㅇ 美側은 供與國 그룹 調整委 會議 運營關聯, 我國의 美側 立場 支持 勢力 役割 期待
   - EC 諸國等의 部分的 異意 提起에 대한 制動 役割 期待(EC 提案 運營委에 我國 參加意思 打診등)
   - 第3次 會議는 11月初 이태리 로마에서 開催키로 決定 (美國만이 아닌 EC, 日本, 사우디등 世界 主要國 망라한 壓倒的 반이라크 勢力 誇示)

4. 第3次 會議 結果 (90.11.5, 로마)

(主要 協議 内容)

가. Kimmitt 美 國務次官 發言 要旨 :

　ㅇ 이라크는 經濟 制裁措置로 150億弗의 損失을 입고 貿易量도 10% 이하
　　 水準으로 激減, 이라크軍이 어려움을 느끼기 始作

　ㅇ 美國은 政治的.平和的 解決을 希望하나, 不可避한 境遇 武力使用의
　　 option 을 생각함.

나. Mulford 美 財務次官 發言中 特記事項

　ㅇ 今番 會議 目的은 25個國에서 100億여弗의 막대한 金額을 動員,
　　 이라크의 쿠웨이트 占領을 容認치 않겠다는 國際的 團結力을
　　 이라크에 誇示하는데 있음.

　ㅇ 總 援助額 128億弗의 供與國 및 配定額 内譯은 適期에 早期 發表

다. 我國代表 發言 要旨

　ㅇ 我國 約束의 早期 履行을 위해 高位 使節團이 前線國家를 訪問中
　　 이며, 이집트, 터키, 요르단에 대한 配定額 및 借款과 現物 比率을
　　 發表

35

0163

○ 我國의 今番 援助 參與 背景으로 韓國戰 당시 UN 旗幟下 16個國의
  귀중한 援助를 想起함.

(特記事項)

가. 美國의 武力使用 可能性

○ 美國의 武力使用 option 에 대한 語調가 第2次 調整會議時(90.10.12)
  보다 强化된 것으로 감지됨. 앞으로 短期間 內에 經濟的 制裁의
  效果가 不充分할 境遇, 蘇.中 等의 協調를 얻어 UN 의 軍事的 制裁
  解決을 採擇할 것으로 보이며, 그럼에도 不拘하고 이라크가 撤收치
  않으면 適切한 武力使用이 不可避할 것으로 觀測됨.

나. 我國에 대한 追加 供與 要請 可能性

○ 第3次 調整委 會議 期間中 我國에 대한 追加 支援 要請은 一切 없었음.

○ 다만 앞으로 武力 行使로 인해 방대한 追加 軍事費 支出이 있을 境遇
  美國에 의한 追加 要請 可能性 있음.

다. Kimmitt 美 國務次官 面談

○ 권 大使는 會議 開催前 Kimmitt 次官에게 Baker-Mubarak 面談時
  이집트에 韓國과의 修交 勸誘를 要望한 바, 同 次官은 기꺼이 建議할
  것을 約束하고 記錄으로 memo 함.

36

0164

5. 第4次 調整國 會議 結果(91.2.5. 워싱턴)

　가. 參席國(28個國)

　　ㅇ GCC 國家 : 사우디 아라비아, 쿠웨이트, UAE

　　ㅇ EC 國家 : 벨지움, 덴마크, 프랑스, 독일, 아일랜드, 이태리, 룩샘부르크, 화란, 폴투갈, 스페인, 영국

　　ㅇ 其他 歐洲國家 : 오스트리아, 핀랜드, 아이슬란드, 노르웨이, 스웨덴, 스위스

　　ㅇ 日本, 韓國, 카나다, 濠洲

　　ㅇ 其他 IMF, IBRD, EC, GCC 代表 參席

　나. 會議 進行

　　ㅇ Mulford 財務部次官, Kimmitt 國務部 政務次官 共同 主宰로 前線國 財政 支援 約束 및 執行現況과 걸프事態의 狀況 설명

　　ㅇ IBRD, IMF 代表의 이집트, 터어키, 요르단 經濟狀況 및 被害規模 評價 설명

　　ㅇ 旣存 約束金額의 執行狀況 및 追加約束 問題에 대한 各國 代表의 發表

0165

다. Kimmitt 및 Mulford 次官 發言要旨

(Kimmitt 次官)

ㅇ 걸프戰의 目的은 이라크의 쿠웨이트 撤收에 있으며 이라크 自體의 破壞에
  있지 않으므로 軍事 施設만을 攻擊 目標로 삼고 있음.

ㅇ 調整國 會議 參席 國家中 18個國이 聯合國에 參戰하고 있으며 軍事同盟
  結束도 그만큼 重要함.

ㅇ 요르단의 政治的 路線에도 不拘하고 財政支援은 계속 必要함.

(Mulford 次官)

ㅇ 現在까지 前線國家에 대한 援助 約束金額 141億弗中 66億弗만 執行되고
  75億弗이 未執行 狀態이므로 조속한 執行이 要請됨.

ㅇ 터키의 경우 30億弗, 요르단의 경우 35億弗이 부족한 狀態에 있는 바,
  조속한 援助執行, 未割當金의 割當 및 追加約束 등 3가지 問題에 대해
  各國, 특히 사우디, 쿠웨이트, UAE, 불란서, 獨逸, 日本, 韓國 代表의
  說明을 要望함.

0166

라.　韓國代表(外務次官) 發言要旨

　○ 韓國은 금번 會議 參席 國家中 유일한 非産油 開發 途上國家(Non-oil
　　producing developing country)로서, 韓國은 財政支援 國家 그룹의
　　一員으로 걸프事態 解決에 寄與하게 된 것을 기쁘게 생각함.

　○ 도표에 韓國의 總 寄與額이 100百万弗로 되어 있으나 115百万弗로 修正
　　되어야 하는 바, 이는 이집트 등 일부 國家가 軍需物資 대신 生必品 現物
　　支援을 要請하여 15百万弗이 財政支援에 追加되었기 때문임.

　○ 財政支援 總 115百万弗中 95百万弗은 이미 韓國 國會에서 豫算措置가
　　끝났기 때문에 援助를 施行하는 데 아무런 問題가 없게 되었음.

　○ 約束金額의 조속한 執行을 위하여 外務次官이 작년 11月 韓國調査團을
　　이끌고 이집트, 요르단, 터키, 시리아를 訪問하여, 이들 國家들과
　　구체적인 援助 필요 분야에 대해 協議를 시작한 바 있으므로, 이에따라
　　대부분의 執行이 ¼分期中 가능할 것으로 예견됨.

　○ 또한 걸프事態로 被害를 입고 있는 東歐圈 國家中 헝가리, 폴랜드,
　　루마니아 및 불가리아에 대하여는 韓國이 別途의 광범위한 經濟協力
　　事業을 施行하고 있음을 밝히고자 함.

0167

○ 非財政分野 軍事支援에 있어서는 지난주 韓國이 280百万弗의 追加 軍事
   支援을 約束하여 總 援助額이 500百万弗에 달하게 되었으며, 그외에
   150여명의 醫療團을 사우디에 旣 派遣하였고, 5臺의 C-130 軍 輸送機
   支援이 원칙 決定되었음.

마. 次期 會議

○ EC 議長國인 룩셈부르크 代表의 提案에 따라 3月 前半期中 유럽에서 開催
   키로 暫定 合意

   예고 : 91. 12. 키 · 일반

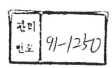

第5次 걸프事態 財政支援 供與國 調整委 會議

代表團 共通 參考資料

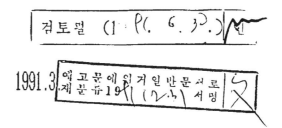

검토필 (1 : PC. 6. 3?.)

1991.3 역고문에 의거 일반문서로 제분류19(2.4) 서명

앙 고 제	부미과 91 3 4	담 당	과 장	심의관	국 장	차관보	차 관	강

美 洲 局

目　次

0170

I. 日 程

1. 航空 日程

日字	時間	出發.到着	航空便	飛行 時間	時 差
3.5(火)	15:00	서울 出發	KE-018	10時間	-17時間
	08:00	LA 到着			
	13:30	LA 出發	AA-36	4時間 46分	+ 3時間
	21:16	D.C. 到着 (Dulles)			
3.9(土)	午後	Shuttle便 뉴욕 向發		1時間	0
	19:55	브랏셀 向發	PA-034	7時間 20分	+ 6時間
3.10(日)	09:15	브랏셀 到着			
	午後	룩셈부르크 到着	車輛便	2時間 30分	0
3.11(月)	午後	룩셈부르크 出發	車輛便	2時間 30分	0
	午後	브랏셀 到着			
3.12(火)	17:00	브랏셀 出發	AE-131	1時間	- 1時間
	17:00	런던 到着 (Gatwick)			
	19:30	런던 出發 (Gatwick)	KE-908	13時間10分	+ 9時間
3.13(水)	17:40	서울 到着			

2. 面談 日程

Ⅱ. 代表團 構成

0174

1. 代表團

o 團　長 : 이정빈 外務部 第1次官補

o 團　員 : 이정보 財務部 經協局長

유명환 駐美大使舘 參事官

왕정중 經濟企劃院 豫算室 行政 豫算 擔當官

허덕행 外務部 中東局 中東2課 書記官

김규현 外務部 美洲局 北美課 事務官

* 91.3.5-8間 李 次官補 訪美時는 김규현 事務官만 遂行

其他 團員은 3.10. Luxembourg에서 合流, 3.11. 現地 解散

2. 宿　所

o 워싱턴 : The Park Hyatt Hotel

(202) 789-1234

* 大使舘 : (202) 939-5600

o Luxembourg :

* 駐 Belgium 大使舘 : (02) 375-39-80

駐 E C　代表部 : (02) 772-3200

Ⅲ. 對美 重點 協議事項

0176

1. 걸프戰 終戰後 中東秩序 再編方案 把握 및 我國의 參與問題 協議

    ◦ 終戰以後 中東秩序 再編에 관한 美側의 構想을 問議

        - 中東地域 集團 安全保障 체제, 유연 平和維持軍 또는 多國籍 平和維持軍

          設置 방안

        - 향후 이라크의 域內 役割에 대한 構想

        - 中東地域 軍縮 推進方向(核 및 化學武器 등 대량 학살武器 減縮 및

          미사일등 移動手段 技術 移轉 제한등)

        - 팔레스타인 問題等 아랍.이스라엘間 和解 摸索방향

    ◦ 상기 構想 및 方案에 대한 我國의 參與 및 役割 가능성에 대한 美國의

      立場과 意見 타진

    ◦ 安保體制 構築에 있어서의 이집트, 시리아의 役割과 對韓 修交促進을 위한

      美國의 居中 役割 요청

2. 戰後 中東建設 計劃 및 我國의 參與支援

    ◦ 美側의 戰後 中東地域 經濟復興計劃을 問議

        - 가칭 中東 經濟開發復興銀行 設立 또는 IMF, IBRD 등 旣存 機構活用

          방안 등

        - 쿠웨이트 및 이라크의 戰後 復舊 構想

        - 걸프戰 前線國 財政支援 供與國 調整會議의 향후 活動계획

7   0177

ㅇ 我國의 參與 및 役割에 대해 協議

    - 新設 또는 旣存 多者間 復興機構에의 參與 방안

    - 쿠웨이트 緊急復舊 計劃 및 이라크 再建 計劃

3. 新世界 秩序 宣言을 위한 頂上會談 開催 計劃 파악

ㅇ 美國이 構想中인 것으로 알려진 多國籍軍 派遣國과 기타 支援國 수뇌간

   頂上會談 開催 計劃과 UN의 향후 役割

    - 同 計劃이 事實일 경우, 我國의 參與 확인

ㅇ 3.6-16間 Baker 長官의 中東地域 巡訪時 中東 各國과의 協議 계획

4. 韓國 軍 醫療支援團 및 軍 輸送團 追加 活動問題

ㅇ 쿠웨이트內 緊急 醫療需要에 부응, 현재 사우디에서 활동중인 韓國軍

   醫療支援團의 쿠웨이트로의 移動問題 協議

    - 당분간 活動 계속 意思를 表明하고 美側 反應 및 立場을 파악

    - 상기 活動地域 移動 및 活動期間 延長은 人道的 堅持에서도 적절

ㅇ UAE 알아인 機地에서 活動中인 軍 輸送支援團(C-130 5臺 및 運營要員 150名)

   活動 계속 協議

    - 中東地域 배치 美軍들에 대한 輸送支援 계속을 위해 당분간 계속 배치할

      計劃임을 통보하고 美側 反應을 파악

5. 걸프事態 관련 我國의 2次 支援 約束額의 執行方案 協議(美側 擧論時 對應)

    ° 1億1千万弗의 執行方案(現金 6千万弗, 輸送 5千万弗)에 대한 美側 立場

    ° 1億7千万弗 규모 軍需物資 支援의 執行方案에 관한 美側 立場
        - 對英國 支援額 3千万弗 捻出
        - 戰爭地域에 콜레라등 傳染病 만연 가능성에 대비한 支援
        - 食水, 醫藥品 등 緊急 人道的 支援
        - 環境汚染 防止對策 支援

6. 外務長官 訪美 日程 協議

    ° 베이커 國務長官과의 會談可能 일정 協議

    ° 부쉬 大統領, 퀘일 副統領, 체니 國防長官, Scowcroft 白堊館 安保補佐官
      등 行政府 高位人士 및 議會 指導者들과의 面談 可能性 파악

    ° 戰後 中東秩序 再編 및 復舊計劃, 韓.美 頂上會談 問題, 韓半島 問題, 通商
      問題 및 亞.太 問題등을 協議하기 위한 韓.美 外相會談 早期 開催 필요성을
      提示하고 美側 反應을 타진

7. 我國의 UN 加入問題와 관련, 美 國務部 關係者들과의 協議   - 끝 -

9

0179

Ⅳ. 걸프事態 關聯 對美 追加 支援

0180

1. 追加 支援 內容

  가. 支援 規模

    ° 追加 支援 規模는 2億8千万弗로함.

      - 이중 1億7千万弗 相當은 國防部 在庫 軍需物資 및 裝備 提供으로
        하고 나머지 1億1千万弗은 現金 및 輸送 支援으로 함.

        * 具體的 執行 用途 및 內譯은 韓.美 兩國間 協議를 거쳐 決定

      - 今番 追加 支援은 多國籍軍(특히 美國)만을 위한 것이며 周邊國 經濟
        支援은 不包含.

      - 我國의 總 支援 規模는 今番 追加 支援으로 昨年 約束額 2億2千万弗을
        包含, 總 5億弗이됨.

  나. 軍 輸送機 支援

    ° 上記 支援과는 別途로 軍 輸送機(C-130) 數臺를 派遣키로 原則的인
      決定(國會 同意 必要)

      - 我國 國防部와 駐韓 美軍間 技術的인 事項에 關한 協議 必要

  다. 91年度 多國籍軍 支援 經費 2,500万弗 全額 對美 輸送支援 配定

    ° 베이커 美 國務長官의 要請(91.1.23)

11   0181

2. 追加 支援 決定 背景

ㅇ 追加 支援을 통한 걸프 事態 解決 努力에의 積極的 參與는 우리의 國際
平和 維持 意志 誇示等 國際的 位相 提高에 크게 寄與

- 今番 걸프 戰爭은 유엔 安保理 決議에 立脚, 유엔 歷史上 最多 會員國이
參與하고 있는 國際社會의 對이라크 膺懲 性格

ㅇ 걸프 戰爭으로 인한 多國籍軍에 대한 追加 支援 必要性 增大

- 500-600億弗 정도의 막대한 戰費 所要에 따라 國際的인 分擔 不可避

- 日本 90億弗, 獨逸 65億弗의 追加 寄與金을 多國籍軍에 提供 約束

ㅇ 我國의 伸張된 國力 및 國際的 地位 等에 비추어, 應分의 寄與를 할 必要

- 我國의 對中東 原油 依存度(75%)도 감안

ㅇ 追加 支援時 國際社會에서 우리의 發言權 等 立地 强化에 效果 多大 期待

- 多國籍軍 活動의 參與 및 支援問題에 美國 等 世界의 耳目이 集中

- 걸프戰爭 終了後 各國의 支援에 대한 評價 效果 長期間 持續 豫想

  ＊ 美國內 與論은 걸프戰爭에 대해 81%라는 壓倒的인 지지 표명

12   0182

3. 追加 支援 決定時 考慮事項

　가. 安保的 考慮事項

　　ㅇ 國際社會의 努力을 적극 支援함으로써 韓半島 有事時 國際社會의 共同
　　　介入을 통한 平和 回復 期待 可能

　　　- 이라크에 대한 成功的인 膺懲時 韓半島에서 武力 挑發 가능성 豫防
　　　　效果도 期待 可能

　　ㅇ 韓.美 安保協力 關係 鞏固化

　　　- 能動的이고 自發的인 支援을 통하여 我國이 信賴할 수 있는 友邦이라는
　　　　認識을 美國 朝野에 提高

　나. 經濟 通商的 考慮 事項

　　ㅇ 安定된 原油 供給 確保 및 戰後 復舊事業 參與 等 對中東 經濟 進出
　　　基盤 마련

　　ㅇ 걸프 戰爭이 我國 經濟에 미치는 影響을 最小化 하는데 寄與

　　　- 事態가 長期化 되어 國際原油價가 上昇할 경우, 我國 經濟에 미치는
　　　　影響 深大(原油價가 배럴당 10弗 上昇時 年33億弗 追加 負擔 發生)

다. 外交的 考慮 事項

    º 6.25 事變時 유엔의 도움을 받은 國家로서 對이라크 共同制裁에
       관한 유엔 決議에 적극 참여해야 할 道義的 의무 履行

    º 我國의 伸張된 國威에 副應하여 國際 平和 維持 努力에 一翼 담당
       - 我國의 支援이 微溫的일 경우, 經濟的 利益만 追求한다는 國際的
         非難 可能性 考慮

    º 걸프戰 終了後 對中東 外交 基盤 强化 布石의 一環
       - 長期的인 觀點에서 사우디, 이집트, UAE 等 中東 友邦國들과의 關係
         增進을 위한 重要한 投資
       - 戰後 樹立될 쿠웨이트, 이라크 兩國 政府와의 즉각적인 關係 强化
         基盤 마련

라. 支援 規模 關聯 考慮

    º 우리의 自發的 支援으로서 伸張된 國力에 알맞는 우리의 成熟한 모습을
       國際的으로 誇示

    º 醫療 支援團 派遣 等을 考慮, 支援 規模는 適正한 水準에서 檢討

14   0184

添附 : 1. 多國籍軍 派遣 現況

2. 各國의 支援 現況

가. 經濟 支援

나. 醫療 支援   끝.

15   0185

<添 附 1>

多國籍軍 派遣 現況

91. 1. 30. 現在

國 家	軍事力 派遣 및 參戰	備 考
美 國	ㅇ 兵 力 : 492,000 名 ㅇ 탱 크 : 2,000 臺 ㅇ 航空機 : 1,300 臺 ㅇ 艦 艇 : 60 隻 (航空母艦 7隻)	
GCC (6個國)	ㅇ 兵 力 : 150,500 名 ㅇ 탱 크 : 800 臺 ㅇ 航空機 : 330 臺 ㅇ 艦 艇 : 36 隻	사우디, 쿠웨이트, 바레인, 오만, UAE, 카타르
英 國	ㅇ 兵 力 : 35,000 名 ㅇ 탱 크 : 170 臺 ㅇ 航空機 : 72 臺 ㅇ 艦 艇 : 16 隻	

16

0186

國　家	軍事力 派遣 및 參戰	備　考
프랑스	ò 兵　力 :　10,000 名 ò 탱　크 :　　　40 臺 ò 航空機 :　　　40 臺 ò 艦　艇 :　　　14 隻	
이집트	ò 兵　力 :　35,000 名 ò 탱　크 :　　　400 臺	
시리아	ò 兵　力 :　19,000 名 ò 탱　크 :　　　300 臺	
파키스탄	ò 兵　力 :　　7,000 名	6千名 追加派遣 豫定
터　키	ò 兵　力 :　　5,000 名 ò 艦　艇 :　　　　2 隻	國境配置 約10万名
방글라데시	ò 兵　力 :　　2,000 名	3千名 追加派遣 豫定

17

0187

國家	軍事力 派遣 및 參戰	備考
카나다	o 兵力 : 2,000名 o 航空機 : 24臺 o 艦艇 : 3隻	
모로코	o 兵力 : 1,700名	
세네갈	o 兵力 : 500名	
니제르	o 兵力 : 480名	
이태리	o 航空機 : 8臺 o 艦艇 : 6隻	
濠洲	o 艦艇 : 3隻	
벨기에	o 艦艇 : 3隻	
네델란드	o 艦艇 : 3隻	
스페인	o 艦艇 : 3隻	
아르핸티나	o 兵力 : 100名 o 艦艇 : 2隻	

18

0188

國　家	軍事力 派遣 및 參戰	備　考
그리스	ㅇ 艦艇 : 　1 隻	
포르투갈	ㅇ 艦艇 : 　1 隻	
노르웨이	ㅇ 艦艇 : 　1 隻	
체　코	ㅇ 兵力 : 　200 名	
總　計 (總 28個國)	ㅇ 兵力 : 760,480 名 ㅇ 탱크 : 3,710 臺 ㅇ 航空機 : 1,774 臺 ㅇ 艦艇 : 154 隻	※ 蘇聯은 艦艇 2隻을 參戰 目的이 아니라 觀察 目的으로 派遣

16

0189

<添 附 2>

各國의 支援 現況

가. 經濟 支援

國　家	戰爭 勃發 前	戰爭 勃發 後
日　本	. 40億弗(20億弗 : 多國籍軍 支援, 20億弗 : 周邊國 支援)	. 90億弗(對美 現金 支援)
獨　逸	. 20.8億弗(33億 마르크)	. 10億弗(1億6千7百万弗의 이스라엘 支援額 및 1億1千4百 万弗의 英國軍 支援額 包含) . 55億弗(對美 支援)
E C	. 19.7億弗	
英　國	. EC 次元 共同 步調	
불란서	〃	
이태리	. 1.45億弗(1次 算定額), 〃	
벨기에	. EC 次元 共同 步調	. 1億1千3百5拾万 BF
네델란드	〃	. 1億8千万弗(戰前 支出 包含)
스페인	〃	
폴투갈	〃	
그리스	〃	

20

0190

國　家	戰爭 勃發 前	戰爭 勃發 後
카 나 다	. 6千6百万弗	
노 르 웨 이	. 2千1百万弗	
濠　洲	. 8百万弗(難民救護)	
G.C.C.國	. 사 우 디 : 60億弗 . 쿠 웨 이 트 : 50億弗 . U.A.E.　: 20億弗	. 사 우 디 : 135億弗 . 쿠 웨 이 트 : 135億弗

21

0191

나. 醫療 支援

國 家	內 譯
美 國	. 사우디 담맘港에 病院船 2隻 派遣(1,000 病床) . 사우디 알바틴에 綜合 醫療團 運營 (專門醫 35 名, 350 病床)

英 國	. 野戰病院 派遣(醫師 200名, 400 病床)
	  (有事時 對備 約 1,500名의 追加 軍 醫療陣
	    派遣 準備中)

濠 洲	. 2個 醫療團 派遣 檢討中
방글라데쉬	. 2個 醫務 中隊 300名 派遣
카 나 다	. 野戰病院 派遣(醫療陣 550名, 225 病床)
덴 마 크	. 軍 醫療陣 30-40名 英國軍에 配置
헝 가 리	. 自願 民間醫療陣 30-40名 英國軍에 配置
체 코	. 自願 醫療陣 150名 派遣
파키스탄	. 1個 醫務 中隊 100名 派遣
오스트리아	. 野戰 앰블란스 1臺 派遣
필 리 핀	. 民間 醫療支援團 270名 派遣

22

0192

國　家	內　　　　譯
폴란드	. 病院船 1隻　派遣 準備中
뉴질랜드	. 民間 醫療陣 50名 , 바레인 駐屯 美 海軍 病院에 勤務 . 軍 醫療團 20名　追加 派遣 決定
싱가폴	. 醫療支援團 30名 , 英國軍 病院에 勤務
벨기에	. 民.軍 自願 醫療 支援團 50名 派遣 . 醫療 裝備 支援(野戰 寢臺 2,800個, 앰블란스 1臺, 負傷兵 護送用 航空機 2臺)

23

0193

V. 걸프 事態 關聯 多國籍軍 및 周邊國 支援 執行 現況

1. 槪要

(單位 : 万弗)

區分 / 年度	多國籍軍 支援	周邊國 經濟支援	計
'90	8,000	9,000	17,000
'91	2,500	2,500	5,000
計	10,500	11,500	22,000

2. 90年度 支援 計劃

(單位 : 万弗)

支援內譯 / 國別	多國籍軍 活動		周邊國 및 國際機構					計	비고
	現金	輸送	EDCF	軍需物資	生必品	쌀	IOM		
美 國	5,000	3,000						8,000	
이집트			1,500	700	800			3,000	
터 키			1,500		500			2,000	
요르단			1,000		500			1,500	
방글라데시						500		500	
시리아				600	400			1,000	
모로코				200				200	
I O M							50	50	
其他(行政費)					50			50	
豫備					200	500		700	
小 計	5,000	3,000	4,000	1,500	2,450	1,000	50	17,000	
計	8,000		9,000					17,000	

24

0194

3. 詳細 執行 現況

　　가. 對美支援 : $85,553,031

　　　　1) 對美 現金 支援 : $ 5,000 万

　　　　2) 對美 輸送 支援 : $ 35,553,031

　　　　　　가) 航空 輸送 支援 : $ 23,533,134

　　　　　　　　- 90年 : $ 10,776,604 ($10,828,773 - $52,169)(24回)

　　　　　　　　- 91年 : $ 12,756,530(30回)

　　　　　　　　　　1月 : 2,536,530(6回)

　　　　　　　　　　2月 : 4,180,000(11回)

　　　　　　　　　　3月 : 6,040,000(總26回)

　　　　　　나) 船舶 輸送 支援 : $ 12,006,397

　　　　　　　　- 三仙海運(1,3,4항차)　 : $5,952,491

　　　　　　　　- 韓進海運(2,5,6 항차)　 : $6,053,906

　　　　　　　　- 軍需物資 輸送 支援 要員 出張 經費(3회) : $13,500

　　　　　　다) 殘　額 : $19,446,969(推定)

걸프사태 재정지원 공여국 조정위원회 회의, 1990-91. 전6권 (V.5 제5차. Luxemburg, 1991.3.11 : 자료) 315

나. 周邊國 經濟 支援 : 總900万弗 執行

　　ㅇ 500万弗 相當의 對터키 支援 品目 發注(91.1.22)

　　　　- 앰블런스, 미니 버스, 트럭等 23個 品目

　　ㅇ 200万弗 相當의 對모로코 支援 品目 發注(91.1.14)

　　　　- 防毒面, 浸透 保護衣, 텐트等 7個 品目

　　ㅇ 200万弗 相當의 對요르단 支援 品目 發注(91.1.30)

　　　　- 설탕, 25人乘 버스 等 2個 品目

　　ㅇ EDCF 4千万弗, 이집트, 요르단, 시리아 支援은 受援國 希望
　　　　project 및 希望品目 檢討中

다. 國際機構 支援 : 總 56万弗 執行

　　ㅇ IOM　　　　: 50 万弗

　　ㅇ UNESCO　　: 3 万弗

　　ㅇ ICRC　　　 : 3 万弗

라. 걸프灣 海上汚染 防除 支援 : 30万弗

　　ㅇ 사우디, 바레인, 카타르에 各 10万弗씩 總 30万弗 規模의 防除 裝備 및
　　　　物資 支援

26　　　　　　　　　　　　　　　0196

마. 對쿠웨이트 의류 緊急 支援 : 70万弗

　o 쿠웨이트軍에 대한 軍服 및 군화 긴급 지원 經費 70万弗 執行 豫定

바. 行政費 : 約 40万弗 執行

　o 1,2次 政府 調査團 中東地域 巡訪

　o 걸프 事態 關聯 2次, 3次, 4次 및 5次 供與國 調整會議 參席

　o 中東地域 我國 公館員用 防毒面 購入

　o 醫療 支援團 派遣 協商團 사우디 訪問

사. 總 執行額 : 9,651万弗(91.3.5. 現在 推定額)

Ⅵ. 걸프戰後 中東秩序 再編 展望과 우리의 對應策

1. 걸프戰 終戰 直後 情勢와 外交的 措置

  가. 終戰直後 情勢

    1) 戰鬪 行爲 終熄

      ㅇ 이라크의 2.28. 걸프 事態 관련 모든 유엔 安保理 決議 受諾通知와
         동일 美國大統領의 戰鬪 行爲 中止 宣言으로 戰鬪 行爲 終熄

        (停戰의 條件)
        - 多國籍軍 捕虜 및 第3國民 卽時 釋放
        - 抑留 쿠웨이트인 전원 卽時 釋放
        - 모든 地雷와 機雷의 位置와 特性通知
        - 유엔 安保理 모든 決議 遵守, 쿠웨이트 合倂 敗消, 被害補償

      ㅇ 多國籍軍, 48時間以內에 이라크軍 指揮官들과의 休戰에 따른 軍事的
         側面 協議要求
        - 3.3. 이라크 南部 샤프완 空軍基地에서 첫 休戰會談 開催 多國籍
           軍側이 提示한 戰爭捕虜 釋放 및 이라크 駐屯 多國籍軍의 撤收
           等에 合意

29

0199

2) 쿠웨이트 亡命政府 本國 復歸準備

　　○ 쿠웨이트 國王은 2.26.부터 3개월간 쿠웨이트 全域에 戒嚴令 宣布

　　○ 亡命 政府는 타이프에서 쿠웨이트 隣近 담밤으로 移動, 3.1. 대부분
　　　閣僚 쿠웨이트로 復歸(王國은 당분간 타이프에서 滯留)

3) 主要國家 戰後 外交協商

　　○ 美, 英, 佛, 獨, 伊 外務長官 워싱턴에서 連鎖 會談(2.27-3.4)

　　○ 베이커 美國務部長官 中東巡訪 豫定(3.6-16)

　　○ 日本 外相 워싱턴 訪問 豫定(3월 중순)

라. 유엔 安保理의 中東 永久 平和 決議案 採擇

　　○ 유엔 事務總長은 戰爭 終熄을 위해 필요한 措置를 向後 유엔 安保理가
　　　취해야 할 것임을 言及하고 유엔 平和維持軍 派遣 希望 表示

　　○ 덴마크, 스웨덴, 노르웨이, 핀란드등 北歐 4開國, 유엔 平和維持軍
　　　240名 共同 派遣 用意 表明

　　○ 3.3. 開催된 UN 安保理는 걸프지역 영구 平和定着을 골자로한 결의안
　　　686호를 採擇

30

0200

- 이라크 政府는 卽刻 受諾意思 發表

- 즉각적인 戰爭捕虜 釋放 및 戰死者 遺骸引渡, 모든 戰鬪 行爲의
  中止, 이라크의 戰爭 賠償責任 認定, 이라크側 休戰條件 違反時
  多國籍軍側의 모든 필요한 수단 使用 承認을 內容

나. 外交的 措置

1) 政府代辯人 聲明 發表(3.2)

2) 對美 措置

 ˚ 부쉬 大統領의 戰鬪 中止 宣言에 대한 外務部 代辯人 支持聲明 發表(2.28)

 ˚ 大統領 閣下의 부쉬 美國 大統領앞 親書 傳達(3.1)

3) 쿠웨이트에 대한 措置

 ˚ 大統領 閣下의 쿠웨이트 國王앞 親書 傳達(2.28)

 ˚ 駐쿠웨이트 大使館 活動 再開
   - 駐쿠웨이트 大使 사우디 派遣(2.23) 亡命政府 接觸中
   - 外務部 長官의 쿠웨이트 外務長官앞 親書 傳達(2.27)
   - 再開要員 3名 派遣

31

0201

ㅇ 쿠웨이트 殘留僑民(9名) 安全確認

4) 其他 友邦國에 대한 措置

ㅇ 사우디, U.A.E., 英, 佛에 대한 大統領 閣下 名義 親書發送

ㅇ 其他 걸프國 및 多國籍軍 派遣國에 대한 外務長官 名義 親書 發送

5) 이라크에 대한 措置

ㅇ 駐 이라크 大使館 活動再開 檢討
   - 友邦國과 協議, 共同交涉
   - 大使 및 公館員 復歸 檢討

ㅇ 殘留僑民(8名) 安全確認

6) 軍醫療 支援團 및 空軍輸送團의 向後 活動

ㅇ 軍醫療 支援團의 쿠웨이트 移動 支援 계속과 관련 사우디 및 미국과 協議

ㅇ 空軍 輸送團 繼續 支援 關聯 美國과 協議
   - 國防部側과 美 國防部와의 協議 側面 支援

32   0202

7) 撤收僑民 復歸 檢討

ㅇ 쿠웨이트, 이라크, 사우디等 撤收僑民 等 勤勞者 復歸時期等

나. 其他 後續 措置

1) 大統領 特使 派遣

ㅇ 사우디, 쿠웨이트, U.A.E., 이란등 派遣 對象國家 檢討

ㅇ 3月 中旬

2) 外務部 第1次官補 派遣

ㅇ 3.5-9.間 豫定

ㅇ 워싱턴 訪問, 美國政府 要路와 戰後 秩序 再編, 經濟 復興 計劃關聯
　　對美 協議 動向 把握

ㅇ 3.11. 룩셈부르크 開催 第5次 財政支援 供與國 調整會議 參席

3) 戰後 復舊 및 經濟 復興 參與 對策

ㅇ 現在 U.A.E., 이집트, 사우디, 요르단 巡訪中인 外務部 第2次官補를
　　團長으로 하는 中東 現地 調査團이 3.9. 歸國하는대로 綜合 對策 樹立

ㅇ 外務次官을 委員長으로 하는 關係部處 對策委員會 構成

33

0203

2. 中東秩序 再編 展望

가. 戰後 中東의 政治構圖

1) 域內 勢力 均衡 變化

ㅇ 戰後에도 中東地域에 있어서 特定國의 主導的 影響力 行使를 방지
한다는 域內 國家間 勢力均衡 原則에는 변화가 없을 것이나 그 구도
에는 變化 豫想

- 이집트, 사우디, 이란, 이라크, 시리아등 中東政治 主役들의 離合
集散을 통한 均衡과 牽制가 戰後에도 勢力關係의 기본 골격이 될
것임.

- 또한 穩健勢力(사우디, 이집트등)과 强硬勢力(이란, 시리아등)間의
對立關係와 아랍富國(GCC 국가)과 貧國(시리아, 예멘, 요르단)間의
反目도 繼續 作用

- 今番 戰爭을 계기로 이라크의 中東政治의 主役으로서의 役割상실,
시리아, 요르단, PLO 등의 立場變化 및 이란, 터어키의 强力한
政治的 軍事的 役割이 새 중동 版圖형성에 새 요소로 작용 豫想

- 이스라엘과 아랍 諸國과의 對決關係는 계속 宿題

3+

2) 美國의 主導的 役割

  o 戰爭中 美國의 壓倒的 役割에 비추어 戰後 美國의 영향력은 크게
    增大될 것으로 豫想되며, 美國 스스로도 中東秩序 再編過程에 있어
    主導的 役割을 수행코자 할 것임.

    - 다만 아랍권 전반의 反美感情 擴大로 美國의 影響力 行使에 도전
      豫想되며 이의 撫摩를 위한 努力 必要

3) 蘇聯, 西歐의 影響力 變化

  o 蘇聯은 今番 戰爭을 契機로 顯著하게 약화된 中東에서의 자국의
    影響力 挽回를 위한 노력 경주 예상

  o 이는 美.蘇間 새로운 葛藤의 要地가 되어 脫冷戰 과정의 장애요인이
    될 可能性

  o 英國, 佛蘭西等 西歐勢力도 中東 國家와의 緣故權과 經濟力을 바탕
    으로 中東地域에 대해 影響力 維持

4) 이라크, 쿠웨이트, GCC 國家의 政治的 變化

  o 이라크

    - 사담 후세인 沒落後 親西方 指導者보다는 反후세인 노선의 國粹的
      性向 指導者 擡頭 可能性

35

0205

- 이라크의 새로운 指導府는 失墜된 國際的 地位回復, 戰後復舊, 民生
  安定을 當面課題로 추진예상

- 戰後 相當期間 域內 軍事 大國으로서의 地位 回復 不能

○ 쿠웨이트

- 戰後 復舊가 王政의 최우선 課題

- 國內 民主化 勢力 摩擦等으로 漸進的 政治改革 추진 예상

- 對外的으로는 安保目的 對美依存度 深化

○ GCC 國家

- 王政 守護 및 軍備 增强을 통한 안보에 최대 力點

- 一般國民의 反王政 感情을 고려한 각종 개혁정책 실시 不可避

○ 유엔의 役割 增大

- 今番 多國籍軍의 전쟁명분이 유엔 決議의 移行에 있었으며 전후
  平和 維持軍도 유엔 主導下에 파견 예상

- 蘇聯도 美國의 직접적인 영향력 排除를 위하여 유엔의 積極 介入을
  希望

나. 地域 安保體制 構策

○ 西方側의 基本構想

- 域內 軍事 覇權國 대두 방지

- GCC 諸國等 親西方 穩健國家의 主導的 役割

- 쿠웨이트 國境線 安全 保障 및 이라크 영토 보전

- 大量 殺傷武器 包含 軍備統制

2) 集團 安保 體制 胎動 可能性

　ㅇ 이라크 및 이란의 野望을 牽制키 위해 美國을 背後勢力으로 하고
　　사우디, 쿠웨이트등 GCC國家와 이집트등을 있는 集團的 安保體制
　　樹立 論議中(시리아, 이란도 參與可能性)

　ㅇ 그러나 集團 安保機構 創設보다는 個別的 安保條約 形態를 통하여
　　集團 安保 效果를 얻는 방식을 취할 가능성도 있음.

다. 팔레스타인 問題 解決 努力

　ㅇ 西方側은 아랍, 이스라엘 紛爭 解決을 위한 努力 倍加 豫想
　　- 특히 이스라엘의 對시리아 關係改善 誘導

　ㅇ 그러나 아랍 占領地 撤收에 대한 兩側의 強硬한 立場과, 이라크 미사일
　　攻擊에 대한 이스라엘의 報復自制等 걸프戰 寄與를 감안할때, 서방측의
　　努力에도 불구 당분간 팔레스타인 問題 解決 可能性은 稀薄

37

0207

3. 戰後 經濟 復興

　가. 戰後 復舊 및 經濟復興

　　ㅇ 쿠웨이트는 戰後 緊急 復舊 計劃에 의거 최대한의 民生 安定事業 完了後
　　　막대한 海外 財産 活用, 大規模 再建 計劃 實施 展望(今後 5년간 600-
　　　1,000억불 投入 豫想)

　　ㅇ 이라크는 戰後復舊에 1,000-2,000억불의 소요가 추정되나 戰後 復舊事業에
　　　많은 어려움 豫想

　　ㅇ 西方은 反美, 反西方 感情緩和 및 이라크의 再挑發 防止를 위하여 이라크의
　　　戰後 復舊, 아랍세계 경제復興 構想

　　ㅇ 地域情勢 安定을 위한 貧富 隔差 해소 및 경제성장 촉진

　　ㅇ 資金調達을 위하여 開發銀行, 復興基金, 中東版 마샬플랜, 경제협력
　　　基金等 擧論

　나. 原油 問題

　　ㅇ 戰爭復舊 資金調達을 위한 生産쿼타 增量 및 價格問題로 域內 原油 生産
　　　國間 不和 可能性

　　ㅇ 戰後 國際 原油價格 調整關聯, 美國 役割 增大 豫想

4. 우리의 對應策

　　가. 基本的 考慮事項

　　　　ㅇ 中東地域에서는 금후에도 각국의 利益關係가 相衝하는 불안정한 정치
　　　　　秩序가 계속되고 이슬람 原理主義 思想, 反王政 感情의 擴散等으로
　　　　　걸프 諸國의 現 政勘 將來 不確實

　　　　ㅇ 西方側은 戰爭의 승리에도 불구 反美, 反西方 感情 惡化, 今後 이스라엘
　　　　　아랍 關係에 있어 이스라엘의 非妥協的 姿勢 및 蘇聯의 牽制等으로
　　　　　對中東政策 遂行에 있어 큰 부담을 지게될 것임.

　　　　ㅇ 中東地域은 世界 石油 埋藏量의 65%를 占함으로써 이 지역이 서방의
　　　　　經濟, 安保 利益을 위해 차지하는 비중은 계속 막중할 것임.

　　　　ㅇ 今後에도 상당한 金額의 石油 收入을 활용한 建設工事와 商品輸入이
　　　　　活潑할 것이므로 戰後 復舊事業, 工事 受注 및 上品輸出을 위한 각국의
　　　　　競爭이 熾烈할 것임.

나. 政治的 對應策

　o 基本 方向

　　- 中東地域의 政治的 特性에 비추어 特定國家에 너무 偏重하는 정책은 回避하고 對中東 均衡 外交遂行

　　- 基本的으로 雙務關係 강화를 위한 노력 계속하되 中東平和를 위한 國際的 努力에도 참여 가능성 모색

　o 域內 個別國과의 關係 强化

　　- 사우디등 GCC 國家와는 旣存友好關係 强化

　　- 이라크와는 國際停戰이 樹立되는 대로 관계강화 노력

　　- 對 이스라엘 關係 調整問題는 中東情勢 推移를 보아 검토

　　- 팔레스타인 問題解決을 위한 國際的 努力 支援

　o 域外國家와의 協調體制 維持

　　- 傳統的 影響力 行使國인 美國, 英國, 佛蘭西, 蘇聯等과의 協調體制 維持

　o 戰後 걸프地域 主要國家에 特使 派遣

　　- 國際政治 舞臺에서의 수적 비중에 비추어 韓半島 問題關聯 아랍권의 支持 確保 努力 계속

40

ㅇ 戰後 걸프지역 安保體制 構築과 관련, 우리의 기여 可能分野를 確認, 支援

　　- 사우디 派遣 軍醫療支援團 쿠웨이트로 이동, 유엔 平和軍 支援

　　- 對中東 武器輸出 統制等 軍備管理體制 參與

ㅇ 팔레스타인 基金, 레바논 支援基金等 各種 中東平和基金 參與 擴大

ㅇ GCC 公館長 會議 定例化 및 中東地域 公館 整備計劃 調整

다. 經濟的 對應策

ㅇ 基本 方向

　　- 戰後 復舊計劃 및 餘他 中東國家의 建設工事, 積極 參與 및 商品
　　　輸出 增大

　　- 原油의 安定的 供給線 確保

　　- 戰後 經濟復興 開發 基金 출연으로 각종 프로젝트 참여

ㅇ 쿠웨이트 復舊 計劃 參與

　　- 協力 可能分野 쿠웨이트측과 협의

　　　· 過去 쿠웨이트에서의 工事 實績, 經驗 및 旣存 裝備 活用

　　　· 電氣, 通信, 上下水道等 技術者로 構成된 緊急 復舊 支援團
　　　　쿠웨이트 派遣, 支援 提供

41

0211

- 사우디 駐屯 醫療 支援團 쿠웨이트로 移動, 戰後 救護 事業 支援

- 我國業體, 단독 受注 또는 美, 英희사등과 共同 受注 및 下請 進出
  積極 推進

- 我國의 工事 可能分野 計劃書 作成, 쿠웨이트측에 제출 필요

- 쿠웨이트 緊急 再建 프로젝트(KERP)팀과의 接觸 强化

○ 이라크 復舊事業

- 이라크의 어려운 財政 事情으로 今後 相當한 期間 國際的 支援에
  의한 復舊 工事 推進 展望

- 戰後 民生安定을 위한 基本施設 工事는 着手될 것임으로 종전 직후
  我側의 참여 計劃案 제시

- 原油를 建設代金으로 受領하는 형태의 복구사업 검토

- 戰後 生必品, 醫藥品等 일부 인도적 지원 제공

○ 商品 輸出 增大

- 戰後 모든 基本物資 大量 購入 不可避

- 我國業體 積極的 輸出 活動 必要

○ 原油의 安定的 供給線 確保

- 戰後 原油生産 과다현상, 선진국의 에너지 節約 傾向 확산으로 아국의
  原油 도입 物量 確保에는 문제 없을 것임.

42   0212

- 그러나 豫測할 수 없는 緊急事態 發生에 대비, 主要 供給國家(오만,
  UAE, 사우디, 이란, 쿠웨이트, 이라크)와의 緊密한 關係 維持
- 中長期的으로는 中東地域 依存度(90년도 73%)를 낮추는 노력 필요
  (我國의 世界 原油 輸入國家中 中東 依存度 최고, 미국도 중동
  依存度 減少 및 代替에너지 개발 중요 과제)

예고 : 91. 12. 31 일반

정 리 보 존 문 서 목 록

기록물종류	일반공문서철	등록번호	2020110048	등록일자	2020-11-13
분류번호	772	국가코드	XF	보존기간	영구
명 칭	걸프사태 재정지원 공여국 조정위원회 회의, 1990-91. 전6권				
생 산 과	북미1과/경제협력2과/중동2과	생산년도	1990~1991	담당그룹	
권 차 명	V.6 1991.4-11월				
내용목차	* 4.8 실무회의(Washington D.C.) 　　- 조정위원회 기능 전환문제 토의 * 제6차 조정위원회 개최 및 참석문제				

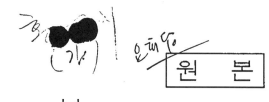

관리
번호 91-902

외　무　부

종　별 : 긴 급

번　호 : USW-1634   일　시 : 91 0405 1956

수　신 : 장관(미북,경이)

발　신 : 주 미 대사

제　목 : 걸프사태 조정위 실무회의

　　　대 : WUS-1079, 0951

　　1. 재무부 DALLARA 국제담당 차관보는 표제회의가 4.8(월) 11:00 재무부에서 개최됨을 알려오며 당관 관계관의 참석을 요청하는 서한을 금 4.5. 당관에 보내왔음.

　　2. 금번 회의에서는 재정지원 약속액에 대한 각국의 집행실적(별첨 의제 Ⅳ 항)과 걸프전 종전에 따라 조정위의 기능을 주변국 재건 및 개발 문제 협의로 전환하는 방안(의제 Ⅴ 항)을 주로 협의하게 될 예정임.

　　3. 이와관련 3.11. 룩셈부르크 개최 조정위 이후의 진전사항을 포함, 현재까지의 아국의 전선국에 대한 지원실적을 국별 상세 지원 내역과 함께 별첨도표 양식 (2 매)에 의거, 회의 개최전까지 통보하여 주시기 바람.

　　4. 또한, 조정위 기능전환 문제에 대한 본부 입장을 아울러 회시 바람.

(IBRD/IMF 가 동 조정위의 요청에 따라 작성한 별첨 "중동지역 개발 원조안" 참조)

첨부:USW(F)-1216 (12 매)

(대사 현홍주- 국장)

91.12.31. 까지

미주국　　장관　　차관　　1차보　　2차보　　중아국　　경제국　　정와대

PAGE 1   91.04.06   10:26
　　　　　　　　　　　　　　　　　　　　　　　외신 2과 통제관 BW
　　　　　　　　　　　　　　　　　　　　　　　　0002

DEPARTMENT OF THE TREASURY
WASHINGTON

April 4, 1991

ASSISTANT SECRETARY

UGW(A)-1246
수신: 장반(미북, 경이)
발신: 주미대사
참부됨 (12매)

Dear Colleague:

To follow up on the meeting of the Gulf Crisis Financial Coordination Group in Luxembourg, Assistant Secretary of State Eugene J. McAllister and I would like to convene the Working Committee on Monday, April 8, at 11:00 a.m. in Room 4121 at the Department of the Treasury. Please arrive at the 15th Street entrance.

At the March 11 meeting of the Coordination Group, the participants asked the Working Committee to conduct some preparatory work on various issues related to the future work of the GCFCG and post-war economic concerns. This subject appears as item V on the proposed agenda for our meeting. The World Bank and IMF distributed a paper on this subject to the Executive Directors on Monday, April 1.

Attached is a proposed agenda and an update of the tables showing commitments and disbursements as well as terms and conditions. We regret the short notice, but look forward to your participation.

Sincerely,

Charles H. Dallara
Assistant Secretary
(International Affairs)

1246-1

0003

GULF CRISIS FINANCIAL COORDINATION GROUP

Working Committee Meeting
April 6, 1991

AGENDA

I.   Introduction by Chair

II.   Political Overview

III. Presentation by the IMF and World Bank

    A.   Update on Economic Issues

IV.   Update from Participants on Commitments and Disbursements

V.   Future Work of the GCFCG and Post-War Economic Issues

    A.   Presentation by the World Bank and IMF on Post-War
        Growth and Development Issues in the Middle East

    B.   Tour de Table

1216-2   0004

4/4/91

TERMS AND CONDITIONS ON GULF CRISIS FINANCIAL ASSISTANCE FOR EGYPT, TURKEY AND JORDAN
(Millions of U.S. Dollars)

	GRANTS						LOANS					NOT SPEC.	TOTAL
	BOP	Human.	Project	In-Kind	Unspec.	Total	BOP	Project	Co-Fin.	Unspec.	Total		
GCC	3360	0	500	1270	0	5130	0	850	0	0	850	188	6168
Saudi Arabia	1000	0	500	1160	0	2660	0	0	0	0	0	188	2848
Kuwait	1540	0	0	110	0	1650	0	850	0	0	850	0	2500
UAE	820					820					0	0	820
EC	843	113	0	13	146	1115	306	517	0	49	872	1048	3034
EC Budget	443	78	0	0	0	521	239	0	0	0	239	45	805
Bilateral:	400	35	0	13	146	594	67	517	0	49	633	1003	2229
Belgium				7		7	26				26		33
Denmark					30	30							30
France	346	14				360	13	517			530	300	1190
Germany												200	200
Ireland				6		6							6
Italy					101	101				49	49	500	650
Luxembourg		6			5	11							11
Netherlands	54				9	63							63
Portugal					1	1						3	4
Spain		9				9	28				28		36
U.K.		6				6							6
OTHER	0	67	33	1	103	204	0	0	9	0	9	37	250
Australia				1		1						13	14
Austria			9		3	12			9		9		21
Finland		16				16							16
Iceland		3				3							3
Norway												24	24
Sweden		28	24			52							52
Switzerland		20			100	120							120
JAPAN		9	21	1		31	1684	194	157	0	2035	60	2126
CANADA	29	37				66					0		66
KOREA				48		48				50	50		98
TOTAL	4232	226	558	1333	249	6593	1990	1561	166	99	3816	1333	11742
% of Total						56.2					32.5	11.4	

0005

걸프사태 재정지원 공여국 조정위원회 회의, 1990-91. 전6권 (V.6 1991.4-11월) 339

GULF CRISIS FINANCIAL ASSISTANCE *
1990-91 COMMITMENTS AND DISBURSEMENTS
(Millions of U.S. Dollars)

	TOTAL			Egypt			Turkey			Jordan			Humanitarian/Unalloc'd 1/			Other States			GRAND TOTAL		
	Commit.	Disb. to Date	Future Disb.	Commit.	Disb. to Date	Future Disb.	Commit.	Disb. to Date	Future Disb.	Commit.	Disb. to Date	Future Disb.	Commit.	Disb. to Date	Future Disb.	Commit.	Disb. to Date	Future Disb.	Commit.	Disb. to Date	Future Disb.
GCC STATES 2/	6168	3463	2705	3423	2663	760	2745	800	1945	0	0	0	0	0	0	3576	2785	791	9744	6248	3496
Saudi Arabia 3/	2848	1788	1060	1688	1388	300	1160	400	760	0	0	0	0	0	0	1773	1403	370	4621	3191	1430
Kuwait	2500	855	1645	1015	555	460	1485	300	1185	0	0	0	0	0	0	1184	763	421	3604	1618	2066
UAE	820	820	0	720	720	0	100	100	0	0	0	0	0	0	0	619	619	0	1439	1439	0
EC budget	3034	1123	1911	1222	398	824	533	294	240	559	369	189	720	62	658	184	1	183	3217	1124	2094
EC total	805	624	181	254	207	48	240	193	48	214	173	41	96	51	45	0	1	0	805	624	181
total:	2229	499	1730	968	191	777	293	101	192	345	196	149	624	11	613	184	0	183	2413	500	1913
Belgium	33	17	16	16	6	10	10	0	10	7	1	6	0	0	0				13	17	16
Denmark	30	10	20	20	4	16	0	0	0	10	6	4	0	0	0				13	10	20
France 4/	200	0	200	50	0	50	30	0	30	20	0	20	100	0	100				220	0	230
Germany	1190	360	830	770	153	617	173	73	100	247	134	113	0	0	0	30	0	30	1334	360	974
Ireland	6	0	6	6	10		0	0	0	27	27		0	0	0				6	17	6
Italy 5/	630	37	614	75	10	65	49	0	49	2	2		500	0	500	144	0	144	689	37	623
Luxembourg	11	2	9	1	0	1	2	0	2	18	18		6	0	6	9		9	2	3	9
Netherlands	63	59	4	18	18	0	18	18	0	0	0	0	9	5	4	1	1	0	13	59	4
Portugal	4	0	4		0		0	0	0				0	0	0				0	0	4
Spain	36	9	27	12	0	12	11	0	11	14	9	5	6		3				36	9	27
U.K.	6	6	6				0	0	0				6						120	16	104
OTHER EUROPE/AUSTRALIA	249	74	175	55	3	52	31	2	29	67	23	44	96	46	50	82	60	22	331	134	197
Australia	14	5	9	1	1	0	0	0	0	9	9	0	13	4	9				14	5	9
Austria	21	2	19	19	0	19	0	0	0	3	3	0	12		10				21	14	19
Finland	16	14	2	0	0	0	0	0	0	1	1	0	13	11	2				16	14	2
	3	2	1	19	2	17	2	0	2	3	3	0	1	1	0				3	2	1
Norway	24	7	17	10	0	10	4	0	4	26	16	10	0	0	0	82	60	22	106	67	39
	52	28	24	25	0	25	25	0	25	25	0	25	12	12	0				52	28	24
Switzerland	120	16	104										45	16	29				120	16	104
JAPAN	2126	800	1326	629	336	293	720	218	502	717	186	531	60	60	0	100	0	100	2226	800	1426
CANADA	66	17	49	22	0	22	4	0	4	23	0	23	17	17	0	0	0	0	66	17	49
KOREA	98	5	93	30	0	30	20	5	15	15	0	15	33	0	33	17	2	15	115	7	108
(a) TOTAL COMMITMENTS	11741	5482	6259	5381	3400	1982	4054	1319	2735	1380	578	802	926	185	741	3959	2848	1111	15700	8330	7370
(b) EST. EFFECT OF GULF CRISIS 6/	13580	13580	-	3375	3375	-	5910	5910	-	4295	4295	-	-	-	-	-	-	-	-	-	-
DIFFERENCE (a minus b)	-1839	-8098	-	2006	25	-	-1856	-4591	-	-2915	-3717	-	-	-	-	-	-	-	-	-	-

* Does not include contributions to the multinational force. Totals may not equal sum of components due to rounding. Based on data submitted to the Coordinating Group. 1/ Unallocated among Egypt, Jordan, and Turkey. Includes general humanitarian assistance. 2/ GCC financing for "Other States" is for Syria, Morocco, Lebanon, Somalia, and Djibouti. 3/ Grant oil to Turkey is $1160 million. 4/ Protocols for $130 million of grand total were signed by the Gulf crisis is $600 million in both 1990 and 1991. Aid to "Other States" is for Morocco. 5/ Italian aid to "Other States" is for Somalia. 6/ IMF/World Bank estimate (oil at $31/barrel) circulated to Group shown for illustrative purposes. Not intended to represent precise figure of impact.

COORDINATION OF DEVELOPMENT ASSISTANCE IN THE MIDDLE EAST REGION

Background

1.   This discussion note has been prepared by the World Bank and IMF staff at the request of the Gulf Crisis Financial Coordination Group (GCFCG). At the March 11, 1991 meeting, participants agreed that the GCFCG had performed a highly useful function and should continue to follow up on existing commitments and disbursements of financial assistance to the three "frontline" countries (Egypt, Jordan and Turkey). Participants also had a preliminary exchange of views about how future financial assistance for reconstruction and development in the region might be coordinated. This note discusses organizational mechanisms for coordinating such financial assistance.

2.   The note first briefly outlines the principal objectives of the economic programs that could be supported by a multilateral development assistance effort. It then discusses the principles that should guide the coordination of such assistance. Finally, possible mechanisms that satisfy these criteria are presented for discussion. The success of the economic program outlined here would obviously also depend on sufficient progress being made in parallel efforts to settle the political issues in the region, as well as to control military expenditures.

3.   Financial assistance to countries in the Middle East region should, as in other cases, seek to facilitate, rather than substitute for, the sustained implementation of sound economic policies. In this regard, it is also important that, as earlier envisaged for the period after an initial phase, resources mobilized via the GCFCG or a successor group would be coordinated with the implementation of comprehensive adjustment policies, including those supported by or otherwise endorsed by the Bank and Fund.

Objectives

4.   Countries in the region have been affected to varying degrees by recent events in the Middle East and face an array of economic challenges. For a few countries in the region, the most immediate task lies in emergency rehabilitation and physical reconstruction. Other countries in the region must respond to the continuing adverse impact of trade disruptions, loss of remittance and tourist receipts and, until recently, higher oil import bills--factors which, in some cases, compounded already serious financial imbalances and deep rooted structural problems. While the external environment has started to return toward pre-crisis conditions, there is a continuing need for economic recovery assistance, as well as financial support for the implementation of economic adjustment and restructuring programs.

5.   However, these efforts need to be set in the context of a number of fundamental problems that have affected countries in the region for many years. The region is characterized by major disparities in resource endowments and income levels. While demographic trends are varied--and some countries have been labor scarce--in most countries, pressures from high population growth rates cause severe social strains, particularly in the rapidly growing urban areas. In the absence of improved economic performance,

0007

2

unemployment is expected to increase in the labor-surplus countries, with the bulk of the unemployed concentrated in the large urban centers. Unfortunately, the Gulf crisis has the potential to result in further restrictions on labor mobility in the region as well as in acceleration of capital flight. Disparities could thus grow even wider than they are today.

6.   A major cause of the economic problems in the region lies in the countries' own domestic economic policies, dirigiste orientation of institutions and administrative governance systems. Past policy failures have often been accompanied by inappropriate expenditure priorities and very high military expenditures. Large capital transfers alone would not be enough to transform these economies and could worsen the situation over the longer term by reducing the incentive for reforms. It is in the interest of both recipient and donor countries, therefore, that post-war aid be structured in a manner that promotes fundamental changes in economic management and leads to a gradual replacement of official assistance by private capital flows. Significant private investments, however, will only occur if a more hospitable business environment is created in the capital-poor countries.

7.   Country level programs will need to stress policy reforms to establish a sound macroeconomic environment and improve the efficiency of resource allocation and use within countries through private sector growth. Individual country programs also can be strengthened and supported by new efforts to nurture better regional economic cooperation. This will not be an easy task and objectives need to be realistic and focussed on steps that can begin to yield results in the near term. A first step might be consultations on policy and regulatory frameworks to promote capital and labor mobility and to reap efficiency gains through the economies of larger markets and increased competition. This could then lead to the exploration and development of common infrastructure projects. Such regional policy should be designed so that it becomes a step towards, and not a substitute for, greater integration with international markets. Initially, one of the benefits and justifications for the regional consultations may be mainly in building a common political consensus in support of the liberalization of economic policies on a region-wide basis. Such region-wide cooperation could produce, over time, substantial economic efficiency and welfare gains.

8.   A sustainable approach would also require attraction of larger, market-based private capital flows for investment from both local and international sources. This again is something that will take time to emerge and will depend on improvements in the policy environment within individual countries as well as greater political stability in the region. These private flows would need to be supported by official assistance to finance government-sponsored activities in reconstruction and economic recovery, the development of physical and social infrastructure, environmental protection, and the setting up of social safety nets in individual countries.

9.   The main focus of official support should thus be on fostering crucial domestic reforms in individual countries through financing of stabilization and adjustment program and priority development projects. The degree of regional and non-regional donor cooperation during the Middle East crisis has been exceptional. Such cooperation could provide a catalyst for renewed

١٤٦-۵

0008

3

efforts by the countries in the region to discuss common economic concerns and move towards region-wide economic liberalization. In addition, financing for regional projects and programs aimed at stimulating regional economic cooperation could play a significant role in the post-war efforts to create a lasting peace in the region. Success in limited and immediately feasible projects of common interest, supported by non-regional as well as regional donors and creditors on a multilateral basis, could prove to be a foundation for broader regional cooperation later.

10. Accordingly, future multilateral development assistance efforts should encompass the following four inter-related and complementary elements:

(i) a reconstruction program that meets the urgent needs of a few countries as well as a development assistance program in support of the ongoing economic recovery programs in many others which are directed at mitigating the impact of the crisis. These programs, implemented within a comprehensive macroeconomic framework, should be designed in a manner that, at the same time, promotes the agenda for the long-term economic growth of the entire region;

(ii) country-level policy and institutional reforms that would increase the productivity and growth of the countries in the region by: reducing and eliminating chronic internal and external imbalances as reflected in large fiscal deficits, excessive domestic liquidity and payments imbalances; improving the incentive environment and eliminating distortions; promoting outward orientation; reducing unnecessary regulations and controls; and, more generally, developing a business environment more conducive for private investment. Initially, this would require support for structural reforms and investment program that several countries are discussing with the Fund and the Bank, and initiation of similar programs in the other countries wishing to participate in the initiative. Over time, these reforms should be deepened and accompanied by further institutional changes as well as increased emphasis on human capital development and on efficient public administration and governance.

(iii) region-wide infrastructure projects and networks to exploit obvious complementarities and foster regional cooperation. Such a program might, provided sufficient political support is forthcoming, incorporate regional or sub-regional projects, for example, for: joint exploitation of riparian waters; environment protection; networks of gas, petroleum and/or water pipelines; and research and training institutions; and

(iv) broadly-based efforts to liberalize economic policies in the region in order to facilitate foreign investment, develop more flexible financial and labor markets, as well as facilitate

1216-8

0003

4

increased market-induced trade--both intra-regional and global--
over the longer term.

11.   An initiative based on the above outward-oriented and efficiency
enhancing policies would require strong political leadership within the
countries of the region, especially as these reforms may result in the social
dislocation of some segments of the population in the short term. However,
the success of such a program and its sustainability over the longer term
would also depend heavily on support from the donor community--both regional
and international. The donor/creditor countries and organizations—from
outside the region will need to provide new financing and facilitate debt
relief, where necessary, to supplement internal resource generation and
transfers within the region. Sustainable growth throughout the Middle East is
of mutual interest to both capital-surplus and labor-surplus countries within
the region as well as the rest of the world. Similarly, the integration of
the region's economies internally and with the international economy is also
highly desirable. Therefore, it is appropriate that official assistance
within the region, including from existing regional institutions, be
complemented with significant contributions by countries outside the region.
Based on country needs, some of the official assistance would need to be on
concessional terms, but it should not come at the expense of development
programs in other regions. Two other areas of action by non-regional parties
that are critical to the success of the program are to: (i) provide the
countries in the region non-discriminatory access to markets outside the
region; and (ii) facilitate transfer of technology and management skills to
both the public and private sector entities.

Principles for the Design of Institutional Mechanisms

12.   These considerations suggest a number of basic principles that might
guide the design of specific arrangements to coordinate future development
assistance in the Middle East, which are discussed below. In addition, given
the need to move rapidly, attention at this time should perhaps be focussed on
approaches that could quickly mobilize resources to meet urgent reconstruction
needs and to support economic reform programs while fostering regional policy
coordination. This would suggest building on the positive experience with
the GCFCG and the use of existing multilateral institutions and coordination
mechanisms in the immediate future--including, importantly, existing regional
institutions--while leaving options open for possible development of more
formal mechanisms over time.

13.   First, renewed emphasis on domestic economic policy and institutional
reforms in an appropriate policy context within the recipient countries,
including efforts to promote private investment in the productive sectors, is
crucial for establishing the basic enabling environment and sound economic
framework. There have been substantial official transfers within and to the
region in the past. All too often, they have either reinforced or failed to
mitigate shortcomings in domestic economic policies within the recipient

126-8

0010

5

countries. While some welfare-oriented transfers are needed and appropriate, the central focus of future assistance should be to support the crucial policy and institutional reforms. Efficiency and performance criteria should guide resource allocation and use decisions. To the extent feasible, official assistance should be linked to the creation of productive assets, associated institutional reforms and human resource development. The disbursement of public funds should be linked to the use of transparent and competitive procurement procedures, with suppliers from countries from within and outside the region participating.

14.   Second, the official assistance, whether within the region or from the outside, would be most effective when coordinated in a multilateral context. The use of assistance in a multilateral context, as far as possible, is desirable to foster the needed domestic reforms, to stimulate regional cooperation and to visibly demonstrate the willingness of the international community to jointly tackle the fundamental problems in the region.

15.   Third, there is the need to retain considerable flexibility to accommodate: (a) changes over time in membership of participating countries both donors and recipients; (b) major differences in the creditworthiness and financial needs of individual recipients; and (c) individual donor preferences on the magnitude and terms of official assistance to be made available to different recipient countries. Due to the diversity of international relations, attitudes, and starting economic environment, the initiative might start initially with a core group of countries committed to common objectives. There should be scope for flexibility and expansion over time in the focus of such aid coordination efforts beyond the initial core group. Countries have very different needs and will clearly not move ahead with adjustment programs and other developmental efforts at the same pace. More importantly, it is likely to be extremely difficult, if not impossible, to define a target group of participants rigidly at the outset. While criteria such as geographic proximity, shared resources, common language and culture may play a role, mutuality of interests and willingness to create an economic environment that will allow effective use of the resources are likely to be the most important considerations. Similarly, the resource mobilization mechanisms would need to recognize that the recipient countries have diverse financial requirements. The forms and terms on which assistance is extended to them should be based on their economic and financial needs. Finally, differences in donor country circumstances and preferences in terms of the size and conditions of official assistance to be made available to the individual recipient countries would have to be accommodated.

16.   Fourth, considering the central importance of countries' own efforts in undertaking far reaching domestic reforms, it would be important that priority in allocation of the official assistance be given to support such policy reform programs, which would generally be expected to be developed in cooperation with the Fund and the World Bank (in addition to meeting the criteria outlined in para. 13).

1216-㉑

0011

6

17.   Fifth, regional economic cooperation and policy harmonization must
remain the responsibility of countries in the region. The non-regional donors
and institutions could only support such efforts. Accordingly, appropriate
arrangements would be needed to provide for enhanced dialogue on an ongoing
basis between countries in the region and between them and the broader
international community.

Possible Coordination Mechanisms

18.   There is a wide variety of potential mechanisms for multilateral
cooperation at the regional level. Based on the objectives of the initiative
and the principles discussed above, as well as the need to act expeditiously
to support the process of recovery and reform, a flexible and less
institutional two-tier arrangement--at the regional and individual country
levels--appears desirable at this time. Under this approach, an umbrella
group consisting of participating donors (including regional institutions) and
recipients, as well as international institutions, would be created.
Similarly to the GCFCG itself or the Special Program of Assistance (for
Africa), but, in either case, with the possible participation of recipient
countries, this group would agree on the objectives, policies and procedures
that donors should collectively support within the region. The chairmanship
and representation--both in terms of seniority of officials and agency
participation--would have to be decided at an early stage. This umbrella
organization would also provide the vehicle for marshalling multi-year (e.g.,
3-year) pledges of financial support for these purposes, based on aggregate
estimates of what would be required by the target group of countries in a
medium-term context. The resources pledged within this group would be made
available to recipient countries as cofinancing of, or in parallel with,
programs developed in cooperation with and supported by the multilateral
institutions. Pledges could also involve commitments to a core multilateral
fund that would be administered under the guidance of the umbrella group (see
para. 20 below). There would also be need for a regular reporting system on
aid commitments and for coordinating and monitoring program implementation by
the recipient country and assuring that the agreed policies and approaches
within the group of donors are followed. This could be accomplished by
appointing the institution(s) providing the policy framework also as the
secretariate to the umbrella group.

19.   The second tier would consist of individual country aid consortia or
consultative groups. The bulk of the bilateral and multilateral assistance
would be channeled through these country level consortia within the policy
framework and overall priorities agreed by the umbrella group. The individual
country consortia would thus allow donor countries and regional and non-
regional institutions to maintain the flexibility associated with their
programs to individual countries, while providing a mechanism for coordinating
and facilitating cofinancing arrangements with the multilateral institutions
in support of economic reform programs and other development purposes. The

146-10

0012

7

emphasis of these programs would vary reflecting the diverse country circumstances. In a few cases, the emphasis would need to be on support for reconstruction and rehabilitation programs, and for most others on stabilization, structural adjustment, and longer-term development. Chairmanship of the individual country consortia would normally be a matter for the recipient countries themselves to decide, in consultation with the principal donors and institutions.

20. In addition, a core multilateral fund could be established to finance domestic reform programs and projects and to support agreed region-wide initiatives. Such a core fund need not represent a large share of the total program of financial assistance and transfers to countries in the region. It could be funded in part by already committed regional resources (e.g., a portion of the recently announced $15 billion program of the Gulf Coordination Committee). As with all of the resources mobilized through the SPA-like umbrella group, the resources of the core fund would be allocated on strict criteria and guidelines consistent with the objectives outlined above. There are alternate ways to set up such a fund—a new institution, a facility of one of the existing institutions, or a trust fund jointly governed by the donors. Some of the alternatives would require that administration be assigned to an existing competent institution. Should such a fund take time to set up, the economic programs in the recipient countries could (and should) nonetheless be supported by associating bilateral and other multilateral financing with the ongoing Fund and Bank programs in the countries. Specific lending operations of the core fund or cofinanced through the country consortia would need to be supervised and administered according to common and generally accepted procedures.

21. Consideration could also be given to the formation of a regional forum in which policy-makers from the participating countries in the region could exchange views on regional development priorities, draw upon the expertise of existing regional and international organizations, and reach agreements on economic goals and certain policies that have regional implications. As needed, sub-groups could be organized to handle special topics of common regional interest, e.g. water management. In addition, depending on the degree to which political factors might enter into the decisions of the umbrella group, it may be necessary to consider establishing parallel mechanisms for coordinating development assistance and for discussing political issues as, for example, is being done in the case of Central America.

22. Given strong political support, a two-tier approach along the preceding lines could be established quite rapidly. Other possible options that have been proposed for managing financial transfers and the policy dialogue include a Middle East Bank for Reconstruction and Development as well as a special World Bank subsidiary. Such approaches could lead to a more permanent institution specialized in the problems of the region, and could provide a capacity to leverage official contributions with borrowings from the financial

1216-1人

0013

8

market. However, current conditions within and outside the region may not be conducive at this time to an early agreement on issues such as decision-making and financial structures, burden-sharing arrangements, operating procedures, etc. Also, there are important legal and policy issues related to the establishment of a World Bank subsidiary which could take considerable time to resolve. Nonetheless, since these proposals merit further study, it may be necessary to adopt a phased approach, treating the permanent institutional mechanisms as longer-term options and to focus at this time on how best to structure immediately feasible coordination mechanisms so that they can be strengthened and evolve, over time, as deemed necessary and desirable.

March 29, 1991

1216-12 (ENO)

0014

발 신 전 보

번 호 : WUS-1394   910407 1341 DF   종별 :

수　신 : 주　　미　　대사．총영사

발　신 : 장　관　(미북)

제　목 : 걸프사태 조정위 실무회의

　　　　　연 : WUS-1079.0951

　　　　　대 : USW-1634

　　1. 대호 2항 GCFCG의 기능 조정 문제는 원칙적으로 찬성하며, 동 입장은
3.11. 제5차 회의시 아국대표가 기조 연설에서 아래와 같이 발표코자 하였으나
당시 전반적 회의 분위기상 적절치 않아 유보했으니 참고 바람.

　　　"본인은 이러한 한국 정부의 지원이 이들 국가의 경제적 피해를 극복하는데
　　　다소 도움이 되기를 희망하면서, 걸프전 종전에 따라 주변 피해국에 대한
　　　보다 효과적인 지원과 장기적으로 중동지역 전체의 경제부흥과 균형있는
　　　경제발전을 위해 지난 5차에 걸친 조정위회의를 보다 발전적인 장치로
　　　전환하는 방안을 검토할 시점이 도래했음을 지적코자 합니다.
　　　이 회의가 단순한 정보 고환과 토론장으로서의 성격에서 한걸음 더 나아가
　　　여러 관계국들의 주도에 따라 실효적인 재정지원 장치로 발전될 경우 한국
　　　정부도 이에 적극 참여할 예정입니다."

　　　("I sincerely hope that our contribution to the front-line states will
　　　be helpful to their efforts to recover from the economic losses. Now
　　　that the War is over, it is my view that the time has come for us to

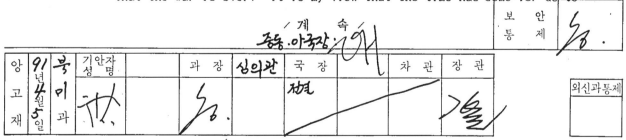

examine the possibility of modifying the Meetings of this Coordination
Group so that they could meet the task of making effective support to
the front-line states and of mapping out a balanced long-term plan to
assist the economic rehabilitation of the entire Middle East region.
When the current series of Meetings, which already is a good forum
of debate and exchange of information, develops into a more efficient
and suitable apparatus with active participation of Member Countries,
Korea will be more than willing to join in their efforts.")

2. 상기 아측 입장은 아직도 유효한 바, 금번 실무회의시 GCFCG 기능전환
방안에 대한 주요 참가국들의 동향을 우선 파악하되, 필요시 동 입장을 비공식
적으로 개진해도 무방함.

3. 이집트, 터키, 요르단 3 전선국만에 대한 지원은 90년도 현물지원
2,500만불(이집트 1,500만불, 터키 500만불, 요르단 500만불), EDCF 4천만불(이집트
1,500만불, 터키 1,500만불, 요르단 1,000만불)이므로 도표1(지원형태 및 조건)은
25,40,25,90(Grants, Loans, Not Spec. Total순)으로 수정되어야 함.

4. Not Spec. 2,500만불(91년도 지원분)의 국별 할당은 상금 미정인 바,
확보된 재원은 물자지원이 가능한 당부예산 500만불과, EDCF 예산 2천만불임을
참고 바람.

5. Table 2(약속 및 기여액 대비)는 소계(98,19,79), 요르단(15,12,3),
인도적 지원 및 미정(33,2,31), 합계(115,21,94)순으로 수정되어야 함.
이는 요르단내 폐수 처리공장 건설을 위한 EDCF 자금 1천만불 지원과 IOM(50만불),
UNESCO(3만불), ICRC(3만불), 대쿠웨이트 군복지원(70만불), 걸프만 오염 방제
(30만불), 이란 난민지원(15만불), 요르단 고아원 설립 지원(15만불)등 예비비
및 행정 경비지출 200만불이 지출되었기 때문임을 참고 바람. 끝.

(미주국장 반 기 문)

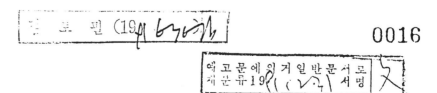

0016

협조문용지

분류기호 문서번호	미북 0160- 969	(720 - 2321)	결 재	담당	과장	심의관
시행일자	1991.4.13					(서명)
수 신	중동아프리카국장	발 신	미주국장			

제 목   걸프사태 재정지원 공여국 조정위 실무회의

　　　　표제에 관한 주미대사 보고 전문 USW-1692호 제2항의

　　"대중동 지역 지원을 위한 새로운 제도장치 마련 방안"에 관한

　　아측입장 수립에 참고코자 하니, 이에 대한 귀국의 검토의견을

　　4.20(토)까지 당국에 통보하여 주시기 바랍니다.

　　　　첨부 : USW-1692 및 1634 사본 각 1부 끝.

검 토 필 (19

0017

협조문용지

분류기호 문서번호	미북 0160- 969	(720 - 2321)	결 재	담 당	과 장	심의관
시행일자	1991.4.13					
수 신	중동아프리카국장	발 신	미 주 국 장 (서명)			
제 목	걸프사태 재정지원 공여국 조정위 실무회의					

표제에 관한 주미대사 보고 전문 USW-1692호 제2항의

"대중동 지역 지원을 위한 새로운 제도장치 마련 방안"에 관한

아측입장 수립에 참고코자 하니, 이에 대한 귀국의 검토의견을

4.20(토)까지 당국에 통보하여 주시기 바랍니다.

첨부 : USW-1692 및 1634 사본 각 1부 끝.

외 무 부

관리
번호 91-936

종 별 : 지 급
번 호 : USW-1692
수 신 : 장관(미북,중동2)사본재무장관
발 신 : 주 미 대사
제 목 : 걸프 사태 재정 공여국 조정위 실무 회의

일 시 : 91 0410 1409

연 USW-1634
대 WUS-1394

1. 연호, 표제 회의는 4.8. 1115-1315 안 재무부에서 25 개 공여국 대표및 EC,
GCC, IMF, IBRD 대표 참석하에 미 재무부 DALLARA 차관보와 국무부 MCALLISTER
차관보 공동 주재로 개최되었음. 당관에서는 장기호 참사관, 허노중 재무관,김중근
서기관이 참석하였는바, 요지 하기 보고함.

가.DALLARA 차관보는 룩셈브르크 조정회의에서 조정위의 기능을 전후 복구 및
평화정책이라는 새로운 목표에 합당하게 변경하도록 합의함에 따라, 연호 첨부
IMF/IBRD 가 - 중동 지역 개발 원조안- 보고서를 작성하였는바, 동 보고서를 중심으로
조정위의 향후 기능을 검토하자고 제의함.

나.MCALLISTER 차관보는 최근 쿠르드족 난민 문제가 중동지역에서 새로운 문제로
등장하고 있으며, 이에 따라 부쉬 대통령이 난민 지원을 위해 4.5 미 공군에 비상
식량, 의복, 의료기구의 긴급 공수를 지시하였고, BAKER 국무 장관을 터키에
파견하는등 미측의 노력을 설명하였음.

또한 동 차관보는 EC 가 난민 구호를 위해 5 백만불 추가 지원을 약속한데 대해
사의를 표명하고 각 원조 공여국의 조속한 원조 이행 특히 터어키에 대해 약속액의
조속한 집행을 촉구하였음.

다.IMF/IBRD 대표는 유가를 17 불로 상정했을때의 전선국에 대한 피해액을 이집트
34 억불, 터어키 59 억불, 요르단 43 억불로 설명하였으며, DALLARA 차관보는 원조 미
집행액에 대한 조속한 이행을 촉구함과 아울러 피해액과 약속액의 차이 즉 터어키의
경우 18 억불, 요르단의 경우 29 억불에 대한 추가 지원이 필요함을 설명하였음.

라. 이어 각국의 약속 및 이행 실적에 대한 보고가 있었는바, 일본은 터어키에

미주국   장관   차관   1차보   2차보   중아국   청와대   재무부

PAGE 1

91.04.11   06:27
외신 2과 통제관 CA
0019

대한 긴급 차관 4 억불을 4.2. 집행하는등 현재까지 14 억불이 집행되었다고 설명하고, 사우디는 레바논에 대해 6 천만불 추가 지원, 스위스는 나민에 대해 2 백만불의 추가 지원을 약속하였음. 장 참사관은 대호에 따라 아국 집행 실적을 수정하는 발언을 하였음.

　　마. 이어 IMF/IBRD 가 작성한 중동 지역 개발 원조안에 대한 검토가 있었는바, 각국 대표는 동 보고서가 4.5(금)배포되어 검토에 시간적인 여유가 없었으나,기본적으로 중동 지역 개발을 위해 새로운 FRAMEWORK 에 대해서는 일응 그 필요성을 인정하면서도 향후 참여국, 검토범위(COVERAGE), 새로운 제도의 기능과 절차상의 문제에 대한 충분한 검토가 있어야할것이라고 언급함.

　　바. 이어 DALLARA 차관보 및 MCALLISTER 차관보는 각 회원국들이 일단 IMF/IBRD 보고서를 긍정적으로 평가하는데 대해 사의를 표하고, 중동 지역의 개발과평화 안정을 위해서는 적절한 기금 마련과 함께 각 원조국들이 정치적인 팀워크를 가지고 협력 하자고 강조함.

　　사. 차기 실무회의는 5 월 초순 개최 예정이며, 동회의에서 차기 조정위 개최 시기를 결정키로 함.

　　2. 차기 실무 회의시에는 연호 IMF/IBRD 작성 보고서의 - 대중동 지역 지원을 위한 새로운 제도 장치 마련 방안-에 대한 우리의 입장을 밝히는것이 필요하리라 사료되는바, 이에 대한 본부 검토 의견 회시 바람. 또한 현재 미국이 크게 관심을 갖고 있는 쿠르드족 난민 지원문제는 향후 국제 문제로 등장하게 되리라 예상되는바, 우리로서도 대미 관계등을 고려하여 지원 방안등 적절한 대책을 검토해 보는것이 좋으리라 사료됨.

　　(대사 현홍주-국장)

　　91.12.31 까지

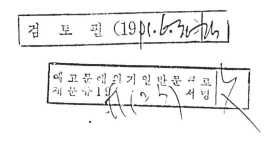

PAGE 2

외 무 부

종 별 : 지 급

번 호 : USW-1692   일 시 : 91 0410 1409

수 신 : 장관(미북,중동2)사본재무장관

발 신 : 주 미 대사

제 목 : 걸프 사태 재정 공여국 조정위 실무 회의

연 USW-1634

대 WUS-1394

1. 연호, 표제 회의는 4.8. 1115-1315 안 재무부에서 25 개 공여국 대표및 EC, GCC, IMF, IBRD 대표 참석하에 미 재무부 DALLARA 차관보와 국무부 MCALLISTER 차관보 공동 주재로 개최되었음. 당관에서는 장기호 참사관, 허노중 재무관, 김중근 서기관이 참석하였는바, 요지 하기 보고함.

가. DALLARA 차관보는 룩셈브르크 조정회의에서 조정위의 기능을 전후 복구 및 평화정책이라는 새로운 목표에 합당하게 변경하도록 합의함에 따라, 연호 첨부 IMF/IBRD 가 - 중동 지역 개발 원조안- 보고서를 작성하였는바, 동 보고서를 중심으로 조정위의 향후 기능을 검토하자고 제의함.

나. MCALLISTER 차관보는 최근 쿠르드족 난민 문제가 중동지역에서 새로운 문제로 등장하고 있으며, 이에 따라 부쉬 대통령이 난민 지원을 위해 4.5 미 공군에 비상 식량, 의복, 의료기구의 긴급 공수를 지시하였고, BAKER 국무 장관을 터키에 파견하는등 미측의 노력을 설명하였음.

또한 동 차관보는 EC 가 난민 구호를 위해 5 백만불 추가 지원을 약속한데 대해 사의를 표명하고 각 원조 공여국의 조속한 원조 이행 특히 터어키에 대해 약속액의 조속한 집행을 촉구하였음.

다. IMF/IBRD 대표는 유가를 17 불로 상정했을때의 전선국에 대한 피해액을 이집트 34 억불, 터어키 59 억불, 요르단 43 억불로 설명하였으며, DALLARA 차관보는 원조 미 집행액에 대한 조속한 이행을 촉구함과 아울러 피해액과 약속액의 차이 즉 터어키의 경우 18 억불, 요르단의 경우 29 억불에 대한 추가 지원이 필요함을 설명하였음.

라. 이어 각국의 약속 및 이행 실적에 대한 보고가 있었는바, 일본은 터어키에

미주국   장관   차관   1차보   2차보   중아국   정와대   재무부

대한 긴급 차관 4 억불을 4.2. 집행하는등 현재까지 14 억불이 집행되었다고 설명하고, 사우디는 레바논에 대해 6 천만불 추가 지원, 스위스는 난민에 대해 2 백만불의 추가 지원을 약속하였음. 장 참사관은 대호에 따라 아국 집행 실적을 수정하는 발언을 하였음.

　마. 이어 IMF/IBRD 가 작성한 중동 지역 개발 원조안에 대한 검토가 있었는바, 각국 대표는 동 보고서가 4.5(금)배포되어 검토에 시간적인 여유가 없었으나,기본적으로 중동 지역 개발을 위해 새로운 FRAMEWORK 에 대해서는 일응 그 필요성을 인정하면서도 향후 참여국, 검토범위(COVERAGE), 새로운 제도의 기능과 절차상의 문제에 대한 충분한 검토가 있어야할것이라고 언급함.

　바. 이어 DALLARA 차관보 및 MCALLISTER 차관보는 각 회원국들이 일단 IMF/IBRD 보고서를 긍정적으로 평가하는데 대해 사의를 표하고, 중동 지역의 개발과평화 안정을 위해서는 적절한 기금 마련과 함께 각 원조국들이 정치적인 팀워크를 가지고 협력 하자고 강조함.

　사. 차기 실무회의는 5 월 초순 개최 예정이며, 동회의에서 차기 조정위 개최 시기를 결정키로 함.

　2. 차기 실무 회의시에는 연호 IMF/IBRD 작성 보고서의 - 대중동 지역 지원을 위한 새로운 제도 장치 마련 방안-에 대한 우리의 입장을 밝히는것이 필요하리라 사료되는바, 이에 대한 본부 검토 의견 회시 바람. 또한 현재 미국이 크게 관심을 갖고 있는 쿠르드족 난민 지원문제는 향후 국제 문제로 등장하게 되리라 예상되는바, 우리로서도 대미 관계등을 고려하여 지원 방안등 적절한 대책을 검토해 보는것이 좋으리라 사료됨.

　(대사 현홍주-국장)
　91.12.31 까지

검토필 (1991. 6. 30. ...)

심의관 :

분류기호	중동이 20005-50	협조문용지	결 재	담 당	과 장	국 장
문서번호		( )		허무행		(서명)
시행일자	1991. 4 . 16.					
수 신	미주국장	발 신	중동아국장			
제 목	중동지역 개발원조를 위한 새로운 제도장치 설립방안					

대 : 미북 0160 - 969 ('91.4.13)

1. 걸프전후 개최된 제5차 걸프재정지원 조정위의 요청에

따라 IMF/IBRD 가 작성한 표제방안에 대하여 검토한 결과, 당국으로서는

하기와 같은 사유로 동방안이 바람직하고 필요한 것으로 사료됨을

통보합니다.

가. 걸프지역의 항구적 평화와 안정을 위해서는 경제부흥 및

개발사업의 추진이 긴요함.

나. 경제재건 및 발전을 위해서 공여되는 원조자금은 이의

효율적 운영 및 배분을 위해 재정공여국 및 수원국이

공동의 목표를 설정하고 조정하는 협의기구의 설립이

필요함.

2. 아국으로서는 동기구가 설립될 경우, 걸프사태 관련

재정지원 실적등을 배경으로 수원국 및 공여국의 협의기구에 계속

참여하여 아국의 과거 개발경험등을 전수할 수 있을 것으로 사료됩니다.

0023/계속.../

검토필(1991. 6. 20.

3. 단 추가재정 부담이 필요한 기본 기금설립시 아국의

참여문제는 재무부등 관계부처와 협의후 아국의 입장을 제시하여야

할 것입니다. //

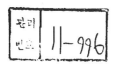

분류기호	중동이 20005-<del>50</del>	협 조 문 용 지	결 재		담 당	과 장	국 장
문서번호		( )					
시행일자	1991. 4 . 16.						
수 신	미주국장	발 신	중동아국장 (서명)				
제 목	중동지역 개발원조를 위한 새로운 제도장치 설립방안						

대 : 미북 0160 - 969 ('91.4.13)

1. 걸프전후 개최된 제5차 걸프재정지원 조정위의 요청에

따라 IMF/IBRD 가 작성한 표제방안에 대하여 검토한 결과, 당국으로서는

하기와 같은 사유로 동방안이 바람직하고 필요한 것으로 사료됨을

통보합니다.

　　가. 걸프지역의 항구적 평화와 안정을 위해서는 경제부흥 및

　　　　개발사업의 추진이 긴요함.

　　나. 경제재건 및 발전을 위해서 공여되는 원조자금은 이의

　　　　효율적 운영 및 배분을 위해 재정공여국 및 수원국이

　　　　공동의 목표를 설정하고 조정하는 협의기구의 설립이

　　　　필요함.

2. 아국으로서는 동기구가 설립될 경우, 걸프사태 관련

재정지원 실적등을 배경으로 수원국 및 공여국의 협의기구에 계속

참여하여 아국의 과거 개발경험등을 전수할 수 있을 것으로 사료됩니다.

0025 /계속.../

3. 단 추가재정 부담이 필요한 기본 기금설립시 아국의

참여문제는 재무부등 관계부처와 협의후 아국의 입장을 제시하여야

할 것입니다. 끝

발 신 전 보

WUS-1664   910422 1706 CV

번   호 : _____   종별 : _____

수   신 : 주   미   대사. 총영사

발   신 : 장   관   (미북, 중동일)

제   목 : 중동개발 원조 조정기구 설립

대 : USW - 1692

1. 아국은 다음과 같은 점에 비추어 IMF/IBRD가 작성한 중동개발 원조
조정장치 또는 기구설립 방안에 대하여 원칙적으로 찬성함.

- 과거 중동지역 국가에 대한 개별적 원조가 소기의 성과를 거두지
  못했던 경험에 비추어 이 지역의 경제재건 및 발전을 위하여 공여
  되는 원조가 효율적으로 배분되고 운영될 필요가 있음.

- 따라서 재정공여국 및 수원국이 산업 및 경제개혁.사회간접자본
  확충 등 공동의 목표를 설정하고, 원조의 사용등에 관해 협의.
  조정할 수 있는 장치 또는 기구의 설치가 필요함.

- 아국으로서는 동 기구가 설립될 경우, 걸프사태 관련 재정지원
  실적등을 배경으로 동 협의기구에 계속 참여하는 한편, 이 기구를
  통하여 아국의 과거 개발경험 등을 전수하므로써 중동지역 진출
  기반을 가일층 확대할 수 있음.

/계   속/

중동아국장:

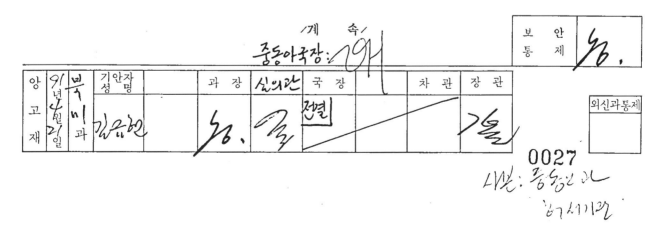

앙 고 재	91 년 4 월 22 일 북미 과	기안자 성 명 김유현	과 장	신의관 국 장	차 관	장 관	보 안 통 제	
				전결			외신과통제	

0027

2. 그러나 새로운 조정기구 또는 장치의 실제 설립은 향후 동 기구에의 참여 대상국, 기구의 기능과 역할, IMF/IBRD 및 GCC등 기존기구와의 관계등 관련사항 등에 대해 보다 충분하고 신중한 검토를 거쳐 추진하는 것이 바람직 하다고 봄.

3. 한편, 추가재정 부담을 필요로 하는 기금설립시 이에대한 아국의 참여문제는 기금의 성격, 참여국가 등을 참작하여 결정될 것임.   끝.

(미주국장 반기문)

예 고 : 91.12.31.일반

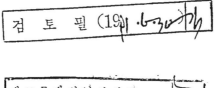

0028

중동지역 개발원조의 조정기구 설립문제

1. 배 경

   o '91.3.11. 제5차 걸프재정지원 조정위의 요청에 따라 IMF/IBRD가
     전후 중동경제부흥 및 개발을 위한 재정원조 조정기구 설립계획서
     작성

2. 경제원조조정의 목표

   o 경제개발 및 복구를 위한 재정지원의 목표는 역내국가의 비효율적
     경제운영 개선을 통한 지역경제 활성화, 복지증진인바, 시장통합,
     경쟁성 제고등으로 노동, 자본이동의 확대가 필요함.

   o 재정원조외에 민간투자 유치를 위한 국내경제 여건조성

   o 재정원조 자금은 수원국의 국내경제 개혁을 위해 하기 4개 분야에
     집중 지원함.

   ① 전후 경제복구 및 부흥

   ② 국내경제 정책의 합리적 개혁

   ③ 지역내 경제통합을 위한 사회간접 부문확충

   ④ 자율적 시장 기능 강화

   o 수원국의 정치적 안정도모

3. 조정기구의 운영지침

   o 수원국의 경제정책 및 제도개혁을 통한 자유시장 경제기능 강화

   o 재정원조시 다자적 조정기능 강화

   o 재정공여국의 정책상 차이를 수용할 수 있도록 탄력적 운용

     - 핵심국가 주도로 설립되나, 조정기능에는 참여 확대가 바람직

   o 원조자금의 배분도 시장경제 원리를 채택하는 국가에 우선 배정

   o 지역 경제 협력은 역내 국가주도로 추진

0029

4. 조정기구의 구상

    o 2원적 구조구상

        - 공여국, 수원국 및 국제기구 대표로 구성된 협의기구

        - 수원국들로 구성된 협의기구

    o 기본 기금설립은 GCC 등의 150억불 공여계획과 같은 기존자금

      활용도 가능

    o 지역정책 협의회 구성, 공동경제정책 추구 및 역내 정치문제 해결

      기능

0030

COORDINATION OF DEVELOPMENT ASSISTANCE IN THE MIDDLE EAST REGION

Background

1.   This discussion note has been prepared by the World Bank and IMF staff at the request of the Gulf Crisis Financial Coordination Group (GCFCG). At the March 11, 1991 meeting, participants agreed that the GCFCG had performed a highly useful function and should continue to follow up on existing commitments and disbursements of financial assistance to the three "frontline" countries (Egypt, Jordan and Turkey). Participants also had a preliminary exchange of views about how future financial assistance for reconstruction and development in the region might be coordinated. This note discusses organizational mechanisms for coordinating such financial assistance.

2.   The note first briefly outlines the principal objectives of the economic programs that could be supported by a multilateral development assistance effort. It then discusses the principles that should guide the coordination of such assistance. Finally, possible mechanisms that satisfy these criteria are presented for discussion. The success of the economic program outlined here would obviously also depend on sufficient progress being made in parallel efforts to settle the political issues in the region, as well as to control military expenditures.

3.   Financial assistance to countries in the Middle East region should, as in other cases, seek to facilitate, rather than substitute for, the sustained implementation of sound economic policies. In this regard, it is also important that, as earlier envisaged for the period after an initial phase, resources mobilized via the GCFCG or a successor group would be coordinated with the implementation of comprehensive adjustment policies, including those supported by or otherwise endorsed by the Bank and Fund.

Objectives

4.   Countries in the region have been affected to varying degrees by recent events in the Middle East and face an array of economic challenges. For a few countries in the region, the most immediate task lies in emergency rehabilitation and physical reconstruction. Other countries in the region must respond to the continuing adverse impact of trade disruptions, loss of remittance and tourist receipts and, until recently, higher oil import bills--factors which, in some cases, compounded already serious financial imbalances and deep rooted structural problems. While the external environment has started to return toward pre-crisis conditions, there is a continuing need for economic recovery assistance, as well as financial support for the implementation of economic adjustment and restructuring programs.

5.   However, these efforts need to be set in the context of a number of fundamental problems that have affected countries in the region for many years. The region is characterized by major disparities in resource endowments and income levels. While demographic trends are varied--and some countries have been labor scarce--in most countries, pressures from high population growth rates cause severe social strains, particularly in the rapidly growing urban areas. In the absence of improved economic performance,

1216-1

0031

2

unemployment is expected to increase in the labor-surplus countries, with the
bulk of the unemployed concentrated in the large urban centers.
Unfortunately, the Gulf crisis has the potential to result in further
restrictions on labor mobility in the region as well as in acceleration of
capital flight. Disparities could thus grow even wider than they are today.

6.   A major cause of the economic problems in the region lies in the
countries' own domestic economic policies, dirigiste orientation of
institutions and administrative governance systems. Past policy failures have
often been accompanied by inappropriate expenditure priorities and very high
military expenditures. Large capital transfers alone would not be enough to
transform these economies and could worsen the situation over the longer term
by reducing the incentive for reforms. It is in the interest of both
recipient and donor countries, therefore, that post-war aid be structured in a
manner that promotes fundamental changes in economic management and leads to a
gradual replacement of official assistance by private capital flows.
Significant private investments, however, will only occur if a more hospitable
business environment is created in the capital-poor countries.

7.   Country level programs will need to stress policy reforms to establish a
sound macroeconomic environment and improve the efficiency of resource
allocation and use within countries through private sector growth. Individual
country programs also can be strengthened and supported by new efforts to
nurture better regional economic cooperation. This will not be an easy task
and objectives need to be realistic and focussed on steps that can begin to
yield results in the near term. A first step might be consultations on policy
and regulatory frameworks to promote capital and labor mobility and to reap
efficiency gains through the economies of larger markets and increased
competition. This could then lead to the exploration and development of
common infrastructure projects. Such regional policy should be designed so
that it becomes a step towards, and not a substitute for, greater integration
with international markets. Initially, one of the benefits and justifications
for the regional consultations may be mainly in building a common political
consensus in support of the liberalization of economic policies on a region-
wide basis. Such region-wide cooperation could produce, over time,
substantial economic efficiency and welfare gains.

8.   A sustainable approach would also require attraction of larger, market-
based private capital flows for investment from both local and international
sources. This again is something that will take time to emerge and will
depend on improvements in the policy environment within individual countries
as well as greater political stability in the region. These private flows
would need to be supported by official assistance to finance government-
sponsored activities in reconstruction and economic recovery, the development
of physical and social infrastructure, environmental protection, and the
setting up of social safety nets in individual countries.

9.   The main focus of official support should thus be on fostering crucial
domestic reforms in individual countries through financing of stabilization
and adjustment program and priority development projects. The degree of
regional and non-regional donor cooperation during the Middle East crisis has
been exceptional. Such cooperation could provide a catalyst for renewed

0032

3

efforts by the countries in the region to discuss common economic concerns and move towards region-wide economic liberalization. In addition, financing for regional projects and programs aimed at stimulating regional economic cooperation could play a significant role in the post-war efforts to create a lasting peace in the region. Success in limited and immediately feasible projects of common interest, supported by non-regional as well as regional donors and creditors on a multilateral basis, could prove to be a foundation for broader regional cooperation later.

10. Accordingly, future multilateral development assistance efforts should encompass the following four inter-related and complementary elements:

   (i)   a reconstruction program that meets the urgent needs of a few
         countries as well as a development assistance program in support
         of the ongoing economic recovery programs in many others which are
         directed at mitigating the impact of the crisis. These programs,
         implemented within a comprehensive macroeconomic framework, should
         be designed in a manner that, at the same time, promotes the
         agenda for the long-term economic growth of the entire region;

   (ii) country-level policy and institutional reforms that would increase
         the productivity and growth of the countries in the region by:
         reducing and eliminating chronic internal and external imbalances
         as reflected in large fiscal deficits, excessive domestic
         liquidity and payments imbalances; improving the incentive
         environment and eliminating distortions; promoting outward
         orientation; reducing unnecessary regulations and controls; and,
         more generally, developing a business environment more conducive
         for private investment. Initially, this would require support for
         structural reforms and investment program that several countries
         are discussing with the Fund and the Bank, and initiation of
         similar programs in the other countries wishing to participate in
         the initiative. Over time, these reforms should be deepened and
         accompanied by further institutional changes as well as increased
         emphasis on human capital development and on efficient public
         administration and governance.

   (iii) region-wide infrastructure projects and networks to exploit
         obvious complementarities and foster regional cooperation. Such a
         program might, provided sufficient political support is
         forthcoming, incorporate regional or sub-regional projects, for
         example, for: joint exploitation of riparian waters; environment
         protection; networks of gas, petroleum and/or water pipelines; and
         research and training institutions; and

   (iv) broadly-based efforts to liberalize economic policies in the
         region in order to facilitate foreign investment, develop more
         flexible financial and labor markets, as well as facilitate

1216-8

0033

4

increased market-induced trade--both intra-regional and global--over the longer term.

11.   An initiative based on the above outward-oriented and efficiency enhancing policies would require strong political leadership within the countries of the region, especially as these reforms may result in the social dislocation of some segments of the population in the short term. However, the success of such a program and its sustainability over the longer term would also depend heavily on support from the donor community--both regional and international. The donor/creditor countries and organizations from outside the region will need to provide new financing and facilitate debt relief, where necessary, to supplement internal resource generation and transfers within the region. Sustainable growth throughout the Middle East is of mutual interest to both capital-surplus and labor-surplus countries within the region as well as the rest of the world. Similarly, the integration of the region's economies internally and with the international economy is also highly desirable. Therefore, it is appropriate that official assistance within the region, including from existing regional institutions, be complemented with significant contributions by countries outside the region. Based on country needs, some of the official assistance would need to be on concessional terms, but it should not come at the expense of development programs in other regions. Two other areas of action by non-regional parties that are critical to the success of the program are to: (i) provide the countries in the region non-discriminatory access to markets outside the region; and (ii) facilitate transfer of technology and management skills to both the public and private sector entities.

Principles for the Design of Institutional Mechanisms

12.   These considerations suggest a number of basic principles that might guide the design of specific arrangements to coordinate future development assistance in the Middle East, which are discussed below. In addition, given the need to move rapidly, attention at this time should perhaps be focussed on approaches that could quickly mobilize resources to meet urgent reconstruction needs and to support economic reform programs while fostering regional policy coordination. This would suggest building on the positive experience with the GCFCG and the use of existing multilateral institutions and coordination mechanisms in the immediate future--including, importantly, existing regional institutions--while leaving options open for possible development of more formal mechanisms over time.

13.   First, renewed emphasis on domestic economic policy and institutional reforms in an appropriate policy context within the recipient countries, including efforts to promote private investment in the productive sectors, is crucial for establishing the basic enabling environment and sound economic framework. There have been substantial official transfers within and to the region in the past. All too often, they have either reinforced or failed to mitigate shortcomings in domestic economic policies within the recipient

126-8

0034

5

countries. While some welfare-oriented transfers are needed and appropriate,
the central focus of future assistance should be to support the crucial policy
and institutional reforms. Efficiency and performance criteria should guide
resource allocation and use decisions. To the extent feasible, official
assistance should be linked to the creation of productive assets, associated
institutional reforms and human resource development. The disbursement of
public funds should be linked to the use of transparent and competitive
procurement procedures, with suppliers from countries from within and outside
the region participating.

14.   Second, the official assistance, whether within the region or from the
outside, would be most effective when coordinated in a multilateral context.
The use of assistance in a multilateral context, as far as possible, is
desirable to foster the needed domestic reforms, to stimulate regional
cooperation and to visibly demonstrate the willingness of the international
community to jointly tackle the fundamental problems in the region.

15.   Third, there is the need to retain considerable flexibility to
accommodate: (a) changes over time in membership of participating countries
both donors and recipients; (b) major differences in the creditworthiness and
financial needs of individual recipients; and (c) individual donor preferences
on the magnitude and terms of official assistance to be made available to
different recipient countries. Due to the diversity of international
relations, attitudes, and starting economic environment, the initiative might
start initially with a core group of countries committed to common objectives.
There should be scope for flexibility and expansion over time in the focus of
such aid coordination efforts beyond the initial core group. Countries have
very different needs and will clearly not move ahead with adjustment programs
and other developmental efforts at the same pace. More importantly, it is
likely to be extremely difficult, if not impossible, to define a target group
of participants rigidly at the outset. While criteria such as geographic
proximity, shared resources, common language and culture may play a role,
mutuality of interests and willingness to create an economic environment that
will allow effective use of the resources are likely to be the most important
considerations. Similarly, the resource mobilization mechanisms would need to
recognize that the recipient countries have diverse financial requirements.
The forms and terms on which assistance is extended to them should be based on
their economic and financial needs. Finally, differences in donor country
circumstances and preferences in terms of the size and conditions of official
assistance to be made available to the individual recipient countries would
have to be accommodated.

16.   Fourth, considering the central importance of countries' own efforts in
undertaking far reaching domestic reforms, it would be important that priority
in allocation of the official assistance be given to support such policy
reform programs, which would generally be expected to be developed in
cooperation with the Fund and the World Bank (in addition to meeting the
criteria outlined in para. 13).

1216-09

0035

6

17.   Fifth, regional economic cooperation and policy harmonization must remain the responsibility of countries in the region. The non-regional donors and institutions could only support such efforts. Accordingly, appropriate arrangements would be needed to provide for enhanced dialogue on an ongoing basis between countries in the region and between them and the broader international community.

Possible Coordination Mechanisms

18.   There is a wide variety of potential mechanisms for multilateral cooperation at the regional level. Based on the objectives of the initiative and the principles discussed above, as well as the need to act expeditiously to support the process of recovery and reform, a flexible and less institutional two-tier arrangement--at the regional and individual country levels--appears desirable at this time. Under this approach, an umbrella group consisting of participating donors (including regional institutions) and recipients, as well as international institutions, would be created. Similarly to the GCFCG itself or the Special Program of Assistance (for Africa), but, in either case, with the possible participation of recipient countries, this group would agree on the objectives, policies and procedures that donors should collectively support within the region. The chairmanship and representation--both in terms of seniority of officials and agency participation--would have to be decided at an early stage. This umbrella organization would also provide the vehicle for marshalling multi-year (e.g., 3-year) pledges of financial support for these purposes, based on aggregate estimates of what would be required by the target group of countries in a medium-term context. The resources pledged within this group would be made available to recipient countries as cofinancing of, or in parallel with, programs developed in cooperation with and supported by the multilateral institutions. Pledges could also involve commitments to a core multilateral fund that would be administered under the guidance of the umbrella group (see para. 20 below). There would also be need for a regular reporting system on aid commitments and for coordinating and monitoring program implementation by the recipient country and assuring that the agreed policies and approaches within the group of donors are followed. This could be accomplished by appointing the institution(s) providing the policy framework also as the secretariate to the umbrella group.

19.   The second tier would consist of individual country aid consortia or consultative groups. The bulk of the bilateral and multilateral assistance would be channeled through these country level consortia within the policy framework and overall priorities agreed by the umbrella group. The individual country consortia would thus allow donor countries and regional and non-regional institutions to maintain the flexibility associated with their programs to individual countries, while providing a mechanism for coordinating and facilitating cofinancing arrangements with the multilateral institutions in support of economic reform programs and other development purposes. The

1216-10

0036

7

emphasis of these programs would vary reflecting the diverse country circumstances. In a few cases, the emphasis would need to be on support for reconstruction and rehabilitation programs, and for most others on stabilization, structural adjustment, and longer-term development. Chairmanship of the individual country consortia would normally be a matter for the recipient countries themselves to decide, in consultation with the principal donors and institutions.

20.   In addition, a core multilateral fund could be established to finance domestic reform programs and projects and to support agreed region-wide initiatives. Such a core fund need not represent a large share of the total program of financial assistance and transfers to countries in the region. It could be funded in part by already committed regional resources (e.g., a portion of the recently announced $15 billion program of the Gulf Coordination Committee). As with all of the resources mobilized through the SPA-like umbrella group, the resources of the core fund would be allocated on strict criteria and guidelines consistent with the objectives outlined above. There are alternate ways to set up such a fund--a new institution, a facility of one of the existing institutions, or a trust fund jointly governed by the donors. Some of the alternatives would require that administration be assigned to an existing competent institution. Should such a fund take time to set up, the economic programs in the recipient countries could (and should) nonetheless be supported by associating bilateral and other multilateral financing with the ongoing Fund and Bank programs in the countries. Specific lending operations of the core fund or cofinanced through the country consortia would need to be supervised and administered according to common and generally accepted procedures.

21.   Consideration could also be given to the formation of a regional forum in which policy-makers from the participating countries in the region could exchange views on regional development priorities, draw upon the expertise of existing regional and international organizations, and reach agreements on economic goals and certain policies that have regional implications. As needed, sub-groups could be organized to handle special topics of common regional interest, e.g. water management. In addition, depending on the degree to which political factors might enter into the decisions of the umbrella group, it may be necessary to consider establishing parallel mechanisms for coordinating development assistance and for discussing political issues as, for example, is being done in the case of Central America.

22.   Given strong political support, a two-tier approach along the preceding lines could be established quite rapidly. Other possible options that have been proposed for managing financial transfers and the policy dialogue include a Middle East Bank for Reconstruction and Development as well as a special World Bank subsidiary. Such approaches could lead to a more permanent institution specialized in the problems of the region, and could provide a capacity to leverage official contributions with borrowings from the financial

1216-14

0037

8

market. However, current conditions within and outside the region may not be
conducive at this time to an early agreement on issues such as decision-
making and financial structures, burden-sharing arrangements, operating
procedures, etc. Also, there are important legal and policy issues related to
the establishment of a World Bank subsidiary which could take considerable
time to resolve. Nonetheless, since these proposals merit further study, it
may be necessary to adopt a phased approach, treating the permanent
institutional mechanisms as longer-term options and to focus at this time on
how best to structure immediately feasible coordination mechanisms so that
they can be strengthened and evolve, over time, as deemed necessary and
desirable.

March 29, 1991

1216-13 (END)

0038

협조문용지

분류기호 문서번호	국연 2031- *186*	(	)	결	담 당	과 장	국 장
시행일자	1991. 5. 8.			재			
수 신	중동아프리카국장	발 신	국제기구조약국장 (서명)				
제 목	걸프사태 피해국 지원						

유엔사무총장은 91.4.29자 외무장관앞 전문을 통하여

걸프사태로 인한 피해국의 지원을 축구하는 안보리의장 명의

성명을 전달하여 온바, 동 전문을 이첩하오니 필요한 조치를

취하여 주시기 바랍니다.

   첨 부 : 유엔사무총장 전문 1부.   끝.

0039

IIX2504721-4168(UNNY:WUCA4168)
TXD807 78724651
 WUCA4168 NYKU027 UNNY:WUCA4168
TLXCAB
78724651 24651

 WUCA4168 MCX9779
SS CABKS
NEWYORK (UNNY) 0346 GMT 05/04/91
ETATPRIORITE
 HIS EXCELLENCY
 THE MINISTER FOR FOREIGN AFFAIRS
 OF THE REPUBLIC OF KOREA
 MINISTRY OF FOREIGN AFFAIRS
 SEOUL (REPUBLIC OF KOREA)
BT
20388-05
    I HAVE THE HONOUR TO TRANSMIT TO YOU HEREWITH
FOR THE ATTENTION OF YOUR EXCELLENCY'S GOVERNMENT THE
TEXT OF THE STATEMENT MADE BY THE PRESIDENT OF THE
SECURITY COUNCIL ON BEHALF OF THE COUNCIL AT ITS 2985TH
MEETING ON 29 APRIL 1991.
QUOTE :
    NOTE BY THE PRESIDENT OF THE SECURITY COUNCIL FOLLOWING
CONSULTATIONS WITH THE MEMBERS OF THE SECURITY COUNCIL, THE
PRESIDENT OF THE COUNCIL MADE THE FOLLOWING STATEMENT, ON BEHALF
OF THE COUNCIL, AT ITS 2985TH MEETING ON 29 APRIL 1991, IN
CONNECTION WITH THE COUNCIL'S CONSIDERATION OF THE ITEM ENTITLED
QUOTE THE SITUATION BETWEEN IRAQ AND KUWAIT UNQUOTE :
    THE MEMBERS OF THE SECURITY COUNCIL HAVE CONSIDERED THE
MEMORANDUM, DATED 22 MARCH 1991 (S/22382) WHICH WAS ADDRESSED TO
THE PRESIDENT OF THE SECURITY COUNCIL BY THE 21 STATES WHICH HAVE
INVOKED ARTICLE 50 OF THE UNITED NATIONS CHARTER OWING TO THE
SPECIAL ECONOMIC PROBLEMS ARISING FROM THE IMPLEMENTATION OF THE
SANCTIONS IMPOSED AGAINST IRAQ AND KUWAIT UNDER COUNCIL
RESOLUTION 661 (1990).
    THE MEMBERS OF THE SECURITY COUNCIL HAVE TAKEN NOTE OF THE
SECRETARY-GENERAL'S ORAL REPORT TO THEM ON 11 APRIL 1991, IN
WHICH HE SUPPORTED THE APPEAL LAUNCHED BY THE 21 STATES THAT HAVE

0040

INVOKED ARTICLE 50. THE SECRETARY-GENERAL FURTHER INFORMED THE COUNCIL ON 26 APRIL 1991 OF THE CONCLUSIONS REACHED BY THE ADMINISTRATIVE COMMITTEE ON COORDINATION (ACC) AT THE SESSION IT HAS JUST HELD IN PARIS, WHERE MEMBERS OF ACC AGREED TO VIGOROUSLY PURSUE THEIR EFFORTS TO RESPOND EFFECTIVELY TO THE NEEDS OF COUNTRIES MOST AFFECTED BY THE IMPLEMENTATION OF RESOLUTION 661. THE SECRETARY-GENERAL WILL COORDINATE THROUGH ACC, WITHIN THE FRAMEWORK OF THIS ASSISTANCE, THE ACTIVITIES OF ORGANIZATIONS OF THE UNITED NATIONS SYSTEM.

THE MEMBERS OF THE SECURITY COUNCIL HAVE TAKEN NOTE OF THE REPLIES FROM A NUMBER OF STATES (AUSTRIA. BELGIUM, DENMARK, FRANCE, GERMANY, GREECE, IRELAND, ITALY, JAPAN, LIECHTENSTEIN, LUXEMBOURG, LUXEMBOURG ON BEHALF OF THE EUROPEAN COMMUNITY AND ITS 12 MEMBER STATES, NETHERLANDS, NEW ZEALAND, NORWAY, PORTUGAL, SPAIN, SWITZERLAND, UNITED KINGDOM, UNITED STATES AND THE USSR) WHICH HAVE FURNISHED SPECIFIC INFORMATION ON THE ASSISTANCE THEY HAVE PROVIDED TO VARIOUS AFFECTED COUNTRIES., THEY HAVE ALSO TAKEN NOTE OF THE REPLIES FROM OFFICIALS OF INTERNATIONAL FINANCIAL INSTITUTIONS, SUCH AS THOSE RECEIVED FROM THE PRESIDENT OF THE WORLD BANK AND THE MANAGING DIRECTOR OF IMF. THEY INVITE OTHER MEMBER STATES AND INTERNATIONAL FINANCIAL INSTITUTIONS AND ORGANIZATIONS TO INFORM THE SECRETARY-GENERAL AS SOON AS POSSIBLE OF THE MEASURES THAT THEY HAVE TAKEN ON BEHALF OF THE STATES WHICH HAVE INVOKED ARTICLE 50.

THE MEMBERS OF THE SECURITY COUNCIL MAKE A SOLEMN APPEAL TO STATES, INTERNATIONAL FINANCIAL INSTITUTIONS AND UNITED NATIONS BODIES TO RESPOND POSITIVELY AND SPEEDILY TO THE RECOMMENDATIONS OF THE SECURITY COUNCIL COMMITTEE, ESTABLISHED UNDER RESOLUTION 661, FOR ASSISTANCE TO COUNTRIES WHICH FIND THEMSELVES CONFRONTED WITH SPECIAL ECONOMIC PROBLEMS ARISING FROM THE CARRYING OUT OF THOSE MEASURES IMPOSED BY RESOLUTION 661 AND WHICH HAVE INVOKED ARTICLE 50.

THE MEMBERS OF THE SECURITY COUNCIL NOTE THAT THE PROCEDURE ESTABLISHED UNDER ARTICLE 50 OF THE CHARTER REMAINS IN EFFECT.
UNQUOTE.
HIGHEST CONSIDERATION.

JAVIER PEREZ DE CUELLAR
SECRETARY-GENERAL
UNITED NATIONS NEW YORK

0041

His Excellency
Mr. Javier perez de Cuellar
Secretary-General
United Nations, New York

                                          11th May, 1991

        With reference to your telex message dated 5th May, 1991
transmitting the text of the statement made by the President of
the Security Council on behalf of the Council at its 2985th Meeting on 29 April, 1991, I have the honour to inform you that the
Korean Government has provided the financial assistance as follows :

                                          (Unit : US dollars)

Country	Total Commitment	Grants	Loans	Disbursements through 30/4/91
Jordan	15,000,000	5,000,000	10,000,000	2,630,000
Syria	10,000,000	10,000,000	-	-
Yemen	100,000	100,000	-	100,000
Bangladesh	100,000	100,000	-	100,000

        I have further the honour to inform you that the Korean
Government is considering additional assistance which will be
reported when the details are decided.
        Accept, Excellency, the renewed assurances of my highest
consideration.

                                          Lee Sang-Ok
                                          Minister of Foreign Affairs
                                          Republic of Korea

                                                    0042

His Excellency
Mr. Javier perez de Cuellar
Secretary-General
United Nations, New York

With reference to
~~I have the honour to acknowledge the receipt of~~ your telex message
dated 5th May, 1991 transmitting the text of the statement made
by the president of the Security Council on behalf of the council
at its 2985th Meeting on 29 April, 1991, I have the honour to inform
you that

~~In compliance with the recommendations of the Security Council Committee~~, the Korean Government has provided the financial
assistance ~~for various affected countries to help ease their economic problems~~ as follows :

(Unit : US dollars)

Country	Total Commitment	Grants	Loans	Disbursements through 4/30/91
Jordan	15,000,000	5,000,000	10,000,000	2,630,000
Syria	10,000,000	10,000,000	-	-
Yemen	100,000	100,000	-	100,000
Bangladesh	100,000	100,000	-	100,000

I have further the honour to inform you that the Korean
Government is considering additional assistance ~~for the other~~ which will
~~affected countries which have invoked article 50.~~ be reported when its details are decided.
~~I would be grateful if your Excellency report the above mentioned assistance to the Security Council.~~

Accept, Excellency, the renewed assurances of my highest
consideration.

Lee Sang-Ok
Minister of Foreign Affairs
Republic of Korea

0042 -1

분류번호	보존기간

발 신 전 보

WUN-1314   910511 1331   FL

번 호 : _____   종별 : _____

수 신 : 주   유 엔   대사. 총영사

발 신 : 장 관   (중동이)

제 목 : 걸프사태 피해국지원

유엔사무총장은 91.5.4자 본직앞 전문을 통해 안보리결의 661호(대이락

경제제재조치)이행에 따른 경제난 문제를 헌장50조에 의거 안보리에 제기한

21개국의 지원요청에 대한 국제사회의 신속, 긍정적 반응을 촉구하는 91.4.29자

안보리의장의 성명을 전달하여온바 별첨 회신을 유엔사무총장에게 적의 전달바람.

첨 부 : 유엔사무총장앞 회신문 1부.   끝.

(중동아국장 이 해 순)

	기안자 성명	과 장	국 장	차 관	장 관	보안 통제
앙고재 91년5월11일 중동2과						

0043

His Excellency
Mr. Javier perez de Cuellar
Secretary-General
United Nations, New York

11th May, 1991

With reference to your telex message dated 5th May, 1991 transmitting the text of the statement made by the President of the Security Council on behalf of the Council at its 2985th Meeting on 29 April, 1991, I have the honour to inform you that the Korean Government has provided the financial assistance as follows :

(Unit : US dollars)

Country	Total Commitment	Grants	Loans	Disbursements through30/4/91
Jordan	15,000,000	5,000,000	10,000,000	2,630,000
Syria	10,000,000	10,000,000	-	-
Yemen	100,000	100,000	-	100,000
Bangladesh	100,000	100,000	-	100,000

I have further the honour to inform you that the Korean Government is considering additional assistance which will be reported to you when the details are decided.

Accept, Excellency, the renewed assurances of my highest consideration.

Lee Sang-Ok
Minister of Foreign Affairs
Republic of Korea

0044

외 무 부

종 별 :

번 호 : UNW-1222

수 신 : 장관(중동이,국연)

발 신 : 주 유엔 대사

제 목 : 걸프사태 피해국지원

일 시 : 91 0513 1830

대:WUN-1314

대호 회신 금 5.13. 자로 사무총장실에 전달하였음을 보고함. 끝

(대사 노창희-국장)

예고:91.12.31. 일반

중아국   국기국

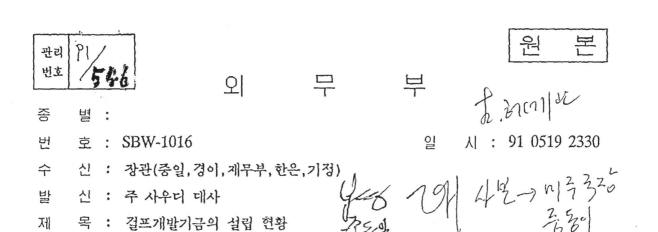

관리
번호 91/546

원 본

외 무 부

종 별 :

번 호 : SBW-1016   일 시 : 91 0519 2330

수 신 : 장관(중일,경이,재무부,한은,기정)

발 신 : 주 사우디 대사

제 목 : 걸프개발기금의 설립 현황

연:SBW-936(91.4.24), 재무부 국기 22257-255(91.4.30)

당관 노훈건 재무관은 5.18 GCC 사무처의 ABDULLA EL-KUWAIZ 경제담당 부총장과 면담하고 걸프개발기금의 설립현황에 관하여 탐문한바를 아래와 같이 보고함

1. 지난 3 월 룩세부르크에서 열린 걸프사태 재정협력단(GFCCG)회의에서 기 출연금의 상설 기금화 방안이 논의되었는바, 미국측은 동 기금을 세계은행 산하에 두기를 희망한 반면 불는 세계은행과 유럽개발은행이 공동으로 관리하는 방안을 제시하였음. 6.10 경에 리야드에서 개최 예정인 차기 GFCCG 회의에서 이문제가 다시 논의될 예정이나 합의에 이르기는 어려울 것이라 함.

2. GCC 국가들은 GFCCG 출연금과는 별도로 작년 12 월 GCC 정상회담에서 합의된 걸프개발기금의 설립을 추진하여 지난 4.22 리야드에서 개최된 GCC 재무장관 회의에서 동 기금의 창설을 승인하였음. 동기금은 GCC 가맹국만의 출자에 의하여 설립하되 최종 출자목표를 100-150 억불로 하고 있으며, 국별 출자비율은 아직 합의에 이르지 못하고 있음. 동기금이 종전의 재기금과 다른점은 주된 지원대상을 정부 부문이 아닌 민간 부문에 둔다는 것과 기존의 개발기금과 협조체제를 유지하면서 운용된다는것임. 사우디의 ABA AL-KHAIL 재무장관은 제다와 워싱턴에서 양차에 걸쳐 가진 BRADY 미 재무장관과의 회담총에서 동구상을 설명하여 미국측으로 부터 긍정적인 반응을 얻었다는 것임

3. 지난 2.7 BAKER 미국무장관의 바(877)(418)(239) 비롯된 중동지역의 개발금융 기구의 신설문제는 중동개발은행의 창설 방안이 대내외적인 지지를 받지 못하였고, GFCCG 의 상설기금화 방안도 일부 참여국의 반대로 성사되기 어려운 실정임에 따라 결국 걸프개발기금의 설립으로 종결될것으로 보임.

그러나 동기금이 출자국에 의하여 독자적으로 운영된다고 하더라도 지원 대상국의

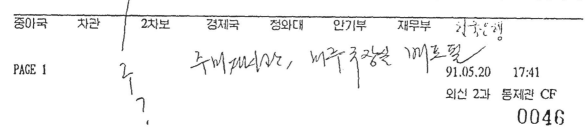

중아국	차관	2차보	경제국	정와대	안기부	재무부	

PAGE 1

91.05.20   17:41

외신 2과 통제관 CF

0046

경제구조 조정등이 수반되어야 하므로 실제 운영에 있어서는 세계은행이나 IMF 의
업무 협조가 불가피할것으로 보임.끝

　　(대사 주병국-국장)

　　예고:91.6.31 까지

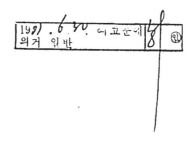

PAGE 2

0047

걸프사태 재정지원 공여국 조정회의 참가문제 검토

91. 5. 29
중동 2과

1. 조정회의 추진현황

   o 걸프사태로 인해 피해를 입고있는 전선국가에 대한 재정지원과 지원국
   의 국제적 단결도모 차원에서 미국 주도로 재정공여국 조정회의가 5차
   개최된바, 주요 협의내용은 다음과 같음.

   - 제 1차 회의 (90. 9. 워싱턴)

     . 지원대상 전선국가를 이집트, 터키, 요르단 3국으로 국한

     . 아측 미참가

   - 제 2차 회의 (90.10. 워싱턴)

     . 한국의 지원계획 발표

     . 수교를 위한 시리아 지원계획, 쌀 지원문제등 협의

     . 아측 대표단 (단장 : 권병현 본부대사, 최영진 주미참사관,

                          홍석규 사무관)

   - 제 3차 회의 (90.11. 로마)

     . 총지원액 128억불의 공여국 및 배정액 발표

     . 미국, 무력사용 가능성 언급

     . 아측 대표단 (단장 : 권병현 본부대사, 최영진 주미참사관,

                          허철 사무관, 재무부 대표)

   - 제 4차 회의 (91. 2. 워싱턴)

     . 공여국의 기존약속 금액의 집행현황, 추가지원계획 발표

     . 총 공여약속액 141억중 66억불 집행

     . 미국, 90년 지원액의 91.2.5한, 91년도 지원액의 90.3월말까지
       집행희망

0048

. 아측 대표단(단장 : 외무차관, 송민순 안보과장, 남관표 비서관,
재무부, 경제기획원 대표)

- 제 5차 회의 (91. 3. 룩셈부르크)

. 총 공여약속액 157억불중 3.8 현재 83억불 집행

. 아국 집행실적 불란서 다음 최하위

. 전후 조정위 기능 재검토 (미측, 지원대상국 확대 언급)

. 향후 GCC 중심 회의 추진

. 아측 대표단 (단장 : 제 1차관보, 유명환 주미참사관, 허덕행
서기관, 김규현 사무관, 재무부, 경제기획원대표)

* 실무회의 (91.4.8 워싱턴)

. IMF/IBRD 작성, 중동지역 개발원조안을 중심으로 조정위의 향후
기능 검토 제의 (미국)

2. 공여국 조정회의의 기능변화

O 조정위의 기능은 대이라크 경제제재를 통한 걸프전의 승리에서 중동
지역의 항구적 평화정착을 위한 정치, 경제적 기능으로 변화되고
있으며 또한 경제재건 및 발전을 위하여 공여된 원조자금의 효율적
운영 및 배분을 위해 재정공여국 및 수원국이 공동의 목표를 설정하고
원조금의 사용등에 관해 협의, 조정할 수 있는 제도적 장치의 마련이
추진되고 있음.

O 항후 동 조정회의 운영은 GCC 각국이 미국과 함께 주요한 역할을 수행
할 것으로 예상됨. (제 6차 조정위 리야드 개최예정)

0049

3. 제 6차 공여국 조정회의 참가 문제 검토

   o 총액 115백만불을 지원하고 있는 아국은 주요한 공여국의 일원인바
     GCC 가맹국이 주로 출자하는 걸프개발 기금을 창설할 경우에도 아국은
     계속 참여하여 원조자금의 효율적 집행을 위한 측면지원을 하고 중동
     진출의 기반을 강화해야 할 것임.

   o 원유등 자원확보 측면에서도 GCC 가맹국과의 관계를 계속 강화하여야
     하므로 동 회의에 계속 참여해야 할 것임.

     - 단, 추가재정부담이 필요할 경우 부담규모는 기금의 성격, 참여국가
       등을 참작하여 결정함.

   o 유엔 가입후 이스라엘과의 관계개선을 위해서도 GCC 와의 관계강화는
     필요하므로 동 회의에 계속 참여해야 함.

   o 6.10경 리야드에서 개최 예정인 제6차 공여국 조정회의에서는 기출연금
     의 상설기금화 방안도 논의될 예정이므로 아국으로서는 제6차 회의에
     당연히 참가해야 함.

   o 제 6차 회의 아국 대표수준은 동 회의의 기능이 변화되는 과도기적
     시기를 감안하고 타공여국의 동향 및 GCC 입장의 정확한 파악을 위해
     국장내지 심의관급 간부가 적절할 것으로 봄.

   o 동 조정회의 기능변화, GCC의 역할 및 관할지역등을 감안 향후 동회의
     관련 업무는 중동아국에서 주관해야 할 것임.

분류번호	보존기간

WUS-2386 발 신 910530 1812 정 보
~~WUS-2385~~ 910530 1813 FL

번 호 :
종별 :

수 신 : 주   미   대사. 총영사////

발 신 : 장   관   (중동이)

제 목 : 걸프 재정공여국 조정회의

연 : SBW-1016

　　　　주 사우디 대사 보고에 의하면 제6차 표제 회의가 리야드에서
6.10경 개최될 예정이라하는 바, 귀 주재국 관계당국에 동 회의 개최
예정일 및 회의 의제, 미측 참가자등 관련사항을 확인 보고바람.　끝.

(중동아국장 이 해 순)

예　　고 : 91.12.31.까지

검토필(. 11. 6.32. 홍)

미주국장 : 서영기훈

	보 안 통 제	玄

앙 고 재	1년5월20일	2등02과	기안자 성명 허미영	과 장 玄	신미관 메	국 장 전결		차 관 1911	장 관	외신과통제

0051

원 본

외 무 부

종 별 :

번 호 : USW-2671   일 시 : 91 0530 1905

수 신 : 장관(중동2, 미북,봉이)

발 신 : 주 미 대사

제 목 : 제6차 걸프 재정공여국 조정회의

대 WUS-2386
연:USW-1634

1. 대호 관련, 당관 김중근 서기관이 5.30. 재무부 TODD CRAWFORD 아주.중동담당과장 에게 전화로 확인한바, 동 과장은 전기 조정 회의시 금번 회의를 중동지역에서 개최하는 방안이 거론되었으나, 관계국간에 이견이 있어, 현재로서는 6.18. 워싱톤에서 개최하는 방안을 검토중에 있다함.

회의 개최 일자 및 장소가 확정되는대로 의제, 미측 참가자등 추보 예정임.

2. 금번 조정회의 이전에 실무회의가 당지에서 개최될 예정이며, 동 실무회의 에서는 조정회의에 제출할 재정지원 약속액에 대한 각국의 집행실적 문제가 협의될것인바, 현재까지의 아국의 지원실적을 연호 도표양식에 의거 국별 상세 지원 내역과 함께 조속 통보 하여 주기 바람.

(대사 현홍주- 국장)

예고:91.12.31. 까지

미주국   1차보   2차보   중아국   통상국

PAGE 1   91.05.31   10:20

분류번호	보존기간

발 신 전 보

WUS-2601   910610 1906 FO

번   호 :   종별 :

수   신 : 주 미   대사. 총영사//

발   신 : 장 관   (중동이)

제   목 : 제6차 걸프재정공여국 조정회의 자료

대 : USW-2671, 1634

표제회의에 대비, 아국의 집행실적 자료를 대호 양식에 따라 하기 통보함.
(항목별, COMMITMENT, DISBURSEMENT, FUTURE DISB.순, UNIT : MILLIONS OF
U.S. DOLLARS)

1) TOTAL   : 100, 7.7, 92.3
2) EGYPT   : 30, 0, 30
3) TURKEY   : 20, 5, 15
4) JORDAN   : 15, 2.7, 12.3
5) HUMANITARIAN/UNALLOCATD : 35, 0, 0
6) OTHER STATES : 15, 4.7, 10.3
7) GRAND TOTAL   : 115, 12.4, 102.6

(중동아국장 이 해 순)

예고 : 91.12.31. 일반

관리 번호	91/706

외 무 부

종 별 : 지 급

번 호 : USW-3657   일 시 : 91 0722 1839

수 신 : 장 관(중동이,미일)

발 신 : 주 미국 대사

제 목 : 걸프전 전선국에 대한 경제 원조 집행 실적

1. 당지 IMF 측은 걸프전 전선국에 대한 경제 원조와 관련, 각국의 원조 집행 현황을 통보하면서 동 일람표를 UPDATE 하여 줄것을 요청하여온바, 이를 별첨송부하니, 아국의 집행 실적을등 일람표에 의거 조속 통보 바람.

2. 또한 동 실무 회의 개최시 회의 준비에 참고코저 하니, 전선국 개별 국가에 대한 원조 내용을 아울러 상세 통보 바람.

첨부 USW(F)-2912

(대사 현홍주-국장)

예고:91.12.31 까지

중아국   미주국

EXECUTIVE DIRECTOR
United States

번호: USW (F) - 2912
수신: 장관 (중동이, 미밀)
발신: 주미 대사
제목: 정부 (3대)

INTERNATIONAL MONETARY FUND
Washington, D.C. 20431

MEMORANDUM   July 16, 1991

TO: Members of the Working Committee of the
           Gulf Crisis Financial Coordination Group

FROM: Thomas C. Dawson II

SUBJECT: Gulf Crisis Financial Assistance

At the April 8 meeting of the Working Committee of the Gulf Crisis Financial Coordination Group, a number of you indicated that you expected significant disbursements during May and June. So that the Group can share the most recent information available, we would like to update the 1990-91 Commitments and Disbursements table and the Terms and Conditions table.

Please fax any changes you have to the attached tables to Dean Kline (fax: 202/633-7640, tel: 202/566-2011). We look forward to your response by end-July, after which we will distribute the revised tables. Thank you for your cooperation.

Attachments

0055

TERMS AND CONDITIONS ON GULF CRISIS FINANCIAL ASSISTANCE FOR EGYPT, TURKEY AND JORDAN
(Millions of U.S. Dollars)

7/12/91

	GRANTS						LOANS					NOT SPEC.	TOTAL
	BOP	Human.	Project	In-Kind	Unspec.	Total	BOP	Project	Co-Fin.	Unspec.	Total		
GCC	3360	0	500	1270	0	5130	0	850	0	0	850	188	6168
Saudi Arabia	1000		500	1160		2660					0	188	2848
Kuwait	1540			110		1650		850			850	0	2500
UAE	820					820					0	0	820
EC	1146	113	64	13	149	1485	306	455	0	49	810	745	3039
EC Budget	443	78				521	239		0	49	239	45	805
Bilateral	703	35	64	13	149	964	67	455	0	49	571	700	2234
Belgium				7		7	26				26		33
Denmark					30	30					0		30
France						0					0	200	200
Germany	649	14	64			727	13	455			468		1195
Ireland		6				6					0		6
Italy					101	101				49	49	500	650
Luxembourg		6				11					0		11
Netherlands	54	9				63					0		63
Portugal				4		4					0		4
Spain		9				9	28				28		36
U.K.		6				6					0		6
OTHER	0	67	33	1	103	204	0	0	9	0	9	37	258
Australia				1		1					0	13	14
Austria		9		3		12			9		9		21
Finland		16				16					0		16
Iceland		3				3					0		3
Norway						0					0	24	24
Sweden		28		24		52					0		52
Switzerland		20			100	120					0		120
JAPAN		9	21	1		31	1684	194	157		2035	60	2126
CANADA	29	37				66					0		66
KOREA				25		25				40	40	33	98
TOTAL	4535	226	618	1310	252	6940	1990	1499	166	89	3744	1063	11747

GULF CRISIS FINANCIAL ASSISTANCE *
1990–91 COMMITMENTS AND DISBURSEMENTS

(Millions of U.S. Dollars)

	TOTAL			Egypt			Turkey			Jordan			Humanitarian/Unallocated 1/			Other States		
	Commit.	Disb. to Date	Future Disb.	Commit.	Disb. to Date	Future Disb.	Commit.	Disb. to Date	Future Disb.	Commit.	Disb. to Date	Future Disb.	Commit.	Disb. to Date	Future Disb.	Commit.	Disb. to Date	Future Disb.
GCC STATES 2/	6168	3863	2305	3423	2663	760	2745	1200	1545	0	0	0	0	0	0	3636	2845	791
Saudi Arabia 3/	2848	2188	660	1688	1388	300	1160	800	360	0	0	0	0	0	0	1833	1463	370
Kuwait	2500	855	1645	1015	555	460	1485	300	1185	0	0	0	0	0	0	1184	763	421
UAE	820	820	0	720	720	0	100	100	0	0	0	0	0	0	0	619	619	0
EC	3039	1225	1814	1225	399	826	533	395	139	560	369	190	721	62	659	177	1	176
EC Budget	805	624	181	254	207	48	240	193	48	214	173	41	97	51	45	0	1	176
Bilateral	2234	601	1633	971	192	779	293	202	91	346	196	150	624	11	614	177	137	40
Belgium	33	17	16	16	6	10	9	9	0	0	0	0	8	2	6	0	0	0
Denmark	30	10	20	20	4	16	0	0	0	0	0	0	10	6	4	30	0	30
France 4/	200	0	200	50	0	50	30	0	30	0	0	0	120	0	120	30	0	30
Germany 4/	1195	462	733	773	154	619	174	174	0	0	0	0	248	134	114	137	137	0
Ireland	6	0	6	6	0	6	0	0	0	0	0	0	0	0	0	0	0	0
Italy 5/	630	37	614	75	10	65	49	0	49	0	0	0	506	27	500	9	0	9
Luxembourg	11	2	9	1	1	0	2	0	2	0	0	0	8	1	7	1	0	1
Netherlands	63	59	4	18	18	0	18	18	0	0	0	0	27	23	4	0	0	0
Portugal	4	0	4	0	0	0	0	0	0	0	0	0	4	0	4	0	0	0
Spain	36	9	27	12	0	12	11	0	11	0	0	0	13	9	4	0	0	0
U.K.	6	6	0	0	0	0	0	0	0	0	0	0	6	6	0	0	0	0
OTHER EUROPE/AUSTRALIA	249	76	173	55	3	52	31	2	29	67	23	44	96	48	48	82	60	22
Australia	14	5	9	1	1	0	0	0	0	0	0	0	13	4	9	0	0	0
Austria	21	2	19	0	0	0	0	0	0	9	0	9	12	2	10	0	0	0
Finland	16	16	0	0	0	0	0	0	0	3	3	0	13	13	0	0	0	0
Iceland	3	2	1	0	0	0	1	1	0	1	0	1	1	1	0	0	0	0
Norway	24	7	17	19	2	17	2	2	0	0	0	0	0	0	0	62	60	22
Sweden	52	28	24	10	0	10	4	4	0	13	4	9	25	20	5	0	0	0
Switzerland	120	16	104	25	0	25	25	25	0	25	16	33	45	16	33	0	0	0
JAPAN	2126	803	1323	629	336	293	720	218	502	717	189	528	60	60	0	481	0	481
CANADA	66	17	49	22	0	22	4	0	4	23	0	23	17	17	0	0	0	0
KOREA	98	19	79	30	0	30	20	5	15	15	12	3	33	2	31	17	2	15
(a) TOTAL COMMITMENTS	11746	6003	5743	5384	3401	1984	4054	1820	2234	1381	593	788	927	189	738	4393	2908	1485
(b) EST. EFFECT OF GULF CRISIS 6/	13580	13580	–	3375	3375	–	5910	5910	–	4295	4295	–	–	–	–	–	–	–
DIFFERENCE (a minus b)	-1834	-7577	–	2009	26	–	-1856	-4090	–	-2914	-3702	–	–	–	–	–	–	–

* Does not include contributions to the multinational force. Totals may not equal sum of components due to rounding. Based on data submitted to the Coordinating Group. 1/ Unallocated among Egypt, Jordan, and Turkey. 2/ GCC financing for "Other States" is for Syria, Morocco, Lebanon, Somalia, Pakistan, and Djibouti. 3/ Grant aid to Turkey is $1160 million. 4/ Protocols for $130 million of grand total. Includes general humanitarian assistance. Total aid to countries affected by the Gulf crisis is $600 million in both 1990 and 1991. Aid to "Other States" is to "Other States". 5/ Italian aid is for Morocco. 5/ Italian aid (aid at $31/barrel) circulated to Group shown for illustrative purposes. Not intended to represent precise figure of impact. 6/ IMF/World Bank estimates.

0057

	분류번호	보존기간

발 신 전 보

번 호 : WUS-3417   910726 0959 CT   종별 :

수 신 : 주 미 대사.총영사

발 신 : 장 관   (중동이)

제 목 : 걸프전 전선국에 대한 경제원조 집행실적

1. 표제관련, 아국의 집행실적자료를 하기 통보함.

(항목별, COMMITMENT, DISBURSEMENT, FUTURE DISBURSEMENT, UNIT : MILLIONS OF U.S. DOLLARS)

        1) TOTAL : 95, 14.7,80.3

        2) EGYPT : 30,7,23

        3) TURKEY : 20,5,15

        4) JORDAN : 15,2.7,12.3

        5) HUMANITARIAN/UNALLOCATED :30,0,30

        6) OTHER STATES : 20,5,15

        7) GRAND TOTAL : 115,19.7,95.3

2. 전선국 개별국가에 대한 원조내역 상세는 차파편 송부 위계임.

                              (중동아국장 이 해 순)

예 고 : 91.12.31.까지

보 안 통 제	

앙고재	91년 7월	중동 과	기안자 성명		과 장 심의관	국 장		차 관	장 관	외신과통제
						전결				

0058

	분류번호	보존기간

발 신 전 보

WUS-3426 910726 1714 FO

번   호 :   종별 :

수   신 : 주 미   대사 . 총영사

발   신 : 장 관   (중동이)

제   목 : 걸프전 전선국에 대한 경제원조 집행 실적

연 : WUS - 3417

연호 통보 자료를 하기와 같이 수정바람.

6) Other States : 20, 6.4, 13.6
7) Grand total : 115, 21.1, 93.9

(중동아국장 이 해 순)

	보 안 통 제	ち

앙고재	91년 7월 26일	중동2과	기안자 성명 이익행		과 장 ち	심의관 국 장 전결		차 관	장 관 ち

외신과통제

0059

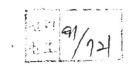
91/7리

분류기호 문서번호	중동이20005- 1864	기안용지 (720-3869)	시 행 상 특별취급	
보존기간	영구·준영구 10. 5. 3. 1	장 관		
수신처 보존기간				
시행일자	1991. 7. 26.	예		

보조 기관	국장	전결	협 조 기 관		문 서 통 제
	심의관				1991. 7. 29
	과장				
기안책임자		허 덕 행			발 송 인

경 유		발신명의		반송 1991. 7. 29 의무부
수 신	주 미 대 사			
참 조				

제 목	걸프사태 주변국 경제지원 현황

대 : USW - 3657 (91.7.22)

아국의 걸프사태 관련 주변국에 대한 경제원조 집행 현황

자료를 별첨과 같이 송부합니다.

첨   부 : 집행현황 자료 1부.   끝.

예   고 : 91.12.31.까지

0060

	분류번호	보존기간

발 신 전 보

번   호 : WUS-3481   910731 1752   FO종별 : _____

수   신 : 주 미   대사 . 총영사/

발   신 : 장 관   (중동이)

제   목 : 걸프사태 전선국에 대한 경제원조

        대 : USW - 3657

        연 : WUS - 3417

        표제관련 아국의 이집트.터키 및 요르단에 대한 원조 형태별 지원
계획을 하기 통보함

                                        (단위 : 백만불)

        1. GRANTS (IN-KIND) : 이집트(15), 터키(5), 요르단(5) 소계 25

        2. LOANS (PROJECT) : 이집트(15), 터키(15), 요르단(10) 소계 40

        3. NOT. SPEC. : GRANTS(8), LOANS(20) 쌀지원(10) 소계 38

        4. TOTAL : 103

                                (중동아국장 이 해 순)

    예   고 : 91.12.31.까지

	보 안 통 제	3/6

앙고재	91년 7월 31일	중동2과	기안자 성명 허덕행	과장	심의관	국장 전결	차관	장관	외신과통제

0061

관리
번호 91/8*6

외 무 부

종   별 :

번   호 : JOW-0607

수   신 : 장 관(중동이, 의전)

발   신 : 주 요 르 단 대 사

제   목 : 외상면담

일   시 : 91 0901 1230

1. 금 9.1. 본직은 김참사관 대동 외무성을 방문, MASARWEH 의전장과 면담한후 ENSOUR 외상을 예방, 전임 박대사의 소환장및 본직의 신임장 사본을 전달함

2. 본직의 신임장 제정 일자는 HUSSEIN 국왕의 외유(9 월 중순경 귀국 예정)로 미정이나 의전장에 의하면 9 월말경 가능할것으로 본다고 말하였음

3. 본직은 ENSOUR 외상과 제반사항등에 관해 약 40 분간 다음과 같이 면담함

가. 외상 발언요지

-의례적인 부임환영, 본직의 부임 계기로 기존의 돈독한 한. 요 관계가 보다 증진되기를 기대함

-2 차대전후 유태인, 팔레스타인간의 역사, 관계의 심각성에 대한 배경

-걸프사태와 관련, 주재국이 대외적으로 취한 중립적인 입장

-걸프사태로 인한 해외 거주 자국 인구 15%의 귀국에 따른 제반 애로사항

-중동 PEACE PROCESS 를 환영하며 일말의 기대를 갖고 있음

-사우디등 GCC 제국의 원조중단, 이라크의 심각한 경제사정등으로 요르단 경제난이 극에 달하고 있음

-나. 분석

-금일 본직의 외상 예방의 신임장 사본전달의 의례적 방문임에도 실질적인 제반문제를 진지하게 거론함으로써 본직에게 대요르단 지원및 협력필요성을 깊이부식하기 위한 의도를 인지하였음

-인근 아랍부국및 서방제국의 대요르단 지원이 중단내지 지연되고 있으며, 현주재국의 경제난이 심각하므로 기존우의를 감안 가능하면 소액이라도 지속적인원조를 제공함이 보도 효과적일것으로 사료됨

(대사 박태진-차관)

중아국   차관   1차보   2차보   의전장

예고:91.12.31 까지

0063

외 무 부

종 별 :

번 호 : USW-5077

일 시 : 91 1016 1950

수 신 : 장 관 (미일,미이,중동일)

발 신 : 주 미국 대사

제 목 : 걸프전 지원금 집행현황

대: WUS-4703

1. 대호, 91.10.11 현재 걸프전 지원금 집행현황을 하기 보고함. (단위 : 백만불)

국명, 기여약속액, 지원액(현금/ 물자등), 잔액(순)

사우디: 16,839, 14,428(10,552/3,876), 2,411

쿠웨이트: 16,006, 13,927(13,890/37), 2,079

UAE: 4,088, 4,088(3,870/218), 0

독일: 6,572, 6,554(5,772/782), 18

일본: 10,072, 9,987(9,416/571), 85

한국: 355, 219(150/69), 136

기타: 26, 26(4/22),

총계: 53,958, 49,229(43,654/5,575), 4,729

2. 상기 잔액관련, 국무부 JOSEPH YUN 담당관에 의하면 주요 잔액 보유국인사우디및 쿠웨이트는 달러 보유고 부족으로 상금 지불치 못하고 있고 독일의 잔액은 90 년에 실시한 물자지원에서 발생한바, 현재 물자지원에 대한 회계 정산을 하고 있고, 일본의 잔액 역시 90 년에 실시한 물자지원에서 발생하였으며, 일본정부와 동 지불에 대한 교섭이 조만간 완료될 것으로 전망하고 있다함.

3. 상기관련, 10.15 자 OBM 걸프전 관련 재정보고서를 별전 FAX(USW(F)-4342) 송부하니 상세 참고바람. 끝.

(대사 현홍주-국장)

예고: 91.12.31. 일반

미주국 안기부	장관	차관	1차보	2차보	미주국	중아국	분석관	정와대

UNITED STATES COSTS IN THE PERSIAN GULF CONFLICT AND FOREIGN CONTRIBUTIONS TO OFFSET SUCH COSTS

Report #8: October 15, 1991

Section 401 of P.L. 102-25 requires a series of reports on incremental costs associated with Operation Desert Storm and on foreign contributions to offset such costs. This is the eighth of such reports. As required by Section 401 of P.L. 102-25, it covers costs incurred during August 1991 and contributions made during September 1991. Previous reports have covered the costs and contributions for the period beginning August 1, 1990, and ending July 31, 1991, for costs, and August 31, 1991, for contributions.

Costs

The costs covered in this and subsequent reports are full incremental costs of Operation Desert Storm. These are additional costs resulting directly from the Persian Gulf crisis (i.e., costs that would not otherwise have been incurred). It should be noted that only a portion of full incremental costs are included in Defense supplemental appropriations. These portions are costs that require financing in fiscal year 1991 or fiscal year 1992 and that are exempt from statutory Defense budget ceilings. Not included in fiscal year 1991 or fiscal year 1992 appropriations are items of full incremental costs such as August-September 1990 costs and costs covered by in-kind contributions from allies.

Table 1 summarizes preliminary estimates of Department of Defense full incremental costs associated with Operation Desert Storm from August 1, 1990, through August 31, 1991. The cost information is shown by the cost and financing categories specified in Section 401 of P.L. 102-25. Tables 2-9 provide more detailed information by cost category. Costs shown in this report were developed by the Department of Defense and are based on the most recent data available.

Through August 1991, costs of $47.1 billion were reported by the Department of Defense. The costs reported so far are preliminary. This report includes an estimate of costs identified to date of equipment repair, rehabilitation, and maintenance caused by the high operating rates and combat use. The report also includes many of the costs of phasedown of operations and the return home of the deployed forces.

While a substantial portion of the costs have been reported, incremental costs are being and will continue to be incurred in subsequent months. These include equipment repair, rehabilitation, and restoration that have not so far been identified, long-term benefit and disability costs, and the costs of continuing operations in the region. About 40,000 military

442-1

0065

personnel were|in the region at the end of August, and
approximately 13,000 reservists were still on active duty at that
time. Significant progress has been made in returning equipment
from Southwest Asia; however, considerable amounts of materiel,
equipment, ammunition and vehicles still had not been shipped
from the area at the end of August. Materiel still in theater
includes some large, heavy pieces of equipment which are costly
and time consuming to prepare and transport. Combat aircraft
continue to fly in the region and the U.S. forces will continue
to remain in the region until all parties are satisfied with long
term security arrangements. The costs through August plus the
other costs not yet reported are expected by the Department of
Defense to result in total incremental costs of over $61 billion.
A Department of Defense estimate of potential total incremental
costs by major category of expense is attached.

        Incremental Coast Guard costs through August in support of
military operations in the Persian Gulf were revised from $34
million to $32 million to reflect actual payroll costs.

Contributions

        Section 401 of P.L. 102-25 requires that this report include
the amount of each country's contribution during the period
covered by the report, as well as the cumulative total of such
contributions. Cash and in-kind contributions pledged and
received are to be specified.

        Tables 10 and 11 list foreign contributions pledged in 1990
and 1991, respectively, and amounts received in September. Cash
and in-kind contributions are separately specified.

        As of October 11, 1991, foreign countries contributed
$8.0 billion of the $9.7 billion pledged in calendar year 1990,
and $41.2 billion of the $44.2 billion pledged in calendar year
1991. Of the total $49.2 billion received, $43.7 billion was in
cash and $5.6 billion was in-kind assistance (including food,
fuel, water, building materials, transportation, and support
equipment). Table 12 provides further details on in-kind
contributions.

Table 13 summarizes the current status of commitments and
contributions received through October 11, 1991.

4542-2

0066

Future Reports

As required by Section 401 of P.L. 102-25, the next report
will be submitted by November 15th. In accord with the legal
requirement, it will cover incremental costs associated with
Operation Desert Storm that were incurred in September 1991, and
foreign contributions for October 1991. Subsequent reports will
be submitted by the 15th day of each month, as required, and will
revise preliminary reports to reflect additional costs as they
are estimated or re-estimated.

List of Tables

Table 1 - Summary, Incremental Costs Associated with Operation
          Desert Storm

Table 2 - Airlift, Incremental Costs Associated with Operation
          Desert Storm

Table 3 - Sealift, Incremental Costs Associated with Operation
          Desert Storm

Table 4 - Personnel, Incremental Costs Associated with Operation
          Desert Storm

Table 5 - Personnel Support, Incremental Costs Associated with
          Operation Desert Storm

Table 6 - Operating Support, Incremental Costs Associated with
          Operation Desert Storm

Table 7 - Fuel, Incremental Costs Associated with Operation
          Desert Storm

Table 8 - Procurement, Incremental Costs Associated with
          Operation Desert Storm

Table 9 - Military Construction, Incremental Costs Associated
          with Operation Desert Storm

Table 10 - Foreign Contributions Pledged in 1990 to Offset U.S.
           Costs

Table 11 - Foreign Contributions Pledged in 1991 to Offset U.S.
           Costs

Table 12 - Description of In-kind Assistance Received to Offset
           U.S. Costs as of September 30, 1991

Table 13 - Foreign Contributions Pledged in 1990 and 1991 to
           Offset U.S. Costs Commitments and Receipts through
           October 11, 1991

0067

Table 1

SUMMARY 1/

INCREMENTAL COSTS ASSOCIATED WITH OPERATION DESERT STORM
Incurred by the Department of Defense
From August 1, 1990 Through August 31, 1991
($ In millions)
Preliminary Estimates

	FY 1990	FY 1991			Period and Preliminary Aug 1990 - Aug 1991
	Aug - Sep	Oct - July	This period August	Total through Aug	
(1) Airlift	412	2,341	103	2,447	2,855
(2) Sealift	235	2,512	74	2,586	2,821
(3) Personnel	229	5,154	214	5,367	5,590
(4) Personnel Support	352	5,525	478	6,003	6,354
(5) Operating Support	1,210	12,929	660	13,809	15,019
(6) Fuel	626	3,901	127	4,028	4,653
(7) Procurement	129	8,329	19	8,348	8,477
(8) Military Construction	11	655		655	666
Total	3,197	42,045	1,897	43,943	47,140 2/

Nonrecurring costs included above 3/	201	12,960	203	13,163	13,364
Costs offset by:					
In-kind contributions	225	5,229	65	5,294	5,519
Realignment 4/	812	58		60	872

1/ Data was compiled by OMB. Source of data -- Department of Defense. This report adjusts earlier estimates to reflect more complete accounting information.

2/ The costs reported so far are preliminary. This report includes an estimate of costs identified to date of equipment repair, rehabilitation, and maintenance caused by the high operating rates and combat use. Additional costs for these categories will be reported as more information becomes available. The report also includes many of the costs of phasedown of operations and the return home of the deployed forces. However, certain long-term benefit and disability costs have not been reflected in the estimates. These costs will be reported in later reports. The costs through August plus the other costs not yet reported are expected by the Department of Defense to result in total incremental costs of slightly more than $61 billion.

3/ Nonrecurring costs includes investment costs associated with procurement and Military Construction, as well as other one-time costs such as the activation of the Ready Reserve Force ships.

4/ This includes the realignment, reprogramming, or transfer of funds appropriated for activities unrelated to the Persian Gulf conflict.

0068

Table 2

AIRLIFT

INCREMENTAL COSTS ASSOCIATED WITH OPERATION DESERT STORM
Incurred by the Department of Defense
From August 1, 1990 Through August 31, 1991
($ in millions)
Preliminary Estimates

	FY 1990	FY 1991			Partial and Preliminary Aug 1990 – Aug 1991
	Aug – Sep	Oct – July	This period August	Total through Aug	
Airlift					
Army	507	1,032	14	1,070	1,253
Navy	65	722	42	764	840
Air Force	114	650	60	660	664
Intelligence Agencies		1		1	1
Special Operations Command	6	27		27	32
Total	412	2,341	106	2,447	2,650

Nonrecurring costs included above		696	14	1,000	1,000
Costs offset by:					
In-kind contributions	7	64		64	101
Realignment 1/	6				6

1/ This includes the realignment, reprogramming, or transfer of funds appropriated for activities unrelated to the Persian Gulf conflict.

This category includes costs related to the transportation by air of personnel, equipment and supplies.

During this period over 550 redeployment missions were flown, transporting over 18,500 people and 5,500 short tons of cargo.

4342 – 5

0069

Table 3

SEALIFT

INCREMENTAL COSTS ASSOCIATED WITH OPERATION DESERT STORM
Incurred by the Department of Defense
From August 1, 1990 Through August 31, 1991
($ in millions)
Preliminary Estimates

	FY 1990	FY 1991			Period css Preliminary Aug 1990 - Aug 1991
	Aug - Sep	Oct - July	This period August	Total through Aug	
Sealift					
Army	189	2,788	46	2,844	2,837
Navy	63	417	21	459	557
Air Force	12	261	7	269	653
Defense Logistics Agency		14		14	14
Special Operations Command	2	2		2	4
Total	255	3,512	74	3,599	3,591

Nonrecurring costs included above	57	1,102	15	1,117	1,174
Costs offset by:					
In-kind contributions	2	142	6	151	169
Realignment 1/	2				2

1/ This includes the realignment, reprogramming, or transfer of funds appropriated for activities unrelated to the Persian Gulf conflict.

This category includes costs related to the transportation by sea of personnel, equipment and supplies.

During this period a total of 60 ships (21 of them foreign flag ships) made redeployment deliveries. Over 599,000 short tons of dry cargo were shipped back to the U.S. and Europe.

4)42 ÷ 6

0070

Table 4

PERSONNEL

INCREMENTAL COSTS ASSOCIATED WITH OPERATION DESERT STORM
Incurred by the Department of Defense
From August 1, 1990 Through August 31, 1991
($ in millions)
Preliminary Estimates

Personnel	FY 1990 Aug – Sep	FY 1991 Oct – July	This period August	Total through Aug	Period End Preliminary Aug 1990 – Aug 1991
Army	120	5,000	147	5,267	6,860
Navy	22	1,189	57	1,170	1,562
Air Force	79	950	50	950	1,005
Total	229	6,154	214	6,367	5,660

Nonrecurring costs included above			46	46	45
Costs offset by:					
In-kind contributions					
Realignment 1/	15				15

1/ This includes the realignment, reprogramming, or transfer of funds appropriated for activities unrelated to the Persian Gulf conflict.

This category includes pay and allowances of members of the reserve components of the Armed Forces called or ordered to active duty and the increased pay and allowances of members of the regular components of the Armed Forces incurred because of deployment in connection with Operation Desert Storm.

The previous October–July estimate has been reduced by $20 million due to a redistribution of active duty pay costs.

At the end of August about 13,000 Reservists were still on active duty and about 40,000 people were still in theater.

-7-   4342–9

Table 5

PERSONNEL SUPPORT

INCREMENTAL COSTS ASSOCIATED WITH OPERATION DESERT STORM
Incurred by the Department of Defense
From August 1, 1990 Through August 31, 1991
(\$ in millions)
Preliminary Estimates

	FY 1990	FY 1991			Partial and Preliminary Aug 1990 – Aug 1991
	Aug – Sep	Oct – July	This period August	Total through Aug	
Personnel Support					
Army	260	4,066	471	4,559	4,760
Navy	104	679	6	685	685
Air Force	84	512	1	512	553
Intelligence Agencies	2	10		10	12
Defense Logistics Agency	12	16	1	17	20
Defense Mapping Agency		6		6	6
Special Operations Command	2	7		7	9
Office of the Secretary of Defense		10	0 1/	10	10
Total	352	5,825	478	6,036	6,654

Nonrecurring costs included above	4	1,242	154	1,508	1,403
Costs offset by:					
In-kind contributions	20	1,634	17	1,651	1,673
Realignment 2/	3				3

1/ Costs are less than $500 thousand.
2/ This includes the realignment, reprogramming, or transfer of funds appropriated for activities unrelated to the Persian Gulf conflict.

This category includes subsistence, uniforms and medical costs.

In August major costs were for subsistence, uniforms, and medical supplies.

0072

Table 6

OPERATING SUPPORT

INCREMENTAL COSTS ASSOCIATED WITH OPERATION DESERT STORM
Incurred by the Department of Defense
From August 1, 1990 Through August 31, 1991
($ in millions)
Preliminary Estimates

| | FY 1990 | FY 1991 | | | Period end Preliminary Aug 1990 – Aug 1991 |
	Aug – Sep	Oct – July	This period August	Total through Aug	
Operating Support					
Army	555	7,461	170	7,631	8,185
Navy	228	8,151	602	8,753	8,976
Air Force	60	2,225	107	2,332	2,403
Intelligence Agencies		1		1	1
Special Operations Command	15	35	2	37	52
Defense Communications Agency		1		1	1
Defense Mapping Agency	8	49		49	57
Defense Nuclear Agency		2		2	2
Office of the Secretary of Defense		3		3	3
Total	1,210	12,929	880	13,809	15,010

Nonrecurring costs included above		623		642	868
Costs offset by:					
In-kind contributions	167	1,676	7	1,684	1,851
Realignment 1/	698	12		12	710

1/ This includes the realignment, reprogramming, or transfer of funds appropriated for activities unrelated to the Persian Gulf conflict.

This category includes equipment support costs, costs associated with increased operational tempo, spare parts, stock fund purchases, communications, and equipment maintenance.

Costs reported during this period were for in-country support and for operating losses in the Navy Industrial Fund that were attributable to Desert Storm.

4342-9

0073

408 걸프 사태 재정지원 공여국 조정위원회 회의 2

Table 7

FUEL

INCREMENTAL COSTS ASSOCIATED WITH OPERATION DESERT STORM
Incurred by the Department of Defense
From August 1, 1990 Through August 31, 1991
($ In millions)
Preliminary Estimates

	FY 1990	FY 1991			Period end Preliminary Aug 1990 – Aug 1991
			This period	Total	
	Aug – Sep	Oct – July	August	through Aug	
Fuel					
Army	10	164	16	181	191
Navy	10	1,393	68	1,550	1,550
Air Force	157	2,483	31	2,514	2,651
Special Operations Command		12	1	13	13
Defense Logistics Agency	469				469
Total	626	3,051	127	4,028	4,653

Nonrecurring costs included above					
Costs offset by:					
In-kind contributions	31	1,222	62	1,284	1,675
Reallignment 1/	60				60

1/ This includes the realignment, reprogramming, or transfer of funds appropriated for activities unrelated to the Persian Gulf conflict.

This category includes the additional fuel required for higher operating tempo and for airlift and sealift transportation of personnel and equipment as well as for the higher prices for fuel during the period.

The previous October–July estimate has been decreased by $69 million to correct double counting of Air Force fuel costs.

About 75 percent of the costs reported during this period were due to higher prices for fuel with the balance due to the higher operating tempo.

4362 –10–

0074

Table 8

PROCUREMENT

INCREMENTAL COSTS ASSOCIATED WITH OPERATION DESERT STORM
Incurred by the Department of Defense
From August 1, 1990 Through August 31, 1991
(S in millions)
Preliminary Estimates

	FY 1990	FY 1991			Period and Preliminary Aug 1990 – Aug 1991
			This period —	—Total	
	Aug – Sep	Oct – July	August	through Aug	
Procurement					
Army	48	2,404	12	2,416	2,465
Navy	47	2,415		2,415	2,463
Air Force	32	3,372	7	3,379	3,411
Intelligence Agencies	1	18		18	19
Defense Communications Agency		0 1/		0	0 1/
Special Operations Command		69		69	69
Defense Logistics Agency		4		4	4
Defense Mapping Agency		1		1	1
Defense Nuclear Agency		0 1/		0	0 1/
Defense Systems Project Office		1		1	1
Office of the Secretary of Defense		21		21	21
Total	128	8,329	19	8,348	8,477
Nonrecurring costs included above	128	8,329	19	8,348	8,477
Costs offset by:					
In-kind contributions		124		124	124
Realignment 2/	118	47		47	165

1/ Costs are less than $500 thousand.

2/ This includes the realignment, reprogramming, or transfer of funds appropriated for activities unrelated to the Persian Gulf conflict.

This category includes ammunition, weapon systems improvements and upgrades, and equipment purchases.

The previous October–July estimates have been increased by $10.8 million to reflect reestimates of costs of equipment to facilitate operations in Southwest Asia and of research and development through finalization of contracts, and to reflect revisions of costs of major end items of equipment lost.

The costs for August result primarily from the cost of Army munitions lost during a fire at Doha, Kuwait on July 17th. August costs for the Air Force reflect the impact on the test program for the Joint Surveillance Target Attack Radar System (Joint STARS) from deployment to Southwest Asia.

4312 -11-

Table 9

MILITARY CONSTRUCTION

INCREMENTAL COSTS ASSOCIATED WITH OPERATION DESERT STORM
Incurred by the Department of Defense
From August 1, 1990 Through August 31, 1991
($ in millions)
Preliminary Estimates

| | FY 1990 | FY 1991 | | Partial and Preliminary Aug 1990 – Aug 1991 |
	Aug – Sep	Oct – July	This period August	Total through Aug	
Military Construction					
Army	7	854		854	860
Navy					
Air Force	4	2		2	6
Total	11	855		855	866

Nonrecurring costs included above	11	855		855	866
Costs offset by:					
In-kind contributions		239		859	859
Realignment 1/	11				11

1/ This includes the realignment, reprogramming, or transfer of funds appropriated for activities unrelated to the Persian Gulf conflict.

This category includes the cost of constructing temporary billets for troops, and administrative and supply and maintenance facilities.

No costs were reported during this period.

6142 -12-

Table 10

FOREIGN CONTRIBUTIONS PLEDGED IN 1990 TO OFFSET U.S. COSTS 1/
($ in millions)

	Commitments			Receipts in September			Receipts through October 11, 1991			Future Receipts
	Cash	In-kind	Total	Cash	In-kind	Total	Cash	In-kind	Total	
GCC STATES	5,844	1,001	6,845				4,256	1,001	5,557	1,808
SAUDI ARABIA	2,474	665	3,339				996	665	1,761	1,609 2/
KUWAIT	2,500	6	2,506				2,660	6	2,660	
UAE	870	180	1,050				870	180	1,050	
GERMANY 3/	272	800	1,072				272	782	1,054	18 4/
JAPAN 3/	1,084	656	1,740				1,084	571	1,655	85 5/
KOREA	50	30	80				50	50	80	
BAHRAIN		1	1					1	1	
OMAN/QATAR		1	1					1	1	
DENMARK		1	1					1	1	
TOTAL	7,250	2,490	9,740				5,662	2,387	8,049	1,690

1/ Data was compiled by OMB. Sources of data: commitments -- Defense, State, and Treasury;
cash received -- Treasury; receipts and value of in-kind assistance -- Defense.

2/ This is reimbursement for enroute transportation through December for the second deployment and for
U.S. in-theater expenses for food, building materials, fuel, and support. Bills for reimbursement have
been forwarded to Saudi Arabia.

3/ 1990 cash contributions were for transportation and associated costs.

4/ An accounting of in-kind assistance accepted by U.S. forces is under way. It is expected that this
accounting will conclude that the German commitment has been fully met.

5/ Resolution of balance is under discussion and should be received shortly.

43 42—18—

0077

Table 11

FOREIGN CONTRIBUTIONS PLEDGED IN 1991 TO OFFSET U.S. COSTS 1/
($ in millions)

	Commitments 2/			Receipts in September			Receipts through October 11, 1991			Future Receipts
	Cash	In-kind	Total	Cash	In-kind	Total	Cash	In-kind	Total	
GCC STATES	26,958	3,180	36,055	1,216	59	1,275	24,858	3,180	27,185	2,098
SAUDI ARABIA	10,489	3,011	13,500	501	57	558	9,666	3,011	12,677	823
KUWAIT	13,469	81	13,550	715	2	717	11,380	81	11,461	2,070
UAE	3,000	69	3,069				3,000	69	3,069	
GERMANY	6,500		6,500				6,535		6,500	
JAPAN 3/	9,632		9,632				9,632		9,632	
KOREA 4/	100	175	275		-3	-3	100	50	150	125
DENMARK		11	11					11	11	
LUXEMBOURG		6	6					6	6	
OTHER	4	5	8				4	8	8	
TOTAL	40,694	3,524	44,218	1,216	59	1,275	57,692	3,153	41,180	2,068

1/ Data was compiled by OMB. Sources of data: commitments — Defense, State, and Treasury; cash received –– Treasury; receipts and value of in-kind assistance — Defense.

2/ 1991 commitments in most instances did not distinguish between cash and in-kind. The commitment shown above reflects actual in-kind assistance received unless specific information is available.

3/ 1991 cash contributions are for logistics and related support.

4/ The reduction of $3 million in September reflects a re-pricing of transportation assistance previously provided.

4342 -14-

0078

Table 12

DESCRIPTION OF IN-KIND ASSISTANCE RECEIVED
TO OFFSET U.S. COSTS AS OF SEPTEMBER 30, 1991
($ in millions)

	Calendar Year 1990	Calendar Year 1991
SAUDI ARABIA .... Host nation support including food, fuel, housing, building materials, transportation and port handling services.	695	5,011
KUWAIT ...... Transportation	0	91
UNITED ARAB EMIRATES ..... Fuel, food and water, security services, construction equipment and civilian labor.	150	60
GERMANY ...... Vehicles including cargo trucks, water trailers, buses and ambulances; generators; radios; portable showers; protective masks, and chemical sensing vehicles	762	
JAPAN ...... Construction and engineering support, vehicles, electronic data processing, telephone services, medical equipment, and transportation.	571	
KOREA ...... Transportation and replenishment stocks	80	60
BAHRAIN ...... Medical supplies, food and water —	1	
OMAN/QATAR ...... Oil, telephones, food and water	1	
DENMARK ...... Transportation	1	11
LUXEMBOURG...... Transportation		6
OTHER ...... Transportation		5
TOTAL	2,297	5,189

-15-

0079

Table 13

FOREIGN CONTRIBUTIONS PLEDGED IN 1990 AND 1991 TO OFFSET U.S. COSTS
COMMITMENTS AND RECEIPTS THROUGH OCTOBER 11, 1991 1/
(\$ in millions)

	Commitments			Receipts 2/			Future Receipts
	1990	1991	Total	Cash	In-Kind	Total	
GCC STATES	6,845	20,038	26,858	28,912	6,188	68,444	4,460
SAUDI ARABIA	3,330	12,500	16,850	10,892	3,676	14,480	2,411
KUWAIT	2,505	13,500	16,000	13,500	67	13,527	2,079
UAE	1,000	3,099	4,099	3,870	218	4,059	
GERMANY	1,072	6,500	6,572	6,772	762	6,654	10 3/
JAPAN	1,740	8,332	10,072	9,416	671	9,667	65 4/
KOREA	80	275	355	150	69	219	136
OTHER	3	23	26	4	22	26	
TOTAL	9,740	44,818	53,858	48,054	6,678	49,228	4,730

1/ Data was compiled by OMB. Sources of data: commitments — Defense, State, and Treasury;
cash received — Treasury; receipts and value of in-kind assistance — Defense.

2/ Cash receipts are as of October 11, 1991. In-kind assistance is as of September 30, 1991.

3/ An accounting of in-kind assistance accepted by U.S. forces is under way. It is expected
that this accounting will conclude that the German commitment has been fully met.

4/ Resolution of balance is under discussion and should be received shortly.

6342 -16

0080

Department of Defense Preliminary Estimate of Full Incremental Desert Shield/Desert Storm Costs
($ in Billions)

	Reported 1 August 1990 - 30 August 1991	DOD Estimate of Additional Potential Exposure	Total Reported Plus Potential Costs a
Airlift	2.9	.1	3.0
Sealift	3.8	1.8	5.6
Personnel	5.6	1.6	7.2
Personnel Support	6.4	.6	7.0
Operating Support	15.0	5.0	20.0
Fuel	4.7	.8	5.5
Investment	8.5	--	8.5
Military Construction	.4	-	.4
Present Value of Long Term Personnel Benefits	-	3.9	3.9
Total	**47.2**	**14.0**	**61.1 a**

(May not add due to rounding)

   Estimating the full incremental cost of Desert Shield/Desert Storm requires assumptions about the scope and extent of operations in the region, the level of activity to occur in the phasedown period, the number of people and time it will take to prepare equipment and material for return, the availability of transportation, and needed equipment repair, rehabilitation and restoration due to combat stress, to name several of the more significant factors. Estimates may change as more information becomes available. It should be noted that substantial numbers of people and quantities of equipment and material remained in theater at the end of August.

   o About 40,000 troops were in the region at the end of August, and approximately 13,000 reservists were still on active duty at that time.

   o Significant amounts of material, equipment, ammunition and vehicles had not been shipped from Southwest Asia at the end of August. Material still in theater includes the large, heavy pieces of equipment which are costly and time consuming to prepare and transport.

   o Combat aircraft continue to fly in the region and U.S. forces will continue to remain in the region until all parties are satisfied with long term security arrangements.

a A substantial fraction but not all of these costs require appropriations.

4542-17 (END)

외 무 부

종 별 :

번 호 : USW-5521

수 신 : 장관 (미일,미이,중동이)

발 신 : 주미대사

제 목 : 걸프전 전비

일 시 : 91 1107 1855

1. 금 11.7 국방부 정례 브리핑시 PETE WILLIAMS대변인은 최근 걸프전비에 관한 GAO보고서 가사실과 다르게 우방국의 걸프전 지원금 총액이 실제전비보다 과다하여 8억불의 잉여금이 발생할것이라는 추측을 불러 일으키고 있다고 지적하면서, 실제로는우방국이 걸프지원금 총액을 전부지불해도 28억불의 부족분이 발생하며, 이는 미정부가 부담해야 한다고 발표함.

2. 동 대변인은 걸프전비 총액은 (1) FY 91/92미 국방예산 추가 소요분 471억불, 걸프전 관련 미군인사에 대한 장기 보조금 39억불, (3) 우방국의 대미 현물등 지원및 주재국 지원분 58억불, (4)FY 90 미국의 걸프전비 사용금 31억불, (5) 대체계획이없는 소모군장비 12억불등 총611억불이며, 이중 FY 91/92 미 국방예산 추가소요분및미군인사에 대한 장기보조금(총액 510억불)은 우방국의 걸프지원 현금총액(현물등 기타지원 제외)인 482억불로 충당되어야 하며, 따라서 28억불의 부족이 발생한다고 부연함.

3. 동 관련 발표문은 금파편 송부함.끝.

(대사 현홍주-국장)

외교문서 비밀해제: 걸프 사태 33
걸프 사태 재정지원 공여국 조정위원회 회의 2

초판인쇄 2024년 03월 15일
초판발행 2024년 03월 15일

지은이 한국학술정보(주)
펴낸이 채종준
펴낸곳 한국학술정보(주)
주 소 경기도 파주시 회동길 230(문발동)
전 화 031-908-3181(대표)
팩 스 031-908-3189
홈페이지 http://ebook.kstudy.com
E-mail 출판사업부 publish@kstudy.com
등 록 제일산-115호(2000. 6. 19)

ISBN   979-11-6983-993-8 94340
       979-11-6983-960-0 94340 (set)